D0233150

The New York Times
Sports
Question
Box

# The New York Times
# Sports Question Box

by S. Lee Kanner
*Assistant Sports Editor*
*The New York Times*

Illustrated by Robert Neubecker

The Rutledge Press
New York, New York

*Published by The Rutledge Press*
*A Division of W. H. Smith Publishers Inc.*
*112 Madison Avenue, New York, New York 10016*

*First printing 1981*
*Printed in the United States of America*


*Edited by Deborah Weiss*
*Designed by Allan Mogel*

**Library of Congress Cataloging in Publication Data**
Kanner, S. Lee.
  The New York times sports question box.
  1. Sports—Miscellanea.   I. Title.
GV706.8.K36      796.02      81-8664
ISBN 0-8317-6500-3                AACR2

# Contents

*To Elsie,*
*who knows little about sports, cares less,*
*and who never dropped a stitch as she*
*watched Roger Maris break Babe Ruth's*
*home-run record in 1961.*

# Preface

Oliver Goldsmith once wrote:

> By sports like these are all their cares beguil'd,
> The sports of children satisfy the child.

How wrong he was. We carry the sports of our childhood into adulthood, into old age, into our grave. Memories of the games we played, or watched as spectators, remain with us forever. A great leaping catch will remind us of a similar catch, oh, how many years ago was it? Who was the player? On what team?

The memory nags at us; we cannot let go of it until we are assured we are right, or almost right, or wrong. For memories play tricks and the only infallible memory is the memory of the record books.

Which is why the mail to this caretaker of The New York Times Question Box column is relentless. Americans are possessed by sports, possessed by a consuming desire to know all about the games and the heroes of their past and of their present. And by a desire to thread their way through the thicket of rules that has enveloped and made complex the once-simple games of their youth.

The mail arrives from all over the country and from all manner of people; there are no class distinctions in the grandstand. The letters come from physicians and lawyers, from professors and chairmen of fine arts departments; from musicians and writers; from clerks and blue-collar workers; from chief executives of large corporations and vice-presidents of small advertising agencies. The letters are neatly typed by secretaries on expensive bond paper, or almost illegibly scribbled by students on cheap note paper. They come from children as young as 6 and from adults as old as 89.

I try to answer them all. If the questions are not good enough for the column—and many of them are not—I answer them personally, if there is a return address. And even if they are good enough, I answer them anyway, because I am not certain which questions will eventually appear in the column, since the week's mail usually brings more usable questions than there is room for in SportsMonday, where the column appears.

The questions are sometimes simple, sometimes complex, sometimes prosaic, sometimes interesting and, often enough to be encouraging, sometimes astute and challenging. But all are a product of that intense American involvement in sports, or of that intense human desire to be published, to see a question in print—even if anonymously.

One young man, whose first few questions were published in the column, became so ambitious that he sent me 77 questions in one letter. An impossible situation, and what made it worse was that I could tell, from the tone of the questions, that he obviously knew the answers. He was working in reverse from the baseball record books—making up questions based on answers he had in front of him. Needless to say, I answered only a few of the questions, and I wrote to the young man explaining why.

Of all the questions I have received in the nearly three years I have been writing the column, my favorite remains one I received from Norway. It is the only question to which I have ever signed the name of the writer, and I did so for obvious reasons. Here is the way the question and answer appeared in The Times on April 16, 1979:

**QUESTION: As a Norwegian stationed in the United States during World War II, I competed in 1944 on the old Olympic ski-jumping hill at Lake Placid. The 1980 Winter Olympics and Lake Placid are now a major topic in Norway, a country of skiers, and I recently told my grandchildren that I had finished third in a jumping event there. My grandchildren refuse, however, to believe that their white-haired "blimp" of a grandfather, now in his middle 60's, sailed through the air for a couple of hundred feet on a pair of boards. Would it be possible to supply proof from your files?**

**PER FUERST**
**Oslo**

To the grandchildren of Per Fuerst of Oslo:
The following appeared in The New York Times on Feb. 23, 1944, as part of a longer article.

"Per Fuerst of New York's Telemark [club], who hadn't jumped since 1936, when he performed in his native Norway, also exhibited a form reminiscent of other Norwegian greats who have been seen at Lake Placid in the past. His style upon landing was flawless, and his telemark riding of the lower slope and finish on the hill's apron were impressive.

"Fuerst was rusty at the all-important 'take-off' and didn't get the lift so necessary for long flights, negotiating 145 and 161 feet for a 132.9 point total. He finished tied for third."

Many of the questions and answers in this book appear exactly as they did in The Times. In others, I have inserted the year to which the question is related. Still others I have "updated" where needed with newer records or statistics.

By and large, however, most of the statistical records are historical and constant. And, of course, so are the questions on rules for the various sports.

Finally, I must express my deep gratitude to the many officials of the various professional leagues and teams and of the National Collegiate Athletic Association for their gracious help in explaining the subtle distinctions and nuances of the rules of the game and in searching out obscure records and statistics.

The questions on professional baseball have been far more numerous than for any other sport—as would be expected. And two men have provided me with unfailing and invaluable help. I would be deeply remiss if I did not mention their names: Jack Redding, Librarian of the Baseball Hall of Fame in Cooperstown, New York, and Barney Deary, Administrator for Umpire Development for Baseball, in St. Petersburg, Florida.

A word of appreciation must be expressed, too, for the efforts of Jim Benagh, a friend and a fine editor for SportsMonday, who oversees the column each week with a painless scalpel.

*S. Lee Kanner*

# Baseball

## Rules of the Game

**QUESTION: If a pitcher touches his lips while on the mound, the umpire automatically calls a ball (except on the fourth ball, which the pitcher must throw to his catcher). So, when strategy dictates an intentional walk, why doesn't the pitcher touch his lips three times and then throw the fourth ball, thus reducing the risk of a wild pitch with all its consequences?**

Because he would not be in the game long enough to do so. The rule book, which states that a pitcher may not "bring his pitching hand in contact with his mouth or lips while in the 18-foot circle surrounding the pitching rubber," goes on to add that the umpire is instructed to call a ball the first time, warn him the second time and eject him from the game for defying the rule the third time.

**QUESTION: What is a spitball and when was it banned by the major leagues?**

The spitball is thrown much like a fastball, but with the ball or fingers moistened with saliva or some other lubricant so that the ball slips from the fingers with little rotation and breaks sharply downward as it nears the plate. The pitch was officially banned in 1920, but 17 active spitball pitchers were exempted from the ban for the balance of their careers.

The eight exempted pitchers in the National League were: Bill Doak, Phil Douglas, Dana Fillingim, Ray Fisher, Marv Goodwin, Burleigh Grimes, Clarence Mitchell and Dick Rudolph. The nine in the American League: Y.W. (Doc) Ayers, Ray Caldwell, Stan Coveleski, Urban Faber, H.B. (Dutch) Leonard, Jack Quinn, Allan Russell, Urban Shocker and Allen Sothoron.

The last legal spitball was thrown by Grimes in 1934, but through the years the pitch has been used, even though it is against the rules.

**QUESTION: A relief pitcher entered a game in the sixth inning with his team winning, 7-2. The final score was 8-2, yet, with so wide a margin, he received credit for a save after having pitched the rest of the way. Why? Also, if a relief pitcher stops a rally after having entered the game with the tying run at bat, on base or in the on-deck circle, and if he is subsequently relieved and the new pitcher finishes the game without ever facing the same situation, who gets credit for the save?**

A player is credited with a save if he is the finishing pitcher in a game won by his club, if he is not the winning pitcher and if further he meets at least one of these three criteria: He entered the game with the tying run represented either by a man already on base or by one of the first two hitters he faces; he entered the game with a lead of no more than three runs and pitched for at least one inning; he pitched effectively (a judgment for the official scorer) for at least three innings, regardless of the score.

In the first instance you cite, the relief pitcher finished the game, was not the winning pitcher and hurled effectively for at least three innings, so he was entitled to a save.

In the second case, the first relief pitcher did not finish the game, so he does not qualify. The second relief pitcher did finish; whether he qualifies depends on his having met the other conditions.

**QUESTION: There are runners on first and second, with one out, and the batter hits a line drive to the shortstop, who unintentionally drops the ball and then picks it up. Can the shortstop tag the nearest runner, who remained on second, and then step on second for a force on the runner from first base?**

Yes. Rule 2.00 of the Official Baseball Rules states in part, "A force play is a play in which a runner legally loses his right to occupy a base by reason of the batter becoming a runner." In this instance the runner on second was required to move to third, and the runner on first to advance to second.

If, however, the fielder *intentionally* drops the ball—presumably in an effort to get a double play—then, according to rule 6.05(1), the batter is out, the ball is ruled dead and the runners return to their bases.

**QUESTION: A batter hits a ground ball that, before passing or touching an infielder, hits a runner standing on second base. What is the ruling?**

Because he deflected the batted ball, the runner is out, the ball is dead and the batter takes first base.

**QUESTION: With runners on first and second and one out, the batter hits a home run. But in rounding the bases, the team in the field is under the impression that he failed to touch first base and third base. The pitcher tosses to first in an appeal play. The umpire there rejects the appeal. The pitcher then tosses to third, but the home plate umpire rules that there is only one appeal allowed for a play. Is this correct for the major leagues? Would the ruling also apply in college baseball? Also, what happens to the two base runners who have scored on the homer?**

In the major leagues, successive appeals may not be made on a runner at the same base, but an appeal is allowed on the same runner at another base, so that the home plate umpire would have been in error. Under the rules of the National Collegiate Athletic Association, "the defensive team receives only one chance on an appeal," so that the umpire would have been correct in this instance. Whatever the ruling, the two runs would have counted, since upholding of the appeal simply meant that there were two out. If the appeal had resulted in the third out, the runs would not have counted.

QUESTION: The bases are loaded, and the batter hits a triple, driving in three runs. The team in the field appeals, contending that the batter never touched first base, and the umpire agrees. How many runs score?

If there were fewer than two out, the three runs count. If the appeal call constitutes the third out, no runs count.

QUESTION: All bases are occupied, two men are out, the batter strikes out, but the catcher drops the ball. Is the batter automatically out and the side retired?

No. The batter must be tagged out or thrown out, or a play be made on one of the base runners. The only time a batter is automatically out when a third strike is dropped by the catcher occurs when first base is occupied before two men are out.

QUESTION: There is a man on third, one out, and a suicide squeeze play is across home as the batter inadvertently pops the ball in the air. The runner, afraid the ball will be caught, runs back toward third. The pitcher and catcher miss the pop up, but the catcher picks up the ball and throws to the third baseman, who tags the runner out. Is he out, or does the run count?

The run counts, since the runner has touched home plate.

QUESTION: With a man on first base, the batter hits a foul ball that appears to be dropping into the stands. The catcher leans far over, however, and grabs it. As he does, he topples into the seats. Does the runner advance?

Yes. The ball is dead, and the runner moves to the next base.

QUESTION: Just as the catcher is about to catch a foul fly near the stands, a fan reaches over the railing and knocks the ball out of his glove. What is the ruling?

"When there is spectator interference with any thrown or batted ball," according to Rule 3.16, "the ball shall be dead at the moment of interference and the umpire shall impose such penalties as in his opinion will nullify the act of interference." In this case, the umpire would declare the batter out.

QUESTION: A player hits a ball that goes into the stands and seems like an obvious home run, but he twists his leg while hitting the ball and cannot run around the bases. Is he out, or is it a home run?

In such an unlikely situation, officials say, the home run would be allowed.

QUESTION: With two men on base, a batter hits a game-winning home run. He stands at home plate, acknowledging the crowd's ovation, instead of running the bases. He does this for an unconscionably long time. Can the umpire call him out for delaying the game? Will the two runs that have already crossed the plate count?

This is a technicality to which few umpires would be likely to resort. The batter would be informed that he should run the bases and then take his bows, and he would do so. However, if for some reason he did insist on delaying the game further, and he was called out, the runs would not count if the batter became the third out without touching first base.

QUESTION: I wonder about the baseball rules concerning a batter "breaking his wrists" on a pitch. Can you shed some light on this?

According to Barney Deary, head of the umpire development program for the major leagues, there is no such thing as "breaking the wrists" and batters have smashed home runs without doing so. Such swings are judgment calls on the part of the umpire. Sometimes a batter is merely trying to get out of the way of a pitch, not hit it, even though the bat comes around. If the umpire calls a ball, and if the bat goes by the ball, the catcher may appeal to the home-plate umpire to ask his partner for help on the decision. If the base umpire rules that the ball was in the strike zone, that ruling will prevail. There can be no appeal if the home-plate umpire called the pitch a strike.

QUESTION: There are men on second and third with one out. The batter hits a long drive that is caught by the center fielder. Both runners, who started to advance at the crack of the bat, attempt to return to their bases. The runner from third makes it back, tags up and again dashes for home. He crosses the plate before the throw to second, which arrives ahead of that runner, resulting in the third out. Does the run count?

Yes, since the runner from third scored before the third out was registered, and since that third out did not occur on a force play.

QUESTION: At one time, in the case of an intentional walk, the catcher appeared to step out of the box prior to each pitch. In what year was the present rule adopted requiring catchers to remain behind the plate until the pitch is released?

Until 1955, the catcher's box was a triangle, and although he had to "stand with both feet within the lines of the catcher's box until the ball leaves the pitcher's hand," he had more room to maneuver before the ball was thrown because he was in the widest part of the triangle. In 1955, the shape of the box was changed to its present rectangle, restricting his movements until the ball is thrown.

**QUESTION:** At the last two major league games I attended, there were two passed balls. It is my understanding that a passed ball is an error on the part of the catcher, but in neither case was an error posted on the scoreboard. Why?

The position of the rules makers is that, because catchers and pitchers handle the ball much more frequently than other players, no error is charged for a passed ball or a wild pitch.

**QUESTION:** With two outs and a man on third base, the batter strikes out, but the catcher drops the ball. He quickly picks it up and pursues the batter toward first base and tags him, but not before the runner on third has scored. Does the run count? If the batter had reached first base safely and the run had scored, would the pitcher be charged with an earned run, would the batter get credit for a run batted in and would the runner from third be credited with a stolen base?

The run would not count, if the batter was tagged out before he reached first. If he had reached first safely, the catcher would be charged with a passed ball, and the pitcher would not be charged with an earned run. The batter would not be credited with a run batted in, nor would the runner be credited with a stolen base.

**QUESTION:** With two strikes on a batter and two men on base, he attempts to bunt a pitch that is in the strike zone. The ball hits his hand, which is holding the lower part of the bat, and rolls out into the infield. The pitcher picks up the ball, throws it over the first baseman's head. One run scores, the man on first goes to third and the batter ends up on second. Is this legal?

No. Since the batter was attempting to hit a third strike, and the ball was in the strike zone, he is out, the ball is dead and the two runners must return to their original bases. A player's hand is not considered part of the bat. Another aspect of this rule states that if a batter is hit by a pitched ball that is in the strike zone, it will be called a strike whether or not the batter attempted to avoid the ball.

**QUESTION: As the runner on first attempts to steal, the batter swings and misses, and the ball gets by the catcher and strikes the umpire. The catcher picks up the ball and throws the runner out at second. Is this legal?**

Yes. If a pitched or thrown ball accidentally touches an umpire, it is still in play.

**QUESTION: If a foul tip hits the umpire and is caught by the catcher before the ball touches the ground, is the batter out?**

In this situation the ball is dead and the batter cannot be called out. The same ruling applies if the ball lodges in the umpire's mask.

**QUESTION: What is the ruling when an umpire is struck by a batted ball? Is the ruling affected if he is positioned in front of an infielder at that time?**

If a ball hits an umpire in fair territory before it "touches an infielder, including the pitcher, or touches an umpire before it has passed an infielder other than the pitcher," the rule book states, the ball is dead. However, if the ball hits an umpire "after having passed a fielder other than the pitcher, or having touched a fielder including the pitcher," the ball remains in play.

**QUESTION: If a batter misses a two-strike pitch and the ball hits him, is he out or does he take first base? What happens if a runner attempts to steal on such a play?**

When a batter attempts to hit the pitch and the ball touches him or his clothing, he is out, the ball is dead and the runner must return to his base.

**QUESTION: A foul tip hits the catcher's mask, goes up about 10 feet in the air and then is caught by the catcher. Is the batter out?**

No. It is not a catch if it is a rebound, unless the ball has first touched the catcher's glove or hand.

**QUESTION: On a play at home, Team A's runner narrowly misses the plate on a slide and Team B's catcher misses in his attempt to tag him. The umpire correctly makes no call because this is an appeal play. After the next pitch has been thrown, Team B's manager suddenly realizes the run has not been registered. Can he then instruct his catcher to go into the dugout and tag the runner out?**

No. In addition, appeals must be made before the next pitch is thrown, and umpires are instructed in such situations not to say anything until that occurs. In this instance, the umpire, once the pitch had been made, would have announced that the run counted because the appeal was not made at the proper time.

**QUESTION: There is no one out (or one man out) in the bottom of the ninth inning, the score is tied and the home team has a man on third.**

The batter attempts a suicide squeeze, which is perfectly executed. The runner from third scores as the pitcher fields the ball cleanly. The pitcher makes no play, since the game is over. In an earlier inning, of course, he would have thrown to first to catch the batter. What is the batter credited with, a sacrifice or a single?

There is no rule that takes this specific circumstance into account, and so this is strictly a judgment for the official scorer. But, since the batter might have beaten the throw in any case, it has been the practice in such situations to credit him with a hit.

QUESTION: With men on first and second and one out, a ground ball is hit between those two bases. The first baseman fields the ball and throws to the pitcher, who is covering the bag. The batter is out, but, as he crosses first base, he knocks the pitcher down and falls on top of him. Before the pitcher can get rid of the ball, both runners score. Shouldn't there be an interference call? If so, shouldn't the base runner closest to home be called out?

The call depends solely on the umpire's judgment, but, if he rules that the batter has hindered the fielder at first base, then the ball is dead, the runner closest to home is called out and any other runners return to their original bases.

QUESTION: In a recent game, the third baseman intentionally failed to catch a pop bunt with a man on first. He then fired the ball to second to start a double play. Shouldn't this have been ruled an infield fly?

No, for two reasons. The rules specifically exempt a line drive or a bunt attempt from the infield-fly rule, and only one base—not two or three—was occupied when the bunt was attempted.

QUESTION: There are men on first and second with one out. The batter hits an exceptionally long fly ball, which is caught. The man from second base comes home, and the man from first advances to third. The team in the field, contending that the runner from first base left too soon, appeals to the umpire. He upholds the appeal, for the third out. Does the run count?

Yes, because the runner from second scored before the appeal was made. This is what is known as a time play.

QUESTION: Television replays sometimes show a "phantom" double play, in which the force is called by the umpire although the infielder did not have the ball when crossing second base or did not touch second before throwing to first. Why is this allowed?

If the infielder does not touch the bag when he has the ball, then technically, of course, the runner should be safe. There is a general understanding among umpires, however, that the pivot man on the double play must be protected to some extent from a runner barreling into second base. Thus the "phantom" double play, except when it is most blatant, is almost always permitted. In fact a call of "safe" on such a play is so unusual that it invariably leads to argument from the team in the field.

**QUESTION:** I have heard television commentators discussing, without reaching any definite conclusion, what could be done if a batter kept turning around to try to steal the catcher's signs. Is there an official, or unofficial, rule governing this?

Once the umpire becomes aware of the situation, either on his own or because of the catcher's protest, he can order the batter to desist.

**QUESTION:** In a recent game I watched on television, the left fielder never touched the ball, and yet he was charged with an error. Why?

The rules clearly indicate that if, in the official scorer's judgment, a fly ball could have been handled with "ordinary effort," an error should be charged.

**QUESTION:** With a runner on first base, the batter hits a foul. The first baseman, in trying to catch the ball near the stands, is interfered with by a spectator. The umpire calls the batter out. Can the runner tag up and advance to second?

According to Rule 3.16 of the Official Baseball Rules, "When there is spectator interference with any thrown or batted ball, the ball shall be dead at the moment of interference and the umpire shall impose such penalties as in his opinion will nullify the act of interference."

The runner cannot advance, because the ball is dead. However, the umpire can, in his judgment, move the runner up a base if he believes the runner could have tagged up and gone to second without the interference.

**QUESTION:** With a runner on first and less than two out, the catcher drops a third strike and the batter runs toward first base in the legal running lane. The catcher picks up the ball and throws to first, hitting the batter-runner, who reaches first. The man on first, who previously had remained on the bag, leaves it before the batter gets there and advances to second. The batter is automatically out because there were less than two out, but can the man on first go to second?

The fact that the batter, although automatically out, runs toward first does not constitute interference with the catcher, who should know not to make the throw. The batter is out, but the player who reaches second base remains there.

**QUESTION:** Is a switch-hitter allowed to change from one side of home plate to the other during the time he is at bat?

Yes, but he cannot switch after the pitcher is set to throw the ball.

**QUESTION:** With the count 3 and 2 on the batter, the runner on first base attempts to steal second. The pitch is called a ball, but the catcher throws to second and the umpire calls the runner out, although he was entitled to the base since the batter had walked. The runner on second leaves the bag, heading for the dugout. The shortstop tags him again, and he is officially called out. Was the umpire correct in his second call?

Yes, because the runner should have been aware of his responsibility, and should have known that he was entitled to second base despite the first ruling. If he had stayed on second base until time was called and the situation clarified, he would have been ruled safe.

**QUESTION:** Fog suddenly rolls in on a major league baseball game as a batter drives a long ball toward the right-field stands. The ball is lost to sight, the team in the field claims it went foul and the team at bat claims it went for a home run. How would the umpire rule?

The umpire would rule that the play was invalid and would have to be repeated, once the fog lifted. If the fog did not lift, the game would eventually be called. In an actual case some years ago, the umpires had some fungoes hit toward the outfield, and since the balls could not be followed, the play was voided and the game was later called.

**QUESTION:** There are two outs, a runner on first and a count of three balls and two strikes on the batter. The runner takes off for second, the pitch is the fourth ball, but the runner is thrown out on his attempted steal. What is the ruling: side retired or men on first and second?

The side is not retired and the runner is entitled to second base because of the walk. However, if the runner had been on second or third and had attempted to steal under the same conditions, the batter would have been credited with a walk but the side would have been retired, since the runner was not entitled to advance.

**QUESTION:** The bases are loaded, the score is tied, and there are no outs in the bottom of the ninth inning. The batter hits a fly ball to the outfield and the runner on third tags up and scores. However, the two other runners, who have not tagged up, are still on the basepaths. If the outfielder throws the ball to the second baseman, who steps on the bag and then throws to the first baseman, who does the same, making it a triple play, does the run still count?

Yes. When the outfielder caught the fly ball, the force was removed and it became a time play, which meant the triple play had to be completed before the runner scored. However, since the runner crossed home plate before the completion of the triple play, the run counted.

**QUESTION:** With two outs and the bases loaded, the count on the batter is three balls and two strikes. The next pitch is a ball, and the batter is entitled to a walk, but the pitch gets away from the catcher. The man on third ambles slowly toward home and the man on second dashes across third, also heading for home plate. However, he sees he cannot make it and tries to return to third. He is thrown out before the man who was on third can cross home plate. Does the run count, since there was a walk with the bases loaded?

No. The run would have counted only if the man on third had touched home plate before the third out.

QUESTION: It is the last of the ninth, or of any extra inning. The score is tied, the bases are loaded and there are two outs. Does a player have to be in the on-deck circle, since whatever the batter does will end the game or the inning? Also, does it constitute interference when a throw from a fielder hits the man in the on-deck circle and the ball bounces away, enabling a runner to score?

The rules require that a man must be in the on-deck circle. On the second part of the question, unless the waiting batter intentionally interferes with the ball, the umpire would allow the ball to remain in play and the run would count, since the errant throw was a defensive lapse.

QUESTION: With less than two out, a runner on first base breaks for second as the batter swings and hits a foul tip that is held by the catcher. Must the runner return to first?

No. Runners need not tag up on a foul tip that is caught. The ball is still alive and they may steal a base. However, if the foul tip is not caught, the runners must return to their bases.

QUESTION: A runner is leading off first base, and the pitcher tries to pick him off. The runner slides back head first, beating the throw, but his hand comes to rest on the first baseman's shoe, which is on the bag. Is the runner out or safe?

Unless he moves his hand to the bag itself before the first baseman tags him, he is out.

QUESTION: On a force play in baseball, the runner is out if the fielder holding the ball steps on the bag or touches it with the hand holding the ball before the runner arrives. Is the runner out, however, if the fielder touches the bag with any other part of his body, say, his knee or the hand not holding the ball? Whatever the answer, is the same true in softball?

The runner is out in both sports. It does not matter how the fielder touches the bag, as long as he does so ahead of the runner.

QUESTION: After a batter fouls off a pitch, must a runner retag his base before play is resumed? That is, what prevents a runner from going to the next base on the foul and then taking only a few steps back before stealing the base after the umpire gives the catcher a new ball?

Rule 5.09 of the Official Baseball Rules states in part:

"The ball becomes dead and runners advance one base, or return to their bases, without liability to be put out, when—

"(e) A foul ball is not caught; runners return. The umpire shall not put the ball in play until all runners have retouched their bases."

QUESTION: With runners on first and second and no one out, the batter hits a sharp grounder to the third baseman. The fielder steps on third for the first out, then throws to the first baseman, who has his foot on the bag, for the second out. The runner on first never left the bag, and the first baseman thereupon tags him. Is this a triple play?

No. By keeping his foot on the bag, the first baseman removed the force at second and the runner on first was entitled to remain there. If the first baseman had tagged the man on first before tagging the batter or the bag, he would have completed the triple play.

**QUESTION: Are there any rules prohibiting an infielder or an outfielder from allowing a playable foul ball to fall to the ground so as to prevent a runner on third from tagging up?**

There is no such rule, and fielders do occasionally allow foul balls to drop in such a situation.

**QUESTION: There are runners on second and third with one out. The batter hits a fly to the center fielder for the second out. The runners try to advance, and the throw nails the man going to third, but not before the runner on third has scored. The third baseman calls for the ball, steps on the bag and appeals to the umpire that the scorer left third before the ball was caught. The umpire upholds the appeal, and there are now four outs. Is such a situation possible, and, if so, does the run count?**

It is possible, and the run does not count. The so-called "fourth out" can erase a run as long as the appeal play develops during the same play in which a third out is made. The appeal play takes precedence.

**QUESTION: With fewer than two out and runners on first and third, a batter hits a fly ball to the outfield. The runner on third tags up and dashes for home; the runner on first, thinking the ball is going to be thrown home, also tags up, and heads for second. The throw is cut off, and he is tagged before he reaches second but after the run scores. Since the batter has hit into a double play, does he get credit for a run batted in?**

Yes, because the run had scored before the double play was completed.

**QUESTION: One man is out, and there is a runner on first base. The batter hits a fly to deep left, and the runner almost reaches third before the ball is caught. Is the runner out if the second baseman receives the ball and then steps on second before the runner arrives back? What if the second baseman tags the runner while the runner is on the bag?**

After a fly ball is caught, the runner is out if he fails to retouch his original base "before he or his original base is tagged," in the words of the rule book. The second baseman must, therefore, either throw on to first or tag the runner—not second base, since in this case second is not the runner's original base.

The runner would be out if he were tagged even while on second base, however briefly, as he made his way back to first, because he was not entitled to second.

**QUESTION: When a designated hitter is inserted into an American League game for defensive purposes, does that team lose the d.h.? Also, what happens to the d.h. during the All-Star game and the World Series?**

The rules state that the designated hitter may be used defensively and continue to bat in the same position in the batting order. However, the pitcher must then bat in the place of the substituted defensive player, unless more than one substitution is made. In that case, the manager must designate their spots in the batting order.

In the All-Star game, the d.h. rule only applies if both teams and both leagues agree to it. In World Series play, the d.h. is used every other year, specifically in all even-numbered years. In exhibition games between teams from the two leagues, the home team decides whether the d.h. will be used.

**QUESTION: What determines the game-winning run batted in, and is it an official statistic now?**

The game-winning r.b.i. became an official statistic in the American League in 1980. It was official in the National League in 1979, when Mike Schmidt of the Philadelphia Phillies was the leader, with 20.

The designation applies to a run batted in that gives a club a lead it never relinquishes, and it does not matter in which inning this occurs. In addition, the run batted in must conform to Rule 10.04, which deals with what constitutes a valid r.b.i. (No r.b.i. is credited on a force double play, for example.) Under these guidelines, there need not be a game-winning run batted in for each game.

**QUESTION: How is the slugging percentage figured?**

A batter's total bases is divided by his total at bats. The total bases figure is arrived at by assigning 1 to a single, 2 to a double, 3 to a triple and 4 to a homer. An example: If batter is at the plate 541 times and has 266 total bases, his average is .492, if you carry the last digit to the highest number.

**QUESTION: Please explain how the major leagues arrive at the earned-run average of a pitcher.**

The e.r.a. is arrived at by multiplying the total earned runs charged against a pitcher by nine, and then dividing the result by the total number of innings pitched, which should be rounded off to the nearest whole number.

**QUESTION: Why 502 plate appearances to win the batting title? Why not 486 (162 games times three), or an even 500? When did plate appearances replace times at bat in calculating batting champions?**

In 1957, baseball adopted a rule that 3.1 plate appearances for each scheduled game were needed to determine a batting champion. Multiply 162 by 3.1, and the 502 figure is the result. The first rule for determining a champion was adopted in 1920, when it was decided a player had to appear in 100 games to be eligible. This was changed in 1950 and a player had to appear in at least two-thirds of his team's games. A year later it was ruled that a player must have at least 400 times at bat. The most recent change came in 1967, when it was ruled that if a player did not have the required 3.1 plate appearances, he could still win the title if he were charged with the required minimum and his batting average was still the highest.

**QUESTION:** With no outs and a runner on first base, a ground ball is hit to the first baseman. The runner stays on the bag and is tagged by the first baseman, who then steps on the bag. Is this a double play?

Yes, because the runner was obliged to advance to second on the play. If the first baseman had stepped on the bag before making the tag, he would have removed the force, and the runner could have remained safely on first base.

**QUESTION:** With two outs, a double steal is attempted, but the lead runner is thrown out to end the inning. Does the other runner, who advanced safely, get credit for a stolen base?

No. The rules state that when a double steal or a triple steal is attempted and one of the runners is thrown out, no other runner can be credited with a stolen base. The same rule applies if there is one out or none out.

**QUESTION:** With men on second and third and one out, the defensive manager, without calling time out, walks toward the mound. The runners each steal a base as he does so. Is this legal?

No. It is the responsibility of the umpire to call time once the manager leaves the dugout, and he would do so.

**QUESTION:** A runner overslides first base as the first baseman, who has fielded the ball and does not have his foot on the bag, misses his attempt to tag him. The runner is then tagged before he can get back to the bag. Is he out or safe?

He is safe. A runner has a right to overrun or overslide first base, as long as he touches it. If he does not touch the bag, the fielder can retire him by tagging him or the base.

**QUESTION:** It is the bottom of the sixth inning, the bases loaded, one out, and the team at bat is losing, 6-2. The manager of the team that is ahead protests that the batter is using an illegal bat. The umpire agrees and calls the batter out. The inning ends without any runs, and the game concludes with the same 6-2 score. The manager of the losing team then protests to the league office that the bat was not illegal, and his protest is upheld. Is the game played over?

No. It would be resumed at the point of the first protest, with same batter up.

QUESTION: The manager of the home team is in control of whether a major league baseball game is to be played until he turns over his lineup card to the umpire in chief. If the day is extremely cold, but if weather conditions do not change, may the umpire in chief subsequently call off the game?

Once the home team signifies that it wishes the game be played, and if the weather does not become worse, the umpire in chief will probably not call off the game. He *may* do so, however, though he must first suspend play for at least 30 minutes.

QUESTION: If a player-manager removes himself for a substitute in a major league game, is he allowed to go to the coaching box? If a third-base coach is used as a pinch-hitter, is he allowed to return to coaching?

Yes, in both instances.

QUESTION: In the major leagues, a pitcher must be removed if a manager makes a second visit to the mound in the same inning. A catcher is not limited in his visits to the mound. What happens if the catcher is also the manager?

The umpire will tell the catcher not to abuse his privilege. It will then be up to the umpire's judgment to determine if the catcher-manager is making too many trips to the mound.

QUESTION: A suspended extra-inning major league game is resumed the next night. As the game continues, Team A inserts the last of its players, but the manager, thinking a relief pitcher used the night before is still available, visits the mound a second time in an inning as Team B threatens to score. Since neither the relief pitcher nor any other player is available, what happens?

The pitcher has to be removed and the game is forfeited to Team B.

QUESTION: What is the ruling if a fielder deliberately throws his glove at a fair batted ball and the glove touches the ball? If a pitcher does the same?

In both instances, the batter is awarded three bases and the ball remains in play.

QUESTION: If a batter only gets three bases when a fielder throws his glove at a ball and hits it, why don't fielders attempt to deflect apparent home runs?

The rules also take that situation into account. If a fielder, with his glove or his hat, deflects a ball that in the judgment of the umpire would have been a home run, the batter will be awarded a home run.

QUESTION: With the bases loaded and two out, the batter hits a sharp grounder to the third baseman, who drops the ball. He quickly picks it up and, instead of stepping on third, tries to tag the runner coming from second. The runner retreats toward second, the fielder chases him and finally tags him, but not before the runner from third has crossed the plate. Does the run count?

No. It is still a force play, and the infielder can make the third out by tagging the base or the runner.

**QUESTION:** Was there ever a time when a fair ball that bounced into the stands was a home run? Was Babe Ruth ever credited with such homers?

Until 1931, a fair ball that bounced through or over a fence, or into the stands, was a home run. The record books do not differentiate between such home runs and those that went directly into the stands, so it is possible that Ruth hit some homers that bounced into the stands.

**QUESTION:** In a National League baseball game, Team A is at bat with a man on first, two outs and the pitcher coming up. He is removed for a pinch-hitter, who soon has two balls and one strike on him. Team B's pitcher then picks the runner off first, for the third out. Team A goes into the field, and a new pitcher quickly retires the side. Team A is again at bat. Does the pinch-hitter of the previous inning come to bat again? If so, what happens to the new Team A pitcher?

Once the new pitcher entered the game, the pinch-hitter was out of it. If the Team A manager wants to have someone hit for the second pitcher, he has to insert a new pinch-hitter. This, of course, means inserting yet another pitcher when Team A returns to the field.

**QUESTION:** When was the foul-strike rule adopted?

In 1901, the National League voted to make any foul ball not caught on the fly a strike, unless the batter had two strikes on him. The American League adopted the rule in 1903.

**QUESTION:** Is an aluminum bat permitted in the major leagues?

No. The rules state that the bat must be "one piece of solid wood" or "formed from a block of wood consisting of two or more pieces of wood bonded together with an adhesive in such a way that the grain direction of all pieces is essentially parallel to the length of the bat."

**QUESTION:** There is one out and a man on third in a major league baseball game. As the pitcher gets set on the rubber and throws the ball, the runner dashes for home in an attempted steal. The catcher jumps in front of the plate, interfering with the batter's swing but successfully tagging the runner. What is the call?

The runner would be safe, because the catcher's interference would have caused a balk to be called on the pitcher, entitling the runner to advance a base. In addition, the batter is awarded first because of the interference.

**QUESTION:** The bases are loaded with one out. The batter hits a ground ball to the shortstop that appears to be a certain double play until the runner from second stops and allows the ball to hit him. What is the ruling?

The runner's action results in two penalties. He is out because the ball hit him, and his interference with the fielder will cause the umpire to call the succeeding runner out, thus nullifying the run scored by the man on third since there are now three outs.

**QUESTION:** What rule, if any, prohibits a second baseman or a third baseman from blocking the bag against a runner, as a catcher is allowed to do?

The rules on obstruction apply to all fielders. According to the Official Baseball Rules: "If a fielder is about to receive a thrown ball and if the ball is in flight directly toward and near enough to the fielder so he must occupy his position to receive the ball he may be considered 'in the act of fielding a ball.' It is entirely up to the judgment of the umpire as to whether a fielder is in the act of fielding a ball." On the other hand, the fielder is considered guilty of obstruction if, "while not in possession of the ball and not in the act of fielding the ball, [he] impedes the progress of any runner."

**QUESTION: With a man on third and less than two outs, a fly ball is hit to an outfielder. The ball momentarily pops out of the outfielder's glove, but he catches it again before it hits the ground. Is the man on third permitted to tag up as soon as the ball touches the glove, or must he wait until the outfielder has control of the ball?**

A catch is legal if the ball is finally held by the fielder, even if juggled. The runner is permitted to leave his base the moment the fielder touches the ball.

**QUESTION: If a major league player has hit safely in, say, 25 straight games and is walked each time he goes to the plate in the 26th game, does his streak continue if he gets a hit the next time out?**

Yes, his streak would then be at 26 games. Rule 10.24 (b) states: "A consecutive-game hitting streak shall not be terminated if all the player's plate appearances (one or more) result in a base on balls, hit batsman, defensive interference or sacrifice bunt. The streak shall terminate if the player has a sacrifice fly and no hit."

**QUESTION: If a pitch bounces before it crosses home plate, and the batter manages to drive it for a hit, is that legal?**

Yes. The batter may hit a pitch even though the ball first touches the ground.

**QUESTION: A pitcher throws a ball that bounces in front of the batter's box, skips up and hits the batter. Does he take first base?**

If the batter makes an attempt to avoid the pitch, he takes first base. If he does not, and the pitch is outside the strike zone, the rules state that it shall be called a ball. If, in the judgment of the umpire, the batter did not have enough time to try to get out of the way of the ball, he will be sent to first base.

**QUESTION: A batter hits a high bouncing ball along the first-base line. As he runs toward first in the three-foot designated lane, which is in foul territory, the ball takes an odd bounce, strikes the batter-runner and drops into fair territory. What is the ruling? Also, what is the ruling if a pop fly lands behind the pitcher's mound, takes an erratic bounce and goes into foul territory between first base and home?**

In the first instance, it is a foul ball, because the batter-runner was hit in foul territory, and the ball is dead. In the second case, a ball that is not touched by a fielder and which bounces into foul territory between home and first, or between home and third, is also a foul ball.

**QUESTION:** There is a man on third and one out and the batter hits a long fly to the outfield. The runner on third, without tagging up, races for home. The outfielder, unaware that the runner left the bag early, throws home; the runner beats the throw, crosses the plate and heads for the dugout. The catcher is aware of the failure to tag up properly and dashes to third and steps on the bag. Is the runner out?

No. Unless the catcher appeals to the home-plate umpire before the next pitch is thrown, the runner is safe and the run counts.

**QUESTION:** In a 1979 game against the Los Angeles Dodgers, the New York Mets took an early 3-0 lead. In the fifth inning, the Dodgers rallied, tied the score and knocked out the starting pitcher, Mike Scott. Dwight Bernard came in and stopped the rally, pitching two-thirds of an inning. In the bottom of the fifth, the Mets sent in a pinch-hitter for Bernard and took the lead, 4-3. Dale Murray then came in and pitched three and two-thirds scoreless innings, and the Mets went on to win, 6-3, although Skip Lockwood had to get the final out. Since Bernard was the pitcher of record when the Mets went ahead, why did Murray get credit for the victory?

Usually the winning relief pitcher is the one who was the pitcher of record when his team assumed a lead that it then maintained until the end of the game. The Official Baseball Rules lists an exception, however: "Do not credit a victory to a relief pitcher who pitches briefly or ineffectively if a succeeding relief pitcher pitches effectively in helping to maintain his team in the lead." Under this guideline, Murray deserved the victory, not Bernard.

**QUESTION:** A baseball player who has been in the majors at least 10 years and with his current club at least five has the right to veto a trade. What are his rights if, say, during 10 years in the majors, all with the same club, he was sent to the team's farm for two or three months?

If he lacks even a month or two of the required 10-year minimum service in the majors, he may not veto a trade.

**QUESTION:** Please explain how the New York Yankees were able to bring Brian Doyle back from the minor leagues so many times. I thought a major league team had only three "options" to call up a player from the minors.

A player can be optioned only three times, but no matter how many times he is called up from the minors during one season, he is credited with only one option. Doyle had two options before the start of the 1980 season, and the third was used during that season, which is one of the reasons the Yankees traded him to the Oakland Athletics.

**QUESTION:** What happens to the statistics when a game is forfteited in professional baseball, football, basketball and hockey?

Baseball: All individual and team efforts up to the time of the forfeit, if the game is official, are included in the records. However, although a forfeited game results in a 9-0 score, the runs do not count in the winning team's statistics. If the forfeit occurs before the game is official, no records are included, only the fact of the forfeit.

Basketball: A forfeited game results in a 2–0 score, but there is no league determination as to what happens to individual records.

Football: The National Football League bylaws do not include any recognition of a forfeited game or a protested game.

Hockey: There is only one precedent for a forfeited game in the National Hockey League. On March 17, 1955, a game between Detroit and Montreal in Montreal was forfeited to Detroit after the first period because of a riot over the earlier suspension of Maurice (The Rocket) Richard, the Canadiens star. Detroit was ahead, 4–1, and the statistics, up to the point of the forfeit, counted.

**QUESTION: When and why did fielders discontinue the practice of leaving their gloves on the grass when they came in to bat?**

In 1954, a rule was passed that now reads: "Members of the offensive team shall carry all gloves and other equipment off the field and to the dugout while their team is at bat. No equipment shall be left lying on the field, either in fair or foul territory." The rule was passed because batted balls were sometimes hitting the gloves, and fielders were stumbling over them.

**QUESTION: Is it true that there once was a dirt path, which resembled a keyhole, from the pitcher's mound to the batter's box?**

Yes. It was believed that catchers, who frequently walked to the mound to consult with pitchers, would wear out the grass. According to the Baseball Hall of Fame, the path went out of vogue in the 1950's.

# For the Record

**QUESTION: Please list all the major league baseball teams that have played in the New York City area since 1870, which leagues they were in and how long the franchises lasted.**

There have been six leagues considered major since 1870: the old American Association, the Union Association, the Players League, the Federal League, the National League and the American League.

Brooklyn had a team in the American Association from 1884 through part of 1890; it also had a team in 1890 in the Players League that then went out of existence, and a team in the short-lived Federal

League for 1914–15. In 1876 there was a Brooklyn team in the National League, but it dropped out after that season. In 1890 a team at first called the Brooklyn Bridegrooms, and later the Superbas and the Dodgers, joined the National League, and it remained through the 1957 season, after which the franchise moved to Los Angeles.

A team called the New York Metropolitans was a member of the American Association from 1883 through 1887. There was also a New York team in the Players League in 1890. In 1883 a National League team in Troy was shifted to New York, where it was called the Gothams and then the Giants. It remained until it too moved west, to San Francisco, after the 1957 season.

Newark had a team in the Federal League in 1915.

The New York Yankees, at first called the Highlanders, joined the American League in 1903. The club had been moved from Baltimore.

The New York Mets began play in 1962 to fill the National League void left by the departed Giants and Dodgers.

**QUESTION: Everybody knows what a fungo is—the act of throwing a ball up in the air and hitting it to outfielders. But how did the term originate?**

The origin of the word has never been precisely traced, but an item in The Sporting News of May 23, 1951, gave this explanation:

"According to Bill Bryson of The Des Moines (Iowa) Register, fungo originally was a children's street game, dating back some 90 years, in which a player catching a certain number of fly balls qualified to replace the batter. The term 'fungo' originated from the childish chant at the batter: 'One go, two go, fun go.' The expression has been used in pro ball since the 1870's and for more than 30 years it has been applied to the pregame practice of hitting fly balls to outfielders."

**QUESTION: What are the origins of signals by baseball coaches?**

According to an article provided by baseball's Hall of Fame and written by John Devaney for the American Legion magazine of June 1968, baseball signals can be traced to the 1870's but came into prominence in 1894. According to Mr. Devaney, John McGraw and Wee Willie Keeler, both then playing for the old Baltimore Orioles, devised signs for a hit-and-run play and so demonstrated the value of such signals. From that point on the system evolved, becoming more and more elaborate.

**QUESTION: In baseball, what does "on the black" mean? How did it originate?**

When a pitched ball crosses the black edge of home plate and it is called a strike, pitchers regard it as being "on the black." The origin of the expression is lost in baseball history.

**QUESTION: Who invented the "donut" weight that batters use when in the on-deck circle?**

Elston Howard, the late Yankee catcher, in conjunction with the General Sportscraft Corporation of Bergenfield, N.J., developed and patented the "On-Deck Bat Weight" in 1969.

**QUESTION: When did numbers begin to appear on the uniforms of major league baseball players? Which team was the first to put the names of players on the uniforms? When did it become mandatory to wear batting helmets?**

In 1916, the Cleveland Indians pinned numbers onto the backs of player uniforms for home games only, then discontinued the practice at the end of the season. In 1924, Branch Rickey had numbers sewn onto the arms of St. Louis Cardinal uniforms, but this too was discontinued after the season. In 1929, the New York Yankees put numbers on the back. This time the practice spread. The rest of the American League had followed suit by 1930, and the National League gradually did so as well. The last of the old teams to begin using numbers was the New York Giants, in 1934.

The Chicago White Sox were the first team to put players' names on the uniforms, in 1960. (Even at present, by the way, neither numbers nor names on uniforms are mandatory.)

The use of batting helmets became required in the National League in 1957. William Harridge, then the president of the American League, personally directed the use of helmets in 1958, but this order was not made official by league rules until 1961.

**QUESTION: On a visit to the Baseball Hall of Fame, in Cooperstown, N.Y., I came across the expression "Lena Blackburne mud," which is used by umpires to take the shine off the baseballs before a game. Who was Blackburne, and why is his name associated with the mud?**

Blackburne, who died in 1968 at the age of 81, was an infielder who played in the major leagues for parts of eight seasons from 1910 to 1929 and also managed the Chicago White Sox in 1928 and 1929. He discovered the mud that did just the right job, in the area near Willingboro in New Jersey's Burlington County.

**QUESTION: What is the origin of the baseball expression "around the horn"?**

The act of throwing the ball from third to second to first, the longest possible way to complete a double play in the infield, is called "around the horn." It derives from the longest possible way to sail around the South American continent—around Cape Horn.

THE BASEBALL SOCK...
TEAM SOCK
STIRRUP
SWEAT SOCK

QUESTION: Why are the colored stockings worn by baseball players over their white ones so drastically cut out fore and aft that they appear as thin ribbons on either side of the ankle and shinbone?

The cutouts are called stirrups and are designed to avoid having to wear two pairs of stockings inside the shoes. The white stockings are sanitary hose; the colored ones are decorative and have long been a tradition in baseball. The stirrups effectively keep the colored socks in place without the discomfort of having two stockings inside a shoe.

QUESTION: What is the origin of the seventh-inning stretch in baseball? Also, do rooters for a visiting team stand at the top of the seventh or the bottom?

There are two versions, according to the Baseball Hall of Fame, as to what led to the widespread habit of stretching in the seventh inning.

One concerns a letter that Harry Wright, who joined the Cincinnati Red Stockings in 1869 as manager of the first professional baseball team, sent to a friend in Boston. He wrote that "the people out here have a peculiar custom of standing up to cheer their team in the seventh inning." What led to this "peculiar" local custom in the first place remains unknown.

Greater detail is provided in the second version, in which Brother Jasper of Manhattan College is credited with originating the stretch in 1882. Brother Jasper, for whom the Jaspers are nicknamed, was the college's first moderator of athletics. He was also the coach of the baseball team and had the additional title of prefect of discipline. At each home game he cautioned the student spectators not to leave their seats or move around until the game was over. One hot day in the spring of 1882 the game was long and drawn out, and by the seventh inning he noticed that the students were becoming restless and unruly. As Manhattan went to bat he walked over to the stands and told the youths to stretch and move about for a minute or two. This stemmed the restlessness, and the practice was continued at all Manhattan games, eventually spreading to New York Giant fans because some of the college's games were played at the Polo Grounds, the Giants' home field.

As for the second part of the question, a fan stands just before his team goes to bat in the seventh. Thus a fan of the visitors stands just before the top of the inning, a fan of the home team before the bottom.

QUESTION: In baseball the field general is referred to as the "manager," while in other sports he is the "coach." In addition the baseball manager wears the team uniform, while coaches do not. How did this come about?

The term "manager" came into use in baseball's early days, because the man who directed the team on the field also handled virtually everything else, including gate receipts and hotel bookings. The term stuck, even when the manager's duties narrowed.

Also in those early days, in the mid-19th century, the manager usually was a player, so he wore a uniform. It is not required, however, and Connie Mack of the Philadelphia Athletics never wore one. Burt Shotton, who managed the Philadelphia Phillies and the Brooklyn Dodgers, rarely wore one.

QUESTION: All of us who have ever played baseball learned early to keep the trademark on the bat facing toward us to avoid breaking the bat. I presume this is still advisable, and yet, watching the World Series on television, it appears as if more bats are being broken these days. Is this true, and if so, why? Also, doesn't a batter get more power by hitting the ball where the grain is strongest?

It is still advisable to hold the bat so that the trademark, which is stamped where the grain is weakest, faces the batter. If this is done, the batter, whether left-handed or right-handed, will hit the ball where the bat is strongest—against the grain. This, of course, would deliver the most power.

No more bats than usual are being broken, according to the Hillerich & Bradsby Company, Inc., manufacturer of the Louisville Slugger. Broken bats occur for a number of reasons: the bat is held the wrong way; the ball hits too close to the handle; the ball hits on the flat of the grain; the ball hits too far out on the end of the bat and the whiplash effect of the swing creates a shock that snaps the bat; and there is a defect inside the wood that does not become apparent until the bat breaks.

QUESTION: How many persons who were not born in the mainland United States are members of the Baseball Hall of Fame?

There are five such members. They are:

Henry Chadwick, a writer and statistician who created the first system of scoring games, was born in England. Elected in 1938.

William Henry (Harry) Wright, an early player and manager who helped organize the game, also was born in England. Elected in 1953.

Tom Connolly, an umpire who was born in England and never saw a baseball game until he was 15 years of age, was also elected in 1953.

Martin DiHigo, an exceptional ball player in the Negro, Latin American and Mexican Leagues, was born in Cuba. Elected in 1977.

Roberto Clemente, elected in 1973, was born in Puerto Rico.

QUESTION: Which player in the Baseball Hall of Fame, not including pitchers, had the lowest batting average?

Ray Schalk, a catcher with the Chicago White Sox for most of his career from 1912 through 1929, holds that distinction. He was elected to the Hall in 1955 as a special committee nominee. He had a batting average of .253, based on 1,345 hits in 5,306 times at bat.

QUESTION: I believe that one of the 1980 members of the Hall of Fame, Al Kaline, once hit two home runs in the same inning. When did he do this, and how many others have accomplished that rarity?

Kaline hit his two home runs on April 17, 1955. Twenty other players have also done it, the last being André Dawson of Montreal on July 30, 1978.

QUESTION: I have long wondered about the two small circles, near the base lines, on either side of home plate. I am not referring to the two larger, on-deck circles, which are on either side of home plate but farther away from it. What are those mysterious circles?

Those small circles are used by coaches for hitting fungoes to the infield and the outfield before the game begins.

**QUESTION: Have there ever been any tripleheaders in major league baseball, and if so, when?**

There have been three tripleheaders, all in the National League: Brooklyn and Pittsburgh on Sept. 1, 1890; Baltimore and Louisville on Sept. 7, 1896, and Cincinnati and Pittsburgh on Oct. 2, 1920.

**QUESTION: Did the Yankees ever use the dugout on the third-base line at Yankee Stadium? If so, when did they change to the dugout on the first-base line?**

From the time Yankee Stadium opened in 1923 through 1945, the Yankees occupied the dugout along third base. In 1946, they shifted to the dugout along first base.

**QUESTION: Did Tris Speaker ever hit .400 or more and not win the league batting championship? Also, has the same thing ever happened to any other major league baseball player?**

It never happened to Speaker. His highest season's average was .389, with Cleveland of the American League in 1925, a year in which Harry Heilmann of Detroit won the batting crown, with .393. In baseball's so-called "modern era"—that is, since 1900—it has happened twice, both times in the American League. Shoeless Joe Jackson of Cleveland hit .408 in 1911, but Ty Cobb of Detroit hit .420. Cobb was involved again in 1922; this time his .401 was topped by the .420 of George Sisler of St. Louis.

**QUESTION: How many times have two players on one team hit a total of 100 homers or more in a season?**

Twice. In 1927, Babe Ruth had 60 homers and Lou Gehrig had 47. In 1961, two more New York Yankee players duplicated the feat when Roger Maris hit 61 and Mickey Mantle hit 54.

**QUESTION: Has a baseball player ever led his league in both batting average and slugging average? Has a player ever led both leagues in these two categories?**

Yes, to both questions, with too many instances to enumerate here. The last man to lead both leagues was Billy Williams of the Chicago Cubs, in 1972. He hit .333, and his slugging average was .606.

**QUESTION: How many players have hit a home run on their first time at bat in the major leagues? Has any player ever hit a home run on the first pitch on opening day?**

As of the end of the 1979 season, 24 players in the National League and 22 in the American had hit home runs in their first time at bat. And two did so on the first pitch thrown to them: Eddie Morgan of the St. Louis Cardinals, on April 14, 1936, connected as a pinch-hitter in the seventh inning of a 12–7 loss to the Chicago Cubs. Chuck Tannner, now the manager of the Pittsburgh Pirates, duplicated Morgan's feat on April 12, 1955, having just started out with the Milwaukee Braves. Tanner, who was also batting as a pinch-hitter, hit his homer in the eighth inning of a 4–2 victory over the Cincinnati Reds.

There is no record of a player's hitting a home run on the first pitch of any major league opening day, however.

**QUESTION: Who has hit the most career grand-slam homers in each league?**

Lou Gehrig of the New York Yankees leads the American League with 23 (1923 through 1939) and Willie McCovey of the San Francisco Giants and the San Diego Padres leads the National League with 18 (1959 through 1980).

**QUESTION: Did Roger Maris and Mickey Mantle ever hit back-to-back home runs in a World Series game?**

Yes. On Oct. 14, 1964, in the sixth game against the St. Louis Cardinals, Maris and Mantle hit consecutive pitches for homers in the sixth inning. The Yankees won the game, 8–3, but lost the next game, 7–5, and the Series.

**QUESTION: Which major league player with 300 or more career home runs has the lowest 1-to-1 strikeout ratio?**

Jo DiMaggio of the New York Yankees, with 361 home runs and 369 strikeouts.

**QUESTION: I recently read that Eddie Murray was the fifth switch-hitter to hit 30 or more home runs in one season. Who were the four others?**

Rip Collins, Mickey Mantle, Reggie Smith and Ken Singleton.

**QUESTION: Which switch-hitter has the most home runs in a career and in a season?**

Mickey Mantle of the New York Yankees, with 536 for his career and 54 in the 1961 season, is the leader in both categories.

**QUESTION: How many years and games did Babe Ruth and Hank Aaron play, and how many times at bat did each have when they reached 714 career homers?**

Ruth played 22 years and 2,503 games. He hit his 714th homer in his last time at bat, 8,399, in 1935. He then was ending his career with the Boston Braves.

Aaron played 23 years and 3,298 games. He hit his 714th home run in his 11,249th at bat at the beginning of the 1974 season. He ended his career in 1976 with 755 homers.

Ruth had 8.5 home runs for each 100 times at bat, while Aaron had 6.1 home runs.

**QUESTION: How many players have hit 500 or more career home runs, and which of those players were under 6 feet tall?**

There are 12 such players, but only Mel Ott (5 feet 9 inches), Willie Mays (5–10½) and Mickey Mantle (5–11½) were under 6 feet. The others were Hank Aaron, Harmon Killebrew and Jimmy Foxx (each 6 feet); Frank Robinson, Eddie Mathews and Ernie Banks (6–1); Babe Ruth (6–2); Ted Williams (6–3) and Willie McCovey (6–4).

**QUESTION: How many times did Babe Ruth hit two or more home runs in a game? When did he hit the last home run of his career?**

Ruth hit two or more home runs on 72 occasions. He hit his last three homers—712, 713 and 714—on the same day, May 25, 1935. He was then with the Boston Braves and the game was played against the Pirates in Pittsburgh's Forbes Field. Ruth retired a few days later.

## QUESTION: Who hit the first World Series home run?

Jimmy Sebring, a Pittsburgh Pirates outfielder, hit a home run in the first game of the first Series in 1903. Sebring hit .367 in the Series, to lead all batters, but the Boston Red Sox won, 5 games to 3.

## QUESTION: Did all nine starting players on a major league baseball team ever hit a home run in one game? If not, what is the record for the most home runs by one team in one game? In one inning?

No, to the first question. Three teams in the American League and four in the National League hold the record with eight homers each in a game: New York Yankees (1939), Minnesota Twins (1963) and the Boston Red Sox (1977) of the A.L.; Milwaukee Braves (1953), Cincinnati Reds (1956), San Francisco Giants (1961) and Montreal Expos (1978) of the N.L.

The New York Giants (1939), the Philadelphia Phillies (1949), the San Francisco Giants (1961) and Minnesota (1966) are tied for the record with five home runs each in one inning.

## QUESTION: Which rookies in the American and National Leagues had the most hits and the most home runs in one season?

Most hits: A.L., Tony Oliva, Minnesota, 217 in 161 games in 1964; N.L., Lloyd Waner, Pittsburgh, 223 in 150 games in 1927.

Most home runs: A.L., Al Rosen, Cleveland, 37 in 155 games in 1950; N.L., Wally Berger, Boston, 38 in 151 games in 1930 and Frank Robinson, Cincinnati, 38 in 152 games in 1956.

## QUESTION: Have any major league players ever hit grand-slam homers in consecutive innings?

Yes, three players. Jim Gentile of the Baltimore Orioles, on May 9, 1961, hit grand-slam homers in the first and second innings. Jim Northrup of the Detroit Tigers, on June 24, 1968, did it in the fifth and sixth innings. Frank Robinson, also of the Orioles, on June 26, 1970, smashed grand-slam homers in the fifth and sixth innings.

## QUESTION: Has any baseball player hit a grand-slam home run in his first time at bat in the major leagues? Of those players who never hit a home run during their careers, who had the greatest number of times at bat?

No modern-era player has hit a grand-slam homer in his first turn at bat in the majors, but one player did in the old era. He was William Duggleby of the Philadelphia Phillies, who connected in the second inning on April 21, 1898.

There is no record of a longtime nonpitcher's failing to hit a home run. However, Tommy Thevenow, a National League infielder who began playing in 1924 and hit two homers in 1926, then went to bat 3,-347 times—the rest of his major league career—without ever hitting another. That's a record.

QUESTION: How many pitchers have hit grand-slam homers in the World Series?

Of the 12 grand-slam homers in World Series games, only the most recent, by Dave McNally of the Baltimore Orioles in 1970, has been hit by a pitcher.

QUESTION: Who holds the record in each major league for the most times at bat in a season without hitting a home run?

National League: Rabbit Maranville of Pittsburgh, 672 times at bat in 155 games in 1922. American League: Doc Cramer of Boston, 658 in 148 games in 1938.

QUESTION: Which pitcher in each league holds the record for the most home runs in a season? Which pitcher in each league is the career leader?

In the American League, Wes Ferrell of Cleveland hit nine home runs in 1931. In the National League, Don Newcombe of Brooklyn hit seven in 1955 and Don Drysdale of Los Angeles, after the Dodgers moved to that city, did it twice, in 1958 and 1965.

Ferrell is the A.L. career leader with 36. He also hit a homer as a pinch-hitter and a homer as a pitcher with Boston of the N.L. Warren Spahn is the N.L. career leader, with 35 homers.

QUESTION: How many major league baseball players have won the triple crown (leading a league in batting average, runs batted in and home runs in a single season)? Did any fail to be selected as most valuable player in his league the year he took the crown? If so, who was selected?

There have been 11 triple-crown winners: Ty Cobb of the Detroit Tigers, in 1909; Heinie Zimmerman of the Chicago Cubs, 1912; Rogers Hornsby of the St. Louis Cardinals, 1922 and 1925; Jimmy Foxx of the Philadelphia Athletics and Chuck Klein of the Philadelphia Phillies, both 1933; Lou Gehrig of the New York Yankees, 1934; Joe Medwick of the Cardinals, 1937; Ted Williams of the Boston Red Sox, 1942 and 1947;

Mickey Mantle of the Yankees, 1956; Frank Robinson of the Baltimore Orioles, 1966, and Carl Yastrzemski of the Red Sox, 1967.

Foxx, Medwick, Mantle, Robinson and Yastrzemski got m.v.p. awards in the years they won the crown.

Cobb's triple-crown season, 1909, preceded the inception of any m.v.p. award. In 1912, the year Zimmerman took the crown, the Chalmers Award, that era's equivalent of the m.v.p. citation, went to Larry Doyle, second baseman for the pennant-winning New York Giants. The Chalmers Award expired after the 1914 season, and there was no National League m.v.p. award again until 1924. Hornsby thus missed out in 1922. He was named m.v.p. in 1925, however, his second triple-crown season. In 1933, Carl Hubbell, the great pitcher for the Giants, who had again won the pennant, was selected instead of Klein. In 1934, Mickey Cochrane, the catcher for the pennant-winning Detroit Tigers, was named instead of Gehrig.

In 1942, Joe Gordon, Yankee second baseman, was named instead of Williams, who lost out again in 1947, to Joe DiMaggio. The Yanks had finished in first place both those seasons.

QUESTION: Which player in each league won the batting championship with the fewest number of at bats? The most at bats?

American League: Ty Cobb of the Detroit Tigers, 345 at bats for .368, in 1914; Tony Oliva, Minnesota Twins, 672 for .323, in 1964.

National League: Gene Hargrave, Cincinnati Reds, 326 for .353, in 1926; Pete Rose, Cincinnati, 680 for .338, in 1973.

QUESTION: In baseball, a triple is much more difficult to achieve than a home run. Who holds the season and career records in each league?

Sam Crawford, who played in both leagues, is the overall career leader, with 312 triples, 62 with Cincinnati from 1899 to 1902 and 250 with Detroit from 1903 to 1917. Ty Cobb is the American League career leader, with 297, of which 286 came with Detroit from 1905 to 1926 and 11 with Philadelphia, 1927–28. The National League leader is Honus Wagner, who hit 21 with Louisville from 1897 to 1899 and 231 with Pittsburgh from 1900 to 1917, for a total of 252.

The season-record holders are, in the National League, Owen Wilson of Pittsburgh, 36 in 1912, and, in the American, Shoeless Joe Jackson of Cleveland, 26 in 1912, and Crawford, 26 in 1914.

QUESTION: Have any major league baseball players hit three triples in one game? Four?

There have been many players in both leagues, too numerous to mention, who have hit three triples in a game, and some of those have been hit in succession. Two players have hit four triples in a game: George Strief of Philadelphia of the American Association (when it was a major league) on June 25, 1885, and Bill Joyce of the New York Giants on May 18, 1897.

QUESTION: Hank Aaron once hit at least 30 home runs and stole at least 30 bases in one season. When did he accomplish this feat, and how many other players have done it?

Aaron hit 44 home runs and stole 31 bases in 1963, when he played for the Milwaukee Braves. Four other players have reached the 30–30 mark a total of nine times. They are Bobby Bonds, five times, with the San Francisco Giants in 1969 (32 home runs, 45 stolen bases) and 1973 (39, 43), the New York Yankees in 1975 (32, 30), the California Angels in 1977 (37, 41) and the Chicago White Sox and Texas Rangers in 1978 (31, 43); Willie Mays, twice with the New York Giants in 1956 (36, 40) and 1957 (35, 38); Tommy Harper of the Milwaukee Brewers in 1970 (31, 38), and Ken Williams of the St. Louis Browns in 1922 (39, 37).

**QUESTION: How many baseball players have hit for the cycle (single, double, triple and home run) in a game? Who holds the major league record for such a feat?**

Including the 1980 season, 98 players in the National League and 78 players in the American League have hit for the cycle. Bob Meusel of the New York Yankees did it three times (1921, 1922 and 1928); Babe Herman is the only other player to match that, hitting for the cycle twice with the Brooklyn Dodgers (1931) and once with the Chicago Cubs (1933).

**QUESTION: Who are the on-base career leaders in the American and National Leagues, and how is the on-base average figured?**

Stan Musial leads the N.L. with 5,282; Ty Cobb is the A.L. leader with 5,179.

The on-base average is calculated by dividing a batter's total number of times he reaches base by his total number of times at bat. Total times at bat differs from the official times at bat because the category includes those instances that are not counted as official times at bat: receiving a base on balls; being hit by a pitched ball; being awarded first base because of interference or obstruction, and, in the National League, hitting a sacrifice fly.

**QUESTION: Why did you give the on-base total leaders and not the on-base average leaders in a recent baseball answer? Also, is the total figure of 5,179 for Ty Cobb correct, since The Baseball Encyclopedia shows he had 4,191 hits and 1,249 walks for a total of 5,440?**

On-base average is still not an official baseball statistic, and it is only in recent years that the American and National Leagues have been providing such averages as a service.

At one time, totals were not kept of a batter's walks, so that the 5,440 total for Cobb, who began his career in 1905, is not official but rather the result of digging through old box scores and adding his walks to his totals that were kept in later years. The 5,179 total is official.

**QUESTION: Which player had the highest batting average in his rookie year: Babe Ruth, Willie Mays, Ted Williams, Mickey Mantle or Hank Aaron?**

Williams, with .327 in 1939, had the highest average. Ruth was mainly a pitcher from 1914 through 1918. In 1919, the first year he played primarily in the outfield, he batted .322. Mays hit .274 in 1951, Mantle .267 in 1951 and Aaron .280 in 1954.

**QUESTION:** Jim Rice of the Boston Red Sox had 406 total bases in 1978, the first time the 400 mark had been reached in the American League since Joe DiMaggio had 418 in 1937. Is DiMaggio's total a record for the major leagues? For the American League?

No, to both questions. Babe Ruth holds the American and major league records, with 457 total bases in 1921. The National League record was set by Rogers Hornsby, with 450 in 1922.

**QUESTION:** Who holds the record for the most hits and the most consecutive hits in a nine-inning game? In an extra-inning game?

Wilbert Robinson, when he was playing for Baltimore of the National League, had seven consecutive hits in a nine-inning game in 1892. That feat was duplicated by Rennie Stennett of the Pittsburgh Pirates in 1975.

In extra-inning games, the record for the most hits, nine in an 18-inning game, was set by Johnny Burnett of the Cleveland Indians in 1932. The record for the most consecutive hits is held by Cesar Guiterrez of the Detroit Tigers, who had seven in a 12-inning contest in 1970.

**QUESTION:** Who got the first pinch hit in a World Series game?

Ira Thomas of the Detroit Tigers. He pinch hit for Charley O'Leary, the shortstop, in the last of the ninth inning of the first game of the 1908 Series against the Chicago Cubs. He came through with a single but the Cubs won the game, 10–6. Thirteen previous Series pinch-hitters—four in 1903, two in 1905, five in 1906, one in 1907 and one earlier in the Tiger half of the ninth in that 1908 game—had failed to get a hit.

**QUESTION:** Who are the five leading career singles hitters in major league baseball?

Ty Cobb, 3,052, Eddie Collins, 2,641, Pete Rose, 2,627, Willie Keeler, 2,534 and Honus Wagner, 2,426. Rose hit 137 singles in 1980 and extended his own National League record.

**QUESTION:** Which batters are the top 10 career leaders in strikeouts?

Willie Stargell (1,903); Lou Brock (1,730); Reggie Jackson (1,728); Bobby Bonds (1,713); Mickey Mantle (1,710); Harmon Killebrew (1,699); Tony Perez (1,628); Richie Allen (1,556); Willie McCovey (1,550); and Frank Robinson (1,532). This includes the 1980 season.

**QUESTION:** What was the highest season batting average for a pitcher in each major league? Also, did a player ever win a Gold Glove award for fielding in two different positions?

Walter Johnson of the Washington Senators batted .440 in 30 games in 1925 and Jack Bentley of the New York Giants batted .406 in 31 games in 1923.

From 1957 through 1960, the outfield awards were given for specific positions. Al Kaline of the Detroit Tigers won the award as a right fielder in 1958 and as a center fielder in 1959. Since 1961, there have been no specific designations for outfield positions; thus, Kaline remains the only player to win the award for two different positions.

QUESTION: Has there ever been a switch-pitcher in either the major or the minor leagues?

There is no record of any, though Paul Richards, who later became a major league catcher and then a major league manager, was supposedly an ambidextrous pitcher while in high school.

QUESTION: Has any pitcher ever been credited with three putouts in one inning? Any other fielder?

Only four pitchers have made three putouts in an inning, but many players in the other positions have accomplished that feat. The pitchers are: Jim Bagby Jr. of the Boston Red Sox in 1940; Bob Heffner of the Red Sox in 1963; Rick Reuschel of the Chicago Cubs in 1975; and Jim Beattie of the New York Yankees in 1978. In the case of a strikeout, the catcher, being the last man to handle the ball, gets credit for the putout.

QUESTION: I know there has been only one World Series no-hitter (Don Larsen's perfect game in 1956), but how many one-hitters have there been in the Series, and in what innings were the hits made?

There have been four one-hitters: Ed Reulbach of the Chicago Cubs against the Chicago White Sox in 1906 (the hit was made with none out in the seventh); Claude Passeau of the Cubs against the Detroit Tigers in 1945 (two out in the second); Floyd Bevens of the New York Yankees against the Brooklyn Dodgers in 1947 (two out in the ninth); and Jim Lonborg of the Boston Red Sox against the St. Louis Cardinals in 1967 (two out in the eighth).

QUESTION: Please name the three pitchers who have the best career percentages as New York Yankees.

On the basis of 100 or more decisions, the top three are: Spud Chandler,109 victories and 43 defeats for .717; Vic Raschi, 120–50 for 706, and Whitey Ford, 236–106 for .690.

QUESTION: Has a major league pitcher led his league in strikeouts and bases on balls in the same season?

Yes, several times. A few examples: Bob Feller of the Cleveland Indians in 1938, with 240 strikeouts and 208 walks, and again in 1941, with 260 and 194; Nolan Ryan of the California Angels in 1976, with 327 and 183, again in 1977, with 341 and 204, and again in 1978, with 303 and 148; and Bob Turley of the Baltimore Orioles in 1954, with 185 and 181.

QUESTION: Which pitchers in baseball's modern era have yielded the most bases on balls in a game and in a season? Which pitcher holds the record for the longest game without a walk?

Game: Bruno Haas of the Philadelphia Athletics, 16, on June 13, 1915 (his first major league game).

Season: Bob Feller of the Cleveland Indians, 208 in 278 innings in 1938.

Longest game without a walk: 21 innings, by Charles (Babe) Adams of the Pittsburgh Pirates on July 17, 1914.

QUESTION: Which pitcher in the major leagues gave the most walks in one inning?

Dolly Gray of Washington set the major league record on Aug. 28, 1909, by walking eight men, seven in succession, in the second inning of the first game of a doubleheader. The National League record is seven, held by Tony Mullane of Baltimore (June 18, 1894) and Bob Ewing of Cincinnati (April 19, 1902). Ewing's poor performance was in his first major league start.

**QUESTION: Which five pitchers are the career leaders in the least hits and the least walks per nine innings?**

On the basis of pitching at least 1,500 innings, the leaders among those who were active after 1900 are (not including the 1980 season):

Least hits: Nolan Ryan, 6.27; Sandy Koufax, 6.79; Andy Messersmith, 6.91; Hoyt Whilhelm, 7.02, and Sam McDowell, 7.03.

Least walks: Deacon Phillippe, 1.25; Babe Adams, 1.29; Addie Joss, 1.43; Cy Young, 1.49, and Jesse Tannehill, 1.55.

**QUESTION: Since 1900, what pitchers hold the record for the most wild pitches in a season and a career? What pitchers hit the most batsmen in a season and a career? What batsman holds the record for having been hit the most times by pitchers in a season and a career?**

Leon Ames of the New York Giants had 30 wild pitches in 1905. Phil Niekro, now with the Atlanta Braves, had 188 wild pitches at the end of the 1980 season.

In 1900, Joe McGinnity of the Brooklyn Dodgers hit 41 batsmen. Walter Johnson of the Washington Senators holds the career record with 206.

Ron Hunt set the season record for being hit by pitches with 50, when he was with the Montreal Expos in 1971. Hunt, who also played for the New York Mets, among other teams, holds the career mark of 243.

**QUESTION: How many pitchers have won two complete games in one day? When was the last time this happened in each league? Who holds the record for losing the most consecutive games?**

Twenty-five pitchers in the National League have won a total of 32 doubleheaders, with Joe (Iron Man) McGinnity of the New York Giants accomplishing the feat three times in 1903. The last National Leaguer to do it was Hi Bell of the St. Louis Cardinals on July 19, 1924. He pitched two nine-inning games, winning 6–1 and 2–1.

Nine pitchers in the American League have accomplished the feat, for a total of 10 times. The last to do so was Dutch Levsen of the Cleveland Indians on Aug. 28, 1926. He hurled two nine-inning games, winning 6–1 and 5–1.

Cliff Curtis of the Boston Braves lost 23 consecutive games between June 13, 1910, and May 22, 1911.

**QUESTION: Have there ever been two no-hit games on the same day? Has there ever been a game in which both pitchers hurled no-hit ball for nine or more innings?**

Once, for both questions. On April 22, 1898, Ted Breitenstein of the Cincinnati Reds beat the Pittsburgh Pirates, 11–0, and Jim Hughes of the Baltimore Orioles defeated the Boston Red Sox, 8–0. On May 2, 1917, Fred Toney, also of the Reds, defeated the Chicago Cubs, 1–0, in 10 innings, with Jim Vaughn, the losing pitcher, giving up only two hits in the 10th.

**QUESTION: How many no-hitters of less than nine innings have there been?** This could happen in case of rain, or where the visiting pitcher is hurling a no-hitter and loses on walks and an error, thus ending the game after 8½ innings.

The record book lists, since 1900, 20 no-hitters of less than nine innings. The last was in 1967, when Dean Chance of Minnesota pitched five perfect innings against Boston, winning 2–0.

**QUESTION: Who pitched the first perfect winning games in the American and National Leagues?**

A.L.: Cy Young of Boston against Philadelphia, 3–0, on May 5, 1904.

N.L.: Jim Bunning of Philadelphia against the New York Mets, 6–0, on June 31, 1964.

There were, however, two perfect games in the N.L. in 1880, before the modern era began with the formation of the American League in 1901.

**QUESTION: Which pitchers lead in each league in opening-day victories?**

Walter Johnson of the Washington Senators tops the American League with nine victories, of which seven were shutouts, in 1910, 1913–17, 1919, 1924 and 1926. He lost five games, in 1912, 1918, 1920–21 and 1923.

In the National League, Juan Marichal of the San Francisco Giants won six times, in 1962, 1964, 1966 and 1971–73. He lost twice, in 1965 and 1967, and had two no-decisions, in 1968–69.

Tom Seaver, when he was with the New York Mets, won six times, in 1971–73 and 1975–77. He had four no-decisions, in 1968–70 and 1974. As a member of the Cincinnati Reds, he lost in 1979, did not pitch the opening-day game in 1980, and failed to get a decision in 1981.

**QUESTION: Since the American League came into existence in 1901, how many 30-game winners have there been in the majors? Have the New York Yankees ever had one?**

John Chesbro of the New York Highlanders, later the Yankees, won 41 games and lost 12 in 1904. He is the only man to win 30 or more games for the New York team.

The other 30-game winners were, in the National League: 1903, Joe McGinnity (31–20) and Christy Mathewson (30–13), both of the New York Giants; 1904, McGinnity (35–8) and Mathewson (33–12); 1905 and 1908, Mathewson (31–9) and (37–11); 1915, Grover Cleveland Alexander, Philadelphia Phillies (31–10); 1916 and 1917, Alexander (33–12) and (30–13); and 1934, Dizzy Dean, St. Louis Cardinals, (30–7).

In the A.L.: 1901, Cy Young, Boston Somersets, later Red Sox (33–10); 1902, Young (32–10); 1908, Ed Walsh, Chicago White Sox (40–15); 1910, Jack Coombs, Philadelphia Athletics (31–9); 1912, Joe Wood, Boston (34–5) and Walter Johnson, Washington Senators (32–12); 1913, Johnson (36–7); 1920, Jim Bagby, Cleveland Indians (31–12); 1931,

Lefty Grove, Philadelphia (31–4); and 1968, Denny McLain, Detroit Tigers (31–6).

**QUESTION: As a follow-up on your recent question about pitchers who won 30 games or more in a season, how many teams with such pitchers failed to win the pennant?**

There have been 13 pitchers in both leagues who have won 30 or more games in a season 21 times. In the American League, the teams that did not win the pennant were Boston in 1901 and 1902 (Cy Young was the pitcher), New York in 1904 (John Chesbro), Chicago in 1908 (Ed Walsh) and Washington in 1912 and 1913 (Walter Johnson).

In the National League, New York in 1903 (Joe McGinnity and Christy Mathewson) and in 1908 (Mathewson) and Philadelphia in 1916 and 1917 (Grover Cleveland Alexander).

**QUESTION: Which pitcher holds the record for the most shutouts in a World Series? Which team scored the fewest runs? Which player batted in the most runs in one Series? Which player holds the Series career record for runs batted in?**

Christy Mathewson of the New York Giants pitched three shutouts in 1905 against the Philadelphia Athletics. The Giants won the Series, 4–1. The Los Angeles Dodgers scored only two runs in 1966, while losing four straight games to the Baltimore Orioles.

Bobby Richardson of the New York Yankees drove in 12 runs in the 1960 series against Pittsburgh, which the Pirates won in seven games. Mickey Mantle, also a Yankee, holds the career record with 40, in 1951–53, 1955–58 and 1960–64.

**QUESTION: In the 1980 World Series, no pitcher for the Philadelphia Phillies or the Kansas City Royals hurled a complete nine-inning game. When did this last occur?**

In the 1974 Series between Oakland and Los Angeles. In the 1976 Series, Catfish Hunter of the New York Yankees, pitched 8⅔ innings before losing to Cincinnati, 4–3, in the bottom of the ninth. He was not relieved, and he was the only one in that Series to come that close to a complete game.

**QUESTION: Tom Seaver was named rookie of the year in the National League in 1967, when the New York Mets finished in last place. Has any other player on a last-place team won that honor? Was a player on a team that finished last ever selected as the Most Valuable Player?**

There have been a number of rookies picked from last-place teams, with the most recent being Alfredo Griffin of the Toronto Blue Jays in 1979. No player on a last-place team has been named the most valuable player.

**QUESTION: How do Nolan Ryan and Tom Seaver rank in career strikeouts?**

Ryan, at the end of the 1980 season, ranked fourth with 3,109 and Seaver was fifth with 2,988. Walter Johnson was first with 3,508, Gaylord Perry second with 3,276 and Bob Gibson third with 3,117.

**QUESTION:** I understand that, since 1972, records have been kept on Nolan Ryan's won-lost ratio when he was ahead in the late innings. What is that record?

From 1972 through 1980, Ryan won 112 games and lost 3 when he was ahead in the eighth inning. In five other games, he did not figure in the decision.

**QUESTION:** Please list the career pitching statistics of Tom Seaver and Don Sutton.

As of the end of the 1980 season, Seaver has pitched 3,622 innings, has allowed 2,895 hits, walked 1,008 and struck out 2,988, won 245 games and lost 141. His earned-run average is 2.60.

Sutton, in 3,728 innings, has given up 3,200 hits and 966 walks, struck out 2,652 and has won 230 games and lost 175. His earned-run average is 3.07.

**QUESTION:** Who holds the records for the most putouts in a nine-inning game and in an extra-inning game? Which pitcher has made the most career errors?

The record for the most putouts in a nine-inning game is 22, held by three players: Tom Jones of the St. Louis Browns (May 11, 1906), Hal Chase, New York Highlanders, later the Yankees (Sept. 21, 1906) and Ernie Banks, Chicago Cubs (May 9, 1963). Walter Holke of the Boston Red Sox had a record 42 putouts in a 26-inning game on May 1, 1920.

Jim Vaughn of the Chicago Cubs committed 64 errors between 1913 and 1921, the career record for pitchers.

**QUESTION:** Which third baseman in each league holds the record for the most errors in a season? For the fewest errors in a season?

Most errors: Charlie (Piano Legs) Hickman of the New York Giants, 91 in 118 games in 1900, and Sammy Strang of the Chicago White Sox, 64 in 137 in 1902.

Fewest errors: Ken Reitz of the St. Louis Cardinals, 8 in 150 in 1980 and Don Money of the Milwaukee Brewers, 5 in 157 in 1974.

**QUESTION:** Since the inception of the Gold Glove awards, which major league player has won the most awards in each position?

The Gold Glove awards began in 1957, when it included both the National and American Leagues in a single listing. The next year the awards were given to the top fielders in each league. The major league leaders in each position are:

Pitcher: Jim Kaat (16 awards); first base: George Scott (8); second base: Bill Mazeroski (8); third base: Brooks Robinson (16); shortstop: Luis Aparicio and Mark Belanger (each 8 times); outfield: Roberto Clemente (12), Willie Mays and Al Kaline (each 9 times), and catcher, Johnny Bench (10).

**QUESTION:** Have there ever been any unassisted triple plays in the major leagues? If so, please list them.

There have been eight, the most famous being the one executed by Bill Wambsganss, Cleveland second baseman, against Brooklyn in the fifth game of the 1920 World Series, the only time this has happened in the Series. The others were executed by Neal Ball, Cleveland second baseman, against Boston in 1909; George Burns, Boston first baseman, against Cleveland in 1923; Ernie Padgett, Boston Braves shortstop, against Philadelphia in 1923; Glenn Wright, Pittsburgh shortstop, against St. Louis in 1925; Jimmy Cooney, Chicago Cubs shortstop, against Pittsburgh in 1927; Johnny Neun, Detroit first baseman, against Cleveland in 1927; and Ron Hansen, Washington shortstop, against Cleveland in 1968. All the triple plays were made with runners on first and second. Another oddity: Cleveland was involved in five of them.

**QUESTION: The recent answer to a question about unassisted triple plays brought to mind the possibility of unassisted double plays by a major league catcher. Have there been any?**

Yes, 38 in the National League and 31 in the American League. (Remember that a strikeout counts as a putout for the catcher.)

Only one catcher, Frank Crossin of the St. Louis Browns, in 1914, has ever made two unassisted double plays in a season. Nine catchers have made two unassisted double plays in a career. They are, in addition to Crossin: Boss Schmidt, with the Detroit Tigers; Mike Gonzalez, St. Louis Cardinals; Clint Courtney, Baltimore Orioles; Yogi Berra, New York Yankees; Bob Rodgers, California Angels; Chris Cannizzaro and Bob (Hawk) Taylor, New York Mets; and Ed Bailey, San Francisco Giants and Chicago Cubs.

**QUESTION: How many errors did Willie Mays make in his career, and what was his lifetime fielding average? Also, how many times did he win the Gold Glove award?**

Mays committed 156 errors and had a fielding average of .981. He won the Gold Glove award 11 times (1958 through 1968).

**QUESTION: Babe Ruth is profusely listed in the record books for his hitting and his pitching. I am told he is also listed for stealing bases. Is this correct?**

Ruth is one of seven men who share the record for stealing two bases in one inning in the World Series. He did it in the fifth inning of the second game in 1921 against the New York Giants. The others are: George Browne, Giants, 1905; Jim Slagle, Chicago Cubs, 1907; Ty Cobb, Detroit Tigers, 1908; Eddie Collins, Chicago White Sox, 1917; Lou Brock, St. Louis Cardinals, 1967; and Davey Lopes, Los Angeles Dodgers, 1974.

**QUESTION: When Lou Brock of the St. Louis Cardinals broke Maury Wills's record of 104 stolen bases in a season, in what game did it occur and which base did he steal? Also, who presented him with the record-breaking base?**

Brock stole two bases on Sept. 10, 1974. The first steal, in the first inning, tied the record of the Los Angeles Dodgers star. In the seventh inning, Brock hit a single and then stole second. The game was stopped and James (Cool Papa) Bell, a leading base stealer in the Negro Leagues and a member of the Baseball Hall of Fame, presented the base to Brock, who went on to finish the season with 118 stolen bases, a record that still stands.

**QUESTION:** Has anyone ever stolen second, third and home in one inning? Did Willie Mays or Maury Wills ever do it? Who were the last players in each league to accomplish it?

Many players have stolen their way home in one inning. The last player to do so in the N.L. was Harvey Hendrick of Brooklyn on June 12, 1928, so obviously Mays or Wills failed to accomplish the feat. Dave Nelson of the Texas Rangers, on Aug. 30, 1974, was the last A.L. player to do it.

**QUESTION:** What are the modern-day league records for stolen bases by one team in a single game?

National League: 11, by the New York Giants against the Boston Braves on June 20, 1912, and the St. Louis Cardinals against the Pittsburgh Pirates on Aug. 13, 1916 (a five-inning game).

American League: 15, New York Yankees against the St. Louis Browns on Sept. 28, 1911.

**QUESTION:** Has there ever been a triple steal in a World Series game? Have there ever been two such sets of steals in any game? When was the last time a triple steal occurred during the regular season?

There has never been a triple steal in a Series game. On July 25, 1930, the Philadelphia Athletics executed two triple steals against the Cleveland Indians, the only time this has happened in baseball history. On May 3, 1980, the Oakland A's pulled a triple steal against the Detroit Tigers in the third inning, with Dwayne Murphy stealing home, Mitchell Page third and Wayne Gross second.

**QUESTION:** What were the shortest and longest nine-inning games, in time elapsed? What were the longest extra-inning games, in time elapsed and in innings?

Shortest nine-inning game: 51 minutes, on Sept. 28, 1919, New York Giants 6, Philadelphia 1.

Longest: 4 hours, 18 minutes, on Oct. 2, 1962, Los Angeles 8, San Francisco 7.

Longest (innings): 26, on May 1, 1920. Brooklyn 1, Boston 1.

Longest (time): 7 hours, 23 minutes (23 innings), on May 31, 1964, San Francisco 8, Mets 6.

**QUESTION:** What is the record for the most men left on bases by one team in a major league season? In a game? Both teams in a game? Also, what is the record for most men left on base by a team that failed to score?

The 1941 St. Louis Browns left 1,334 men on base in 157 games. The New York Yankees left 20 men stranded against the Boston Red Sox on Sept. 21, 1956. The record for two clubs in one game is 30, which has happened four times: Brooklyn Dodgers 16, Pittsburgh Pirates 14, on June 30, 1893; Yankees, 15, Chicago White Sox 15, on Aug. 27, 1935; New York Giants 17, Philadelphia Phillies 13, on July 18, 1943, and Los Angeles Angels 15, Washington Senators 15, on July 21, 1961.

Four teams in the American League hold the record of 15 men stranded in shutout defeats: the Yankees against the Browns on May 22, 1913; the Senators against the Cleveland Indians on July 29, 1931; the

Browns against the Yankees on Aug. 1, 1941, and the Kansas City Royals against the Detroit Tigers on May 12, 1975.

**QUESTION: What is the record for most runs scored by a team in one inning in the American League and in the National League? By two clubs in a game? What is the record in each league for the most runs scored in an inning with two out?**

The Boston Red Sox hold the American League record with 17 runs, scored in the seventh inning against the Detroit Tigers on June 18, 1953; the Brooklyn Dodgers hold the National League record with 15, in the first inning against the Cincinnati Reds on May 21, 1952.

The record for both teams in an inning in the A.L. is 19, with the Cleveland Indians accounting for 13 and Boston 6 in the eighth inning on April 10, 1977; in the N.L., the record is 17, with the Boston Braves scoring 10 and the New York Giants 7 in the ninth inning on June 20, 1912.

The American League record for the most runs scored with two out is 13. Cleveland did it against Boston in the sixth inning on July 7, 1923, and the Kansas City A's did it against the Chicago White Sox in the second inning on April 21, 1956. In the National League, the record is 12, with Brooklyn hammering Cincinnati twice: in the first inning on May 21, 1952, and in the eighth inning on Aug. 8, 1954.

**QUESTION: Which team in the major leagues has the best won-lost record since 1900?**

The New York Yankees, as of the end of the 1980 season, had the best record, 6,890 victories and 5,139 defeats for a .573 winning percentage.

**QUESTION: How many teams in the major leagues have won 100 games or more and have not won the pennant? Who did finish first in those years?**

Eight teams failed to win the pennant under those circumstances. The eight and the teams they finished behind were:

1909: Chicago Cubs, 104–49 (finished behind the Pittsburgh Pirates, 110–42).

1915: Detroit Tigers, 100–54 (Boston Red Sox, 101–50).

1942: Brooklyn Dodgers, 104–50 (St. Louis Cardinals, 106–48).

1954: New York Yankees, 103–51 (Cleveland Indians, 111–43).

1961: Detroit, 101–61 (Yankees, 109–53).

1962: Los Angeles Dodgers, 102–63 (San Francisco Giants, 103–62).

1980: Yankees, 103–59 and Baltimore Orioles, 100–62. The Yankees won the American League East title, with the Orioles second, and the Yankees were then beaten by the Kansas City Royals (97–65) in the championship series for the pennant.

**QUESTION: What were the biggest margins between the pennant winners and the second-place teams in both major leagues?**

In the National League, the 1902 Pittsburgh Pirates finished first with 103 games won and 36 games lost, for a percentage of .741. The Brooklyn Dodgers were 27½ games behind with a 75–63 record and .543 percentage.

In the American League, the 1936 New York Yankees finished 19½ games in the lead with a 102–51 record and .667 percentage, compared with the Detroit Tigers' 83–71 record and .539 percentage.

**QUESTION: Which World Series winner had the lowest won-lost percentage in capturing the pennant?**

The Oakland A's, in 1974, finished the season with a record of 90–72, for a .556 average, and then defeated the Los Angeles Dodgers in the Series, four games to one.

The Philadelphia Phillies almost duplicated that in 1980, winning the pennant with a 91–71—.562 record and then defeating the Kansas City Royals in the Series, 4–2.

**QUESTION: Pittsburgh came back to win the 1979 World Series, 4–3, after trailing Baltimore, 3 games to 1. How many other teams have accomplished this feat, and when?**

In 1903, the Boston Red Sox defeated Pittsburgh in a best-of-nine series, 5 games to 3.

In 1925, Pittsburgh against the Washington Senators.

In 1958, the New York Yankees against the Milwaukee Braves.

In 1968, the Detroit Tigers against the St. Louis Cardinals.

**QUESTION: How many teams have come back from a 3–1 deficit in the World Series to tie it, and then lost the seventh game?**

This has occurred only twice. In 1967, the Boston Red Sox tied the St. Louis Cardinals after trailing 3–1, then lost the decisive game at home, 7–2. In 1972, the Cincinnati Reds tied the Oakland Athletics, then lost, 3–2, also at home.

**QUESTION: Has any team ever come from behind to win the World Series in the bottom of the last inning of the seventh game?**

In 1912, the Boston Red Sox scored twice in the bottom of the 10th inning to defeat the New York Giants, 3–2, thus winning the Series, four games to three. Since there was one tie during that Series, the final game was actually the eighth.

**QUESTION: Which league has won more World Series? Which teams have never won a Series since opening in their current cities, including 1980?**

The American League leads the National League, 45 to 32. The following teams have never won a Series: Toronto, Milwaukee, Texas, Kansas City, Minnesota, Seattle and California in the A.L.; Montreal, Houston, Atlanta, San Diego and San Francisco in the N.L.

**QUESTION: Which major league teams have had three or more 20-game winners in a season?**

In the National League, the Chicago Cubs (1903), the New York Giants (1904, 1905, 1913 and 1920), the Pittsburgh Pirates (1902) and the Cincinnati Reds (1923) each have had three pitchers winning at least 20 games in a season. The 1906 Cubs also had three, but one of them, Jack Taylor, won 9 of the 20 with the St. Louis Cardinals.

48

In the American League, the Chicago White Sox (1920) and the Baltimore Orioles (1971) each have had four 20-game winners in a season. Clubs with three such winners were: the Boston Red Sox (1903 and 1904); the White Sox (1907); the Cleveland Indians (1906, 1920, 1951, 1952 and 1956); the Detroit Tigers (1907); the Philadelphia Athletics (1931); the Orioles (1970), and the Oakland A's (1973).

**QUESTION: The Cincinnati Reds have had the National League's most valuable player six times between 1970 and 1978: Johnny Bench, 1970 and 1972; Pete Rose, 1973; Joe Morgan, 1975 and 1976; and George Foster, 1977. Has any other team equaled or come close to that domination of the award? Has any team had three double-winners on their roster at the same time?**

Within a 10-year period, 1954–63, New York Yankee players won the American League's m.v.p. award eight times. They were Yogi Berra, 1954 and 1955; Mickey Mantle, 1956, 1957 and 1962; Roger Maris, 1960 and 1961, and Elston Howard, 1963.

Berra had also won in 1951. Thus the 1963 Yankees had three multiple winners (Berra, Mantle and Maris) on the same team.

**QUESTION: Has a member of a losing team ever been selected as the Most Valuable Player in the World Series?**

Yes. In 1960, Bobby Richardson, the New York Yankees second baseman, was named. The Pittsburgh Pirates won the Series, 4–3. Richardson, a light hitter with a career average of .266, batted .367, with 11 hits in 30 times at bat. One of his hits was the seventh grand slam in Series competition. He also set records, still standing, for the most runs batted in for a game, six, and the most for a Series, 12.

**QUESTION: How many years has the most-valuable-player award been given in the World Series? Which team has the most winners? Has any player ever won it twice?**

The honor was instituted in 1955 by Sport magazine, which continues to award it. The New York Yankees lead, with seven winners. Three players have won the award twice: Sandy Koufax of the Los Angeles Dodgers in 1963 and 1965; Bob Gibson of the St. Louis Cardinals in 1964 and 1967, and Reggie Jackson in 1973, as an Oakland A, and in 1977, as a Yankee.

**QUESTION: I always hear about the good old days in the Polo Grounds and Ebbets Field, where the old New York Giants and Brooklyn Dodgers played, in which there were impossible fences and short porches for batters. But I can never get the real dimensions of the fields. Would you please list them, and also those of Yankee Stadium before it was remodeled?**

Polo Grounds: left field, 279 feet; center field, 483 feet; right field, 257 feet 8 inches.

Ebbets Field: left field, 343 feet; center field, 393 feet; right field, 297 feet.

Yankee Stadium: left field, 301 feet; center field, 461 feet; right field, 296 feet.

QUESTION: When was Fenway Park in Boston rebuilt, and what were the dimensions of the field then as compared with today's? The Philadelphia Phillies used to play in Baker Bowl. When did they stop playing there, and what were the field's dimensions?

Fenway Park was rebuilt in 1934. The dimensions before the rebuilding: right field, 325 feet; left field, 318 feet; center field, 593 feet. The dimensions now: right field, 302 feet; left field, 315 feet; center field, 390 feet.

The Phillies moved to Shibe Park on July 4, 1938. Baker Bowl's dimensions: right field, 280 feet 6 inches; left field, 341 feet 6 inches; center field, 408 feet.


QUESTION: Which team in the American League and in the National League holds the record for the most consecutive games without being shut out? Which player in each league holds the record for hitting safely in the most games in a season?

The New York Yankees, from Aug. 3, 1931, through Aug. 2, 1933, went 308 games without being shut out. The Philadelphia Phillies, from Aug. 17, 1893, through May 10, 1895, went 182 games without being blanked.

Rod Carew of the Minnesota Twins, in 1977, hit safely in 131 games. Chuck Klein of the Phillies, in 1930, hit safely in 135 games.


QUESTION: When did the St. Louis Browns leave that city? Who was the last manager, what ball park did the team play in, and what were the colors of the team's uniform?

The Browns moved to Baltimore after the 1953 season. Marty Marion was the last manager. The team played in the old Sportsman's Park and wore brown and orange uniforms.


QUESTION: Has any major league baseball team ever gone through an entire season without being shut out?

Yes, the New York Yankees in 1932 in 156 games, two more than the normal 154-game schedule in those years. The Brooklyn Dodgers, in 1953, were shut out only once in 155 games, and the Cincinnati Reds, in 1970, after the schedule had been increased to 162 games, also were shut out only once.


QUESTION: In each major league, which team holds the record for most double plays in a season?

The American League record was set by the old Philadelphia Athletics, who made 217 double plays in 1949.

In the National League, there are two marks. The Los Angeles Dodgers completed 198 double plays in 1958, a 154-game season. The 162-game record is 215, set by the Pittsburgh Pirates in 1966.


QUESTION: Everyone talks about the "home-team advantage," but how often did the home team in the major professional sports—baseball, football, basketball, hockey and soccer—win in the most recent full season in each sport?

Baseball (1980): In the American League, the home teams won 582 games and lost 547; in the National League, 556–416.

National Football League (1979): 131–93.

National Basketball Association (1979–80): 588–314.

National Hockey League (1979–80): 427–271 and 142 ties.

North American Soccer League (1980): 251–133.

To further emphasize the home-team advantage, Montreal is the only active club in the N.H.L. to show a career record of winning more games on the road than it has lost (765–726 and 325 ties).

**QUESTION: In the four major professional sports—baseball, football, basketball and hockey—which teams have won the most championships?**

Baseball: The New York Yankees have won the World Series 22 times, the St. Louis Cardinals and the Philadelphia-Oakland A's, each eight times.

Football: The Green Bay Packers have won the National Football League championship or the Super Bowl 11 times, the Chicago Bears seven times and the Cleveland Browns, the Detroit Lions, New York Giants and Pittsburgh Steelers, each four times.

Basketball: The Boston Celtics have won the National Basketball Association title 14 times, the Minneapolis–Los Angeles Lakers seven times.

Hockey: The Montreal Canadiens have won the Stanley Cup 22 times, the Toronto Maple Leafs 11 times and the Detroit Red Wings seven times.

**QUESTION: Which major league team has had the most players with 3,000 or more hits?**

The Pittsburgh Pirates have had three: Honus Wagner, 3,430; Paul Waner, 3,152; and Roberto Clemente, 3,000. However, only Clemente played his entire career with Pittsburgh. But the two others spent most of their careers with the Pirates and are primarily identified with that team.

**QUESTION: Who holds the record for having played for the most teams in a major league career? Who holds the record for having managed the most teams?**

Since 1900, three players each have been on 10 teams: Dick Littlefield, who pitched between 1950 and 1958; Bob Miller, who pitched between 1957 and 1974, and Tommy Davis, who played the outfield and the infield between 1959 and 1976.

Since 1900, Jimmy Dykes managed six teams—Chicago, Philadelphia, Baltimore, Detroit and Cleveland in the American League, and Cincinnati in the National League—from 1934 through 1961.

**QUESTION: Which man managed the longest in the major leagues without ever winning a pennant?**

Two managers are tied for that dubious honor. Jimmy Dykes managed for 21 seasons in both leagues, starting in 1934 and ending in 1961, and Gene Mauch also managed for 21 seasons in both leagues, beginning in 1960 and ending in 1980.

QUESTION: How many players in the major leagues have appeared in 500 or more games consecutively? Not including active players like Steve Garvey of the Los Angeles Dodgers, who are the top ten?

Twenty-seven players have reached that plateau. The top ten are: Lou Gehrig (2,130 games); Everett Scott (1,307); Billy Williams (1,117); Joe Sewell (1,103); Stan Musial (895); Eddie Yost (829); Gus Suhr (822); Nellie Fox (798); Richie Ashburn (730); and Ernie Banks (717).

Charlie Gehringer is the only player with two such streaks during his career, one of 511 games and one of 504.

QUESTION: Which major leaguers since 1900 have played the most games at each of the nine positions?

First base: Mickey Vernon, 2,237 (1939–59, with time out for military service in 1944–45); second base: Eddie Collins, 2,651 (1908–28); third base: Brooks Robinson, 2,870 (1955–77); shortstop: Luis Aparicio, 2,581 (1956–73); outfield: Ty Cobb, 2,943 (1905–28); Willie Mays, 2,843 (1951–73), with military service in 1953) and Hank Aaron, 2,760 (1954–76); catcher: Al Lopez, 1,918 (1928–47, except for 1929); and pitcher: Hoyt Wilhelm, 1,070 (1952–72).

QUESTION: Which team, including before 1900, holds the record for the longest winning streak in the major leagues? The longest losing streak?

The New York Giants, in 1916, won 26 straight games, including a tie, all at home. The Cleveland Indians, in 1899, lost 24 straight games, three at home and 21 on the road.

QUESTION: What is the record in each major league for the most extra-inning games played by a team during one season?

National League: 27, Boston, won 14, lost 13 (1943) and Los Angeles, 10–17 (1967).

American League: 31, Boston, won 15, lost 14, tied 2 (1943).

QUESTION: Since the major leagues introduced divisional play in 1969, how often have all four divisional leaders repeated the following year? How often have none of the leaders repeated the following year?

The four divisional winners of 1977, Philadelphia and Los Angeles in the National League East and West, and the New York Yankees and Kansas City in the American League East and West, repeated in 1978. That was the only time this happened.

None of the 1978 winners, the Yankees and Kansas City in the A.L. East and West, and Philadelphia and Los Angeles in the N.L. East and West, repeated in 1979. And the 1979 winners, Baltimore and California in the A.L. East and West, and Pittsburgh and Cincinnati, in the N.L. East and West, did not repeat in 1980, when the Yankees and Kansas City, and Philadelphia and Houston were victors.

QUESTION: Why is a baseball team from New York called the Yankees, a name usually applied to New Englanders?

The club was formed in 1903 as the New York Highlanders, who played at Hilltop Park, on Broadway between 165th and 168th Streets.

The name was changed after they had moved to the Polo Grounds in 1913. The reason, according to legend, was that Jim Price, sports editor of The New York Press, felt he needed a nickname with fewer letters, so that he could identify the team in a one-column headline. According to some accounts, Price chose "Yankees" not just because it has only seven letters but also because it offered an added advantage: The name could be shortened even further, to "Yanks."

**QUESTION: In a 1980 series in The Times on the New York Yankee farm system, it was mentioned that the first professional minor league was the International Association, organized in 1877. What cities had charter franchises in that league?**

There were seven original members: Allegheny of Pittsburgh; Buckeye of Columbus, Ohio; Manchester, N.H.; Rochester, N.Y.; Live Oak of Lynn, Mass.; Maple Leaf of Guelph, Ontario; and Tecumseh of London, Ontario. Tecumseh won the pennant in that year, using players from the United States. The league disbanded after the 1881 season.

**QUESTION: What are the New York Yankees' club records for the most hits, the most home runs and the most runs in a game?**

Most hits: 30, against the Boston Red Sox on Sept. 28, 1923.

Most homers: eight, against the Philadelphia Athletics on June 28, 1939.

Most runs: 25, against the Athletics on May 24, 1936.

**QUESTION: Have all the professional teams in New York, in a given season, each won the championship of its league?**

No. There have been two champions innumerable times. One year, 1956, three teams won titles: the New York Yankees in the American League, the Brooklyn Dodgers in the National League and the New York Giants in the N.F.L. The Rangers and the Knicks did not win that year.

**QUESTION: Is there any team currently playing in the American League that has a winning record against the New York Yankees?**

Yes, Baltimore. Since the franchise (the old St. Louis Browns) was shifted there before the start of the 1954 season and through 1980 the Orioles have won 253 games and lost 238 against the Yankees.

QUESTION: Reggie Jackson was on two different teams that won the World Series, the Oakland A's in 1973 and 1974 and the New York Yankees in 1977 and 1978. Was he the first player to accomplish this feat? If not, please name all the other players.

Jackson was not the first. In fact, there have been too many to list them all. A few: Eddie Collins of the Chicago White Sox in 1917 and the Philadelphia Athletics in 1929; Mickey Cochrane of the Athletics in 1929 and the Detroit Tigers in 1935; Babe Ruth of the Boston Red Sox in 1915, 1916 and 1918 and the Yankees in 1923, 1927, 1928 and 1932; Paul Blair of the Baltimore Orioles in 1966 and 1970 and the Yankees in 1977 and 1978; and Don Gullett of the Cincinnati Reds in 1975 and 1976 and the Yankees in 1977.

QUESTION: How many pennants did Casey Stengel win as a major league manager? Has any manager won more pennants and not been elected to the Baseball Hall of Fame?

Stengel was a manager for 25 years with four teams, the Brooklyn Dodgers, the Boston Braves, the New York Yankees and the New York Mets. He won ten pennants with the Yankees and seven World Series. Only John McGraw of the New York Giants won as many pennants, and he, too, is in the Hall of Fame.

QUESTION: How many owners have the New York Yankees had, and in what years has the ownership changed?

The first owners were Frank Farrell and Bill Devery, who bought the Baltimore franchise for $18,000 in 1903 and moved it to New York City. In 1915, Col. Jacob Ruppert and Col. Tillinghast L'Hommediue Huston paid $460,000 for the Yankees. In 1922, Ruppert bought out his partner for $1.5-million. In 1945, Dan Topping, Del Webb and Larry MacPhail paid $2.8-million for the club. In 1964, CBS paid $11.2-million for 80 percent of the Yankees, and later bought the remaining 20 percent. In 1973, a group headed by George Steinbrenner bought the Yankees from CBS for $10-million.

QUESTION: Since the New York Mets came into existence, what is the club's record in regular-season and post-season play? How many times have the Mets finished first, second, third, etc.?

The Mets have won 1,324 games and lost 1,649 since they joined the National League in 1962 and through 1980. They have finished tenth on five occasions and ninth twice (before the league was split into East and West divisions). They finished first in the East twice, third three times, fifth twice and sixth three times.

In 1969, the Mets beat Atlanta for the pennant, 3 games to 0, and then defeated Baltimore in the World Series, 4–1. In 1973, the Mets stopped Cincinnati for the pennant, 3–2, then lost the World Series to Oakland, 4–3.

QUESTION: Some time ago the Cincinnati Reds hit three consecutive home runs in one inning. What is the record in this category?

The major league record for consecutive home runs in an inning is four, held by three teams: the Milwaukee Braves (against the Reds in the seventh inning on June 8, 1961); the Cleveland Indians (against the Los

Angeles Angels in the sixth inning on July 31, 1963), and the Minnesota Twins (against the Kansas City A's in the 11th inning on May 2, 1964).

QUESTION: Which teams in the National and American Leagues committed the most errors in a season? In a game?

The Brooklyn Dodgers, in 1905, made 408 errors in 155 games; the Detroit Tigers, in 1901, made 425 in 136 games. Two teams in the N.L. hold the record with 11 errors each in one game: St. Louis (April 19, 1902) and Boston (June 11, 1906). In the A.L., two teams are tied with 12 errors each in a game, Detroit (May 1, 1901) and Chicago (May 6, 1903).

QUESTION: The Boston Red Sox, in two consecutive games in 1979, scored a total of 31 runs and 41 hits. Was that a record? If not, what is?

The Red Sox do hold the modern record (since 1901), but it was established in two different games. In 1950, on June 7 and 8, Boston scored 49 runs on 51 hits.

QUESTION: In a 1979 game, the Boston Red Sox had 12 extra-base hits: seven doubles, a triple and four home runs. Is this a record?

No. The Red Sox hold the major league record, but it was set on June 8, 1950, when they smashed 17 extra-base hits against the St. Louis Browns.

# Memorable Games and Players

QUESTION: I keep reading about the "Merkle boner" in baseball, but have no idea of exactly what happened and why it was so important. Please explain.

On Sept. 23, 1908, the New York Giants and the Chicago Cubs were tied, 1–1, in the bottom of the ninth with the Giants at bat. Moose McCormick was the runner on third base, Fred Merkle was on first and Al Bridwell was at bat. Bridwell smashed a hit into center field, and McCormick raced home for the supposedly winning run. Merkle, however, instead of going to second, ran into the Giant dugout. Frank Chance, the Cub first baseman and manager, called for the ball, but a Giant pitcher, Joe (Iron Man) McGinnity, threw the ball into the grandstand. Chance appealed to the umpire as spectators rushed out into the field. The spectators became rowdy and threatening, and could not be cleared from the field, so the umpire called Merkle out and ruled the game a tie. It cost the Giants the pennant, since they ended the season a game behind the Cubs.

QUESTION: In what year did Rube Marquard, a pitcher for the New York Giants, win 19 straight games? Which team broke the streak, and who was the opposing pitcher?

Marquard's streak was ended by the Cubs on July 8, 1912, in Chicago. Marquard left the game with the score 6–2, and the Cubs eventually won, 7–2. The opposing pitcher was Jimmy Lavender. Marquard ended the year with 26 victories and 11 losses and Lavender finished with 15–13.

QUESTION: When was Babe Ruth traded to the New York Yankees by the Boston Red Sox, and what was involved in the deal? Also, when did Ruth play his first game for the Yankees, and how did he do?

The Yankees bought Ruth on Jan. 3, 1920, for $525,000 in cash, a record sum at the time. Of this, $400,000 was considered a loan from Col. Jacob Ruppert, a Yankee owner, to Harry Frazee, the Red Sox owner, who was in financial difficulty. Through the next several years the loan was reduced as a number of Red Sox players, including Carl Mays, a pitcher, were sent to the Yankees.

Ruth played his first regular-season game for the Yankees on opening day, April 14, 1920, in Philadelphia. He had two singles in four times at bat, but he muffed a fly ball in the bottom of the eighth that permitted the Athletics to win the game, 3–1.


QUESTION: When was the first All-Star baseball game played, who won it and who drove in the first run?

The first game was played on July 6, 1933, in Comiskey Park in Chicago. The American League won the game, 4–2, and Lefty Gomez, the New York Yankee pitcher, drove in the first run with a single in the second inning. Gomez was also the winning pitcher and Babe Ruth, also of the Yankees, drove in two runs with a homer in the third inning.


QUESTION: In a celebrated doubleheader between the New York Giants and the St. Louis Cardinals at the old Polo Grounds, the Giants won the first game, 1-0, in 18 innings with Carl Hubbell pitching, and won the second game by the same score in nine innings. When were those games played, how did the Giants score their two runs, who was the winning pitcher in the second game, and who were the losing pitchers in each game?

The doubleheader was played on July 2, 1933. The Giants scored in the first game this way: Joe Moore singled off Jess Haines, the losing pitcher who had replaced Tex Carleton in the 17th inning. Gus Mancuso sacrificed. Travis Jackson, batting for Blondy Ryan, was purposely passed. Hubbell forced Jackson at second, but Moore reached third, from where he scored on a single by Hughie Critz.

The second game was won on a fourth-inning homer by Johnny Vergez.

Roy Parmelee was the winning pitcher for the Giants in the second game. Dizzy Dean, pitching with one day of rest, was the loser.


QUESTION: Carl Hubbell, the great New York Giant pitcher, won his last 16 games in 1936, ending the season with a 26-6 won-lost record. Who beat him in 1936, and which team was the first to defeat him in 1937? Also, when Hubbell pitched a one-hitter against the Brooklyn Dodgers in 1940, who got the hit?

Hubbell's losses in 1936 were to the St. Louis Cardinals, 2–1, in 17 innings (April 29); the Cincinnati Reds, 1–0 (May 4); the Philadelphia Phillies, 5–3 (May 9); the Pittsburgh Pirates, 3–2 (June 11); the Chicago Cubs, 3–0 (June 28); and Chicago again, 1–0 (July 13). Hubbell won eight in a row in 1937 before the Dodgers snapped his 24-game streak, 10–3, on May 31 at the Polo Grounds.

Hubbell's one-hitter against the Dodgers, on May 30, 1940, was marked by Johnny Hudson's single in the third inning, but a double play on a grounder by Gus Mancuso, the next batter, erased him. Hubbell did not permit another man to reach first base, thus facing the minimum of 27 batters.

QUESTION: After Carl Hubbell struck out Babe Ruth, Lou Gehrig, Jimmy Foxx, Al Simmons and Joe Cronin in succession during the first two innings of the 1934 All-Star Game, what did the next batter do?
Bill Dickey, the New York Yankee catcher, hit a single to left. Lefty Gomez, Yankee pitcher, then fanned, for Hubbell's sixth strikeout in two innings.

QUESTION: When Johnny Vander Meer of the Cincinnati Reds pitched his two consecutive no-hit games in 1938, how many no-hit innings did he have before and after those games? How many scoreless innings did he have before and after?
Vander Meer tossed ⅓ of a hitless inning before the games and 3⅓ after, for a total of 21⅔ consecutive hitless innings. That is a National League record, but Cy Young of the Boston Red Sox, in 1904, pitched 24⅓ straight hitless innings.
Vander Meer recorded eight scoreless innings before his double no-hitter and six after, for a total of 32, which is far from the record, held by Don Drysdale of the Los Angeles Dodgers with 58⅔ innings in 1968. The American League record is 56, accomplished by Walter Johnson of the Washington Senators in 1913.

QUESTION: As the 1940 baseball season neared its end, the Cleveland Indians and the Detroit Tigers were battling for the American League pennant when Floyd Giebell, a Tiger rookie, outpitched Bob Feller in a crucial game. What was the score, and what were the pitching statistics?
The game was played Sept. 27, and the Tigers won, 2–0, as Rudy York hit a two-run homer in the fourth inning. The victory put Detroit three games ahead, with two games to play, thus clinching the pennant. Giebell yielded three hits, walked two men and struck out six; Feller gave up three hits, walked three and struck out four.

QUESTION: In The Times of June 15, 1980, an obituary on Paul Althaus Smith, a mathematician, reported: "During World War II, as part of a fund-raising effort for war bonds, Mr. Smith used his mathematical ability to work out a way for New York's three major league baseball teams, the Yankees, Giants, and Dodgers, to play each other simultaneously at the Polo Grounds." What rules did he work out for the three-way game, and what was the result?
Professor Smith's formula had each team batting six times and fielding six times, with no team batting or fielding for more than six successive outs. The formula worked like this:

| INNING | | 1 2 3 4 5 6 7 8 9 |
|---|---|---|
| TOP | AT BAT | Y G G D D Y Y G G |
| | FIELD | D D Y Y G G D D Y |
| BOTTOM | AT BAT | D D Y Y G G D D Y |
| | FIELD | Y G G D D Y Y G G |

The game, played on June 26, 1944, was witnessed by 50,000 fans. When it ended, the Dodgers had scored five runs, the Yankees one, and the Giants none.

**QUESTION: In an All-Star game, Ted Williams once hit a "blooper" pitch for a home run. What was the year, who was the pitcher and which league won the game?**

Williams hit a blooper pitch from Rip Sewell, who had just entered the game, for a home run in the eighth inning of the 1946 contest, which was played at Williams's home field, Fenway Park in Boston. The blooper pitch was a lob to the plate that faintly resembled a shotput. Sewell, who was with the Pittsburgh Pirates, had had some success with it in the National League. The homer was Williams's second of the game, won by the American League, 12–0.

**QUESTION: In that memorable third playoff game in 1951, in which the New York Giants defeated the Brooklyn Dodgers for the National League pennant, who went to bat for the Giants in the ninth inning and how did those hitters fare?**

The Dodgers were leading, 4–1, when the Giants went to bat in the bottom of the ninth at the Polo Grounds. Alvin Dark, the shortstop, singled off the glove of Gil Hodges, at first. Don Mueller, the right fielder, singled to right. Monte Irvin, the left fielder, popped out. Whitey Lockman, the first baseman, doubled to left, driving in Dark. Mueller sprained his ankle running to third, and Clint Hartung ran for him. Chuck Dressen, the Dodger manager, decided to replace Don Newcombe, his starting pitcher, with Ralph Branca. Bobby Thomson, the third baseman, was the next batter. After one strike, Thomson smashed the ball into the left-field stands, and the Giants, 5–4 winners, had earned the dubious right to face the mighty New York Yankees in the World Series, which the Giants lost, four games to two.

**QUESTION: When the old Brooklyn Dodgers won their first World Series against the New York Yankees in 1955, I recall that the Dodgers used a lot of different pitchers, including a couple of surprises. Who were the pitchers and was a record set?**

The Dodgers used six different starting pitchers in beating the Yankees, 4 games to 3. The starters were: Don Newcombe, Billy Loes, Johnny Podres (who also started the seventh game), Carl Erskine, and the two surprises, both rookies, Roger Craig and Karl Spooner.

The six starters equaled a record for a single series, set by the Dodgers against the Yankees in 1947 and later tied by the Pittsburgh Pirates against the Baltimore Orioles in 1971.

**QUESTION: When Don Larsen of the New York Yankees pitched his perfect game against the Brooklyn Dodgers in the 1956 World Series, how many pitches did he throw and how many times did he reach a three-ball count on a batter?**

Larsen threw 97 pitches and only went to three balls (and two strikes) to one batter, Pee Wee Reese, in the first inning. The Yankees won the game, 2–0, and eventually captured the Series, 4–3.

QUESTION: The death of Walter F. O'Malley, who engineered the shift of the Brooklyn Dodgers and the New York Giants to the West Coast, brought back memories of Ebbets Field and the Polo Grounds, the parks in which those two teams played. Who hit the last home run in each park and who drove in the last run in each before the Dodgers and Giants left New York City?

Duke Snider of the Dodgers hit the last homer in Ebbets Field on Sept. 22, 1957. It was one of two he smashed that day in a 7–3 victory over the Philadelphia Phillies. In the final game at Ebbets Field, on Sept. 24, Gil Hodges drove in the last run as the Dodgers beat the Pittsburgh Pirates, 2–0.

On Sept. 29 that year, in the last game played by the New York Giants, Johnny Powers, a rookie outfielder for the Pirates, came up in the top of the ninth at the Polo Grounds and hit the final home run, also driving in the final run, as the Pirates beat the Giants, 9–1.

QUESTION: The New York Giants baseball team moved to San Francisco for the 1958 season, and played in the old Seals Stadium until the 1960 season, when they opened in the new Candlestick Park. Who were the first Giants to hit home runs in those two parks?

Daryl Spencer hit the first homer in the stadium on opening day, April 15, 1958, as the Giants defeated the Los Angeles Dodgers, 8–0, in the Western debut for both clubs.

Willie Kirkland hit the first Giant home run in Candlestick Park on April 13, 1960, the second day of the season, as the St. Louis Cardinals were defeated, 6–1. The first homer in Candlestick, however, was hit on opening day by Leon Wagner of the Cardinals.

QUESTION: When was the last major league game played at the Polo Grounds and what was the result? When was the Polo Grounds torn down?

The New York Giants left the Polo Grounds for San Francisco after the 1957 season, but the New York Mets used the field as their home for their first two seasons—1962 and 1963. In the last game there, which ended at 4:21 P.M. on Sept. 18, 1963, the Mets lost to the Philadelphia Phillies, 5–1, before 1,752 spectators. Chris Short was the winning pitcher, Craig Anderson the loser.

Demolition of the Polo Grounds for a housing project began on April 10, 1964, and the first 30 families of the eventual total of 1,614 moved in on April 16, 1968.

QUESTION: I recently read that John Paciorek, who played one major league game in 1963, accomplished one of the greatest baseball feats. What was that feat and why did he play only one game?

Paciorek, who was also a football and basketball star, signed with the Houston Colt 45's in 1962, when he was 17 years old. He played on a Houston farm club in 1963, but was brought up for the final game of the season. He got three hits in three official times at bat, walked twice, scored four runs and drove in three. He was returned to the minors for the 1964 season. In June, Paciorek, who had a back abnormality at birth and also a torn muscle in his back, underwent a spinal fusion operation. He played two more years for Houston farm clubs and two for Cleveland farm clubs, finally retiring in 1968. Paciorek, a brother of Tom Paciorek of the Seattle Mariners, is now teaching and coaching at a private school in San Marino, Calif.

**QUESTION: When did Whitey Ford of the New York Yankees retire and against which team did he score his final victory?**

Ford retired on May 30, 1967, citing an injury to his elbow. His last victory was over the Chicago White Sox, 11–2, on April 25 at Yankee Stadium. He pitched a complete game, gave up eight hits, and at that point had won 2 games and lost 1. He was beaten three more times before he retired.

**QUESTION: Has any pitcher hurled a no-hitter and hit two home runs in the same game? If so, please give details.**

Rick Wise of the San Diego Padres, but then with the Philadelphia Phillies, is the only one to do so. On June 23, 1971, he beat the Cincinnati Reds, 4–0, issuing only one walk and facing only 28 batters. He hit two home runs that day, and also hit two homers in another game, which was not a no-hitter, later in that season.

**QUESTION: Did Jim (Catfish) Hunter ever win 20 games or more in a season for the New York Yankees? If so, who was the losing pitcher in his 20th victory and what was the score of the game?**

Hunter won 23 games and lost 14 for the Yankees in 1975, his only 20-game season with them. That was the fifth and last 20-game season of his career. Jim Palmer of the Baltimore Orioles was the losing pitcher when Hunter won No. 20 by 2–0 on Sept. 7. The six-hit shutout was Hunter's seventh and last of the season.

**QUESTION: An incident in a 1979 New York Yankees game, when a batter was hit on his foot by a pitched ball and took first base, recalled a World Series game in which shoe polish was found on a ball and a batter was awarded first base. When did that happen and who was involved?**

The incident referred to took place in the sixth inning of the fifth game in the 1969 Series between the New York Mets and the Baltimore Orioles. Cleon Jones was the batter hit by the ball. The late Gil Hodges, the Met manager, pointed it out to Umpire Lou DiMuro, who had originally called the pitch a ball. Jones was awarded first, Donn Clendenon followed with his third homer of the Series, and the Mets went on to win the game, 5–3, and the championship, four games to one.

**QUESTION: The name of Benny Kauff, an outfielder for the old New York Giants, came up the other day. It was recalled that he was barred from baseball, by then Commissioner Kenesaw Mountain Landis, but no one could remember why. Can you help?**

Kauff, who played in the major leagues for eight years, the last five with the Giants, was indicted in 1920 on the charge of stealing and selling an automobile. On April 7, 1921, Landis declared him ineligible to play major league baseball. A jury acquitted him of the charges in less than an hour on May 13, 1921. Kauff sought an injunction later in that year to be reinstated. The injunction was denied on Jan. 17, 1922, and a suit for reinstatement was dismissed on Sept. 12, 1922. He never played major league baseball again. Kauff died on Nov. 17, 1961, in Columbus, Ohio.

**QUESTION: A long time ago I worked for a man called Bugs Raymond. When I asked him why he was called Bugs, he said he was named after a ballplayer. I let it pass, but recently, in Red Smith's column, I saw a mention of such a ballplayer. Just who was Bugs Raymond?**

Arthur L. (Bugs) Raymond was a major league pitcher with the Detroit Tigers in 1904, the St. Louis Cardinals in 1907 and 1908 and the New York Giants from 1909 through 1911. He won 44 games, lost 54 and had an earned-run average of 2.49. His best year was 1909, when he won 18 and lost 12 for the Giants. After he finished playing in the major leagues, Raymond got into a fight during a sandlot game in Chicago, was beaten with a bat and was found dead in his hotel room on Sept. 7, 1912. He was 30 years old.

**QUESTION: I have a souvenir menu that was used at a Circus Saint and Sinners luncheon that honored Al Schacht, the "Clown Prince of Baseball." What was the reason for the luncheon and when was it held? Where is Schacht now and what is he doing? Is he still involved with his restaurant that was located on East 52nd Street?**

Schacht was initiated into membership of the club on May 25, 1948, an affair that was attended by many celebrities. Schacht, who was born on Nov. 12, 1894, pitched for the Washington Senators for three years, 1919 to 1921, winning 14 games and losing 10. He was more noted for his comedy act, first developed with Nick Altrock, at baseball games, and which he carried on for many years after splitting with Altrock. He sold his restaurant late in 1971 and is now living in Heritage Village, a retirement community in Connecticut.

QUESTION: Many years ago, before World War I, a major league player caught a baseball dropped from the top of the Washington Monument. Who was he and when did he accomplish this feat?

Gabby Street, a catcher with the Washington Senators, caught the ball on Aug. 21, 1908. He was the first one to do so. Street, who made his reputation as Walter Johnson's catcher while with the Senators from 1908 through 1911, was only in the majors as a player for eight years. However, he was connected with organized baseball for more than 40 years, as a player and manager in the minor leagues, as a manager of the St. Louis Cardinals from 1929 until mid-1933 and as a manager for the St. Louis Browns in 1938. He died on Feb. 6, 1951, in Joplin, Mo., at the age of 68.

QUESTION: Did Josh Gibson, the great black catcher, ever hit a ball out of Yankee Stadium?

Many legends have grown up around Gibson's hitting prowess, and this is one of them, but there is nothing on record to substantiate that Gibson, or anyone else, has ever hit a ball out of the stadium.

QUESTION: What was Ralph Branca's won-lost record in 1951, the year the Brooklyn Dodgers lost the pennant to the New York Giants in a playoff? How many Dodger pitchers had better records than Branca? What were his career statistics?

Branca won 13 games and lost 12 in 1951. Four Dodger pitchers had better records: Preacher Roe (22–3), Don Newcombe (20–9), Carl Erskine (16–12) and Clyde King (14–7). Branca, in the major leagues for 12 seasons, pitched in 322 games, winning 88 and losing 68. He had 71 complete games and an earned-run average of 3.79. He struck out 829 batters, walked 663 and allowed 1,372 hits. His best year was 1947, when he finished 21–12.

QUESTION: Ever since I first heard the expression "It's great to be young and a Yankee," I have naturally assumed that the sentiment was originally voiced by some New York Yankee player. Now a friend of mine tells me that the original expression was actually "It's great to be young and a Giant," that it was voiced by a member of the old New York Giants. Who is right?

Your friend, by all accounts. The remark is attributed to Lawrence Joseph (Laughing Larry) Doyle, a Giant second baseman from 1907 to 1920, with time out for service with the Chicago Cubs for part of 1916 and all of 1917. Doyle was just turning 21 years of age when he started playing for the Giants, who were managed then by John McGraw and who, in the years Doyle played for them, won the National League pennant three times.

Besides starting out young and enthusiastic, by the way, Doyle was a pretty good player, and he finished with a career batting average of .290.

QUESTION: How long did it take Joe DiMaggio to be voted into the Baseball Hall of Fame? I have been told that he did not make it until the third year after he became eligible, and I cannot believe this happened to the great DiMaggio. If it's true, who was elected in the two years he did not make it?

DiMaggio did fail twice, in election by the baseball writers. He finally succeeded in 1955, having finished his career in 1951 and become eligible in 1953. (At that time a player had to have been out of baseball only a full year. The five-year rule became effective Jan. 1, 1954, with an exception made for any player who had received 100 votes or more in previous elections.)

In 1953, when 198 votes were needed for election, DiMaggio received 117 and ranked eighth in the balloting. Elected that year were Dizzy Dean, with 209 votes, and Al Simmons, with 199.

In 1954, when 189 votes were needed, DiMaggio received 175 and finished fourth. Three men were elected: Rabbit Maranville, 209; Bill Dickey; 202, and Bill Terry, 195.

In 1955, when again 189 votes were needed, DiMaggio was the top vote-getter, with 223. Elected with him were Ted Lyons, 217; Dazzy Vance, 205, and Gabby Hartnett, 195.

**QUESTION: When Joe DiMaggio's hitting streak was stopped at 56 games, who was the pitcher and what did DiMaggio do at bat in that game?**

DiMaggio's streak was halted on July 17, 1941, in a night game at Cleveland that the Yankees won, 4–3. Al Smith was the starting Indian pitcher. In the first inning, DiMaggio was thrown out by Ken Keltner, the third baseman. In the fourth inning, DiMaggio walked. In the seventh inning, he again was thrown out by Keltner. In the eighth inning, with Jim Bagby on the mound, DiMaggio grounded into a double play.

**QUESTION: What major league baseball player was the first to earn $100,000 or more for a season?**

Joe DiMaggio in 1949.

**QUESTION: Please compare the career batting statistics of Joe DiMaggio and Mickey Mantle, and also list how many errors each made.**

DiMaggio played 13 years for the New York Yankees and appeared in 1,736 games, not including the World Series. He was at bat 6,821 times, had 2,214 hits, 361 homers and 1,537 runs batted in, and finished with a batting average of .325.

Mantle was with the Yankees for 18 years and appeared in 2,401 regular-season games. He was at bat 8,102 times and had 2,415 hits, 536 homers, 1,509 r.b.i.'s and a batting average of .298.

Mantle was at bat 1,281 times more than DiMaggio but had 28 fewer r.b.i.'s and only 201 more hits. Mantle had 175 more homers and his homer percentage (the number of homers per 100 times at bat) also was better, 6.6 to 4.0.

They made the same number of fielding errors, 105. DiMaggio's worst year was 1937, with 17, and his best was 1947, with only one. Mantle's worst year was his last, 1968, when he made 15 errors, and his best was 1966, when he was flawless.

Mantle, however, played several games in the infield during his career, including his last 262 games, at first base, and that added to his error total. DiMaggio played only one game at a position other than the outfield.

QUESTION: When did Roger Maris hit his season's-record total of 61 home runs? Did he retire after that year? If not, when?

Maris hit 61 homers in 1961 and continued playing with the New York Yankees through 1966. He finished his career with the St. Louis Cardinals in 1967 and 1968.


QUESTION: How many major league teams did Phil Rizzuto play for? What were his career statistics?

Rizzuto played only for the New York Yankees, from 1941 through 1956, with time out for military service. He appeared in 1,661 games, was at bat 5,816 times, had 1,588 hits, including 38 homers, and had a batting average of .273. He drove in 562 runs, drew 650 walks, struck out 397 times and stole 149 bases. Rizzuto holds a number of World Series records for shortstops, including most Series played (9), most games (52), most consecutive errorless games (21), most career putouts (107), most career assists (143) and most career chances accepted (250).


QUESTION: Did Bob Lemon, the former manager of the New York Yankees, ever play the outfield, in addition to pitching? If so, where and when?

Lemon was primarily an outfielder and an infielder in his early years of professional ball.

In 1938, his first season, he played both infield and outfield with Springfield of the Middle-Atlantic League and Oswego of the Canadian-American. He pitched only one inning that season. With Springfield the next year he was a shortstop and an outfielder, and with New Orleans of the Southern Association an outfielder and a third baseman. In 1940 and 1941, with Wilkes-Barre of the Eastern League, he played third base, shortstop and the outfield. Also in 1941 he pitched one inning for Wilkes-Barre and played five games at third base for the Cleveland Indians.

Lemon was a third baseman and a shortstop with Baltimore of the International League in 1942. That season he once more played five games at third base for Cleveland.

After three years of military service he returned to Cleveland and in 1946 and 1947 was a pitcher and an outfielder. Then, as strictly a pitcher, he embarked on one of the most successful careers in major league history, and he did not play another position again until Cleveland sent him to San Diego of the Pacific Coast League in 1958, his last season as a player. At San Diego he was both a pitcher and an outfielder.


QUESTION: Is it true that the number 37, worn by Casey Stengel, has been retired by both the New York Yankees and the New York Mets? What other numbers have been retired by those teams?

Stengel's number has been retired by both clubs. The Yankees have also retired the numbers of Babe Ruth (3), Lou Gehrig (4), Joe DiMaggio (5), Mickey Mantle (7), Yogi Berra and Bill Dickey (8), Thurman Munson (15) and Whitey Ford (16). The only number retired by the Mets besides Stengel's is that of Gil Hodges (14).

**QUESTION:** What are the career statistics of Bob Shawkey, the former New York Yankee pitcher, who died in 1980?

Shawkey pitched for 15 years, two with the Philadelphia Athletics and the rest with the Yankees. He won 198 games and lost 150 for a winning percentage of .569. He appeared in 488 games, started 333 and completed 194. His earned-run average was 3.09. In his one year as manager of the Yankees in 1930, the team finished third.

**QUESTION:** How many years did Tony Lazzeri, the great New York Yankee second baseman of the 1920's and the 1930's, play professional ball? What were his primary career statistics in the major leagues? What were his best years for hitting home runs in the minor leagues and the major leagues?

Lazzeri was in pro ball for 18 seasons—in the minors from 1922 through 1925, with the Yankees from 1926 through 1937, with the Chicago Cubs in 1938, and with the Brooklyn Dodgers and the New York Giants in 1939.

In his major league career, he was at bat 6,297 times, had an average of .292, hit 178 homers and batted in 1,191 runs.

His best season's total for major league home runs was 18, which he achieved on four occasions. In the minors, he hit 60 homers in 1925, while with Salt Lake City of the Pacific Coast League, and was the first player in either the majors or the minors to reach that plateau.

**QUESTION:** I remember Art Jorgens and Charley Silvera as second-string Yankees catchers for a good many years behind Bill Dickey and Yogi Berra. How many regular-season games did they catch during their careers? Did they ever appear in a World Series game?

Jorgens was with the Yankees for 11 years, from 1929 to 1939. He appeared in 306 games but never caught in the World Series, for which he was eligible in 1932, 1936, 1937, 1938 and 1939, a total of 23 games.

Silvera was with the Yankees from 1948 through 1956. He appeared in 201 games and in one Series contest, in 1949. He did not appear in any Series games in 1950, 1951, 1952, 1953, 1955 and 1956, when he was eligible for 37 games. In the one game he did play, he failed to get a hit in two times at bat.

**QUESTION:** Did Babe Ruth ever attend high school or college?

No. Ruth, at the age of eight, was placed in the St. Mary's Industrial School, a reform school for incorrigible boys, in Baltimore. He was generally considered an orphan because his parents paid little attention to him. He remained at St. Mary's until he entered professional baseball, at 19.

**QUESTION:** Are Tony Lazzeri and Bob Meusel, former New York Yankees greats, members of the Baseball Hall of Fame? What are their major career statistics?

Neither has been elected to the Hall of Fame. Lazzeri's batting average for his 14 major league seasons was .292, with 178 home runs and 1,191 runs batted in. Meusel hit .309 for 11 seasons, with 156 homers and 1,067 r.b.i.'s.

**QUESTION:** Bob Turley, Don Larsen, Ralph Terry, Bobby Shantz and Tom Sturdivant all once pitched for the New York Yankees. How long did they play for the Yankees, when did they stop pitching and what are they doing now?

Turley pitched for the Yankees from 1955 through 1962; his last year in the majors was 1963. He lives in Dunwoody, Ga., and has his own home-planning business with offices in Savannah.

Larsen, remembered for his perfect game against the Brooklyn Dodgers in the 1956 World Series, was with the Yankees from 1955 through 1959. He pitched in the majors till 1967. He is retired and relaxing in Morgan Hill, Calif.

Terry was with the Yankees in 1956 and part of 1957, returned in 1959 and stayed through 1964. His last year as a pitcher was 1967. He is a golf professional and in the oil business in Hutchinson, Kan.

Shantz was with the Yankees from 1957 through 1960, and he finished his career in the majors in 1964. He owns a dairy bar in Chalfont, Pa.

Sturdivant pitched for New York from 1955 through part of 1959, and his last year in the majors was 1964. He lives in Oklahoma City, where he owns a truck-leasing firm.

**QUESTION:** What specifically was the operation performed on the left arm of Tommy John, the New York Yankee pitcher? Why the label "bionic arm"? What physical therapy did he go through before he could resume pitching?

John ruptured a tendon in his pitching arm during the 1974 season, when he was with the Los Angeles Dodgers. He underwent surgery in September of that year for the transplant of a tendon from his right arm. It was this virtual reconstruction of his injured limb that prompted the term "bionic arm."

According to John himself, his therapy consisted of the following:

"I'd go to the ball park early and jog six or seven miles, then soak my arm in the hot whirlpool for three minutes, then put it in ice for 30 seconds. I'd take eight of those hot-then-cold treatments, then take ultrasound treatments. And when I wasn't doing anything else I'd squeeze Silly Putty to strengthen my arm."

John did not pitch during the 1975 season but successfully resumed his career in 1976.

**QUESTION:** What American League records did Ron Guidry of the New York Yankees break or tie during his incredible 1978 season? How many times was he involved in no-decision games and against whom? How many games did he win in a row and who holds the pitching record in this category in each major league?

Guidry, in winning 25 games and losing 3, posted an .893 percentage, the highest by any 20-game winner in major league history. The previous record-holder was Lefty Grove of the Philadelphia Athletics, who in 1931 won 31 and lost 4, for .886. There have been pitchers who achieved higher percentages than Guidry's, but none who did so with a 20-victory season.

Guidry also fanned 18 California Angels on June 17, 1978, at Yankee Stadium, setting an American League record for most strikeouts by a left-hander in a nine-inning game. And his nine shutouts for the season tied a league record set by Babe Ruth in 1916.

He started 35 times in 1978, and his no-decision games were against Minnesota (twice), Texas, Baltimore, Boston, Chicago and Seattle.

He won 13 straight games, three short of the league record, which is held by Walter Johnson, Washington Senators (1912); Joe Wood, Boston Red Sox (1912); Grove (1931) and Schoolboy Rowe, Detroit Tigers (1934). The longest winning streak in a season in the National League is 19, accomplished by two New York Giant pitchers, Tim Keefe (1888) and Rube Marquard (1912).

QUESTION: It was reported that Jim Kaat, acquired in 1979 by the New York Yankees, was the only currently active baseball player to have played with the old Washington Senators. Wasn't Aurelio Rodriguez, now with the Detroit Tigers, also a Senator, and wasn't he involved in the big Joe Coleman–Denny McLain trade?

Kaat played briefly in 1959 and 1960 with the original Washington Senator team, which in 1961 became the Minnesota Twins. Rodriguez appeared in 1970 with the Washington team that lasted from 1961 to 1971 and that then became the Texas Rangers. Rodriguez, having been sent to the Senators from the California Angels, was traded to the Tigers after the 1970 season, along with Coleman, Ed Brinkman, shortstop, and Jim Hannan, pitcher. In exchange the Senators acquired McLain; Don Wert, third baseman; Elliott Maddox, outfielder, and Norm McRae, pitcher.

QUESTION: Whose numbers have been retired by the New York–San Francisco Giants, and what were those players' career statistics?

When the Giants were based in New York, before 1958, they retired Carl Hubbell's 11 and Mel Ott's 4. In San Francisco they have retired Willie Mays's 24 and Juan Marichal's 27.

Hubbell, a southpaw known as the Meal Ticket, pitched 16 years, from 1928 to 1943, won 253 games, lost 154 and had an earned-run average of 2.97.

Ott, the Boy Wonder, who began his career with the Giants at the age of 17, lasted 22 years as a player, until 1947. He also managed the team from 1942 to 1948. He finished with a career batting average of .304 and with 511 home runs and 1,860 runs batted in.

Mays, who was voted into baseball's Hall of Fame in 1979, his first year of eligibility, also played for 22 years, most of them with the Giants. He played part of the 1972 season and all the 1973 season with the New York Mets. He had a career batting average of .302, with 660 home runs and 1,903 runs batted in.

Marichal, a right-hander, pitched for 16 years, from 1960 to 1975. The last two were with the Boston Red Sox and the Los Angeles Dodgers. He won 243 games, lost 142 and had an earned-run average of 2.89.

QUESTION: Is it part of baseball lore that Bill Wambsganss made the only unassisted triple play in a World Series game? When and how did he do it?

Wambsganss, the Cleveland Indians' second baseman, accomplished his triple play against the Brooklyn Dodgers on Oct. 10, 1920, in the fifth game of the Series. He caught Clarence Mitchell's line drive, stepped on second to retire Pete Kilduff and then tagged Otto Miller coming in from first.

**QUESTION: I recall two unassisted triple plays happening one day after the other. When did they occur and who was involved?**

On May 30, 1927, in the fourth inning of a morning game, Jim Cooney, a Chicago Cubs shortstop, caught a liner by Paul Waner of the Pittsburgh Pirates, stepped on second to retire Lloyd Waner and then tagged Clyde Barnhart off first. The Cubs won the game, 7–6.

On May 31, in the ninth inning, Johnny Neun, the Detroit Tigers first baseman, caught a liner hit by Homer Summa of the Cleveland Indians, ran over and tagged Charlie Jamieson between first and second and then touched second base before Glenn Myatt could return. The triple play choked off an Indian rally, and the Tigers won, 1–0.

**QUESTION: I recently watched a television show about Willie Mays. At the end of the program, a poem about baseball was recited. It was a beautiful poem, and I had never heard it before. One line—"Time is of the essence"—is repeated a few times. What is the name of the poem, and who wrote it?**

The poem is "Polo Grounds," written by Rolfe Humphries. It was included in a collection of his poems, "Summer Landscape," published by Charles Scribner's Sons. Humphries, who died on April 22, 1969, won a number of poetry awards and was elected to the National Institute of Arts and Letters.

**QUESTION: How long did Johnny Antonelli pitch in the major leagues and what were his career statistics? Also, he was a good long-ball hitter for a pitcher, so please list his home-run total.**

Antonelli was in the majors for 12 years, from 1948 until 1961, most of which he spent with the New York and San Francisco Giants. He won 126 games, lost 110, for a .534 percentage and an earned-run average of 3.34. He hit 15 home runs in his career.

**QUESTION: Please list Juan Marichal's pitching statistics and the date and the result of the last game in which he appeared.**

Marichal pitched for the San Francisco Giants from 1960 through 1973, for the Boston Red Sox in 1974 and for the Los Angeles Dodgers in 1975. He won 243 games and lost 142 for .631. His earned-run average was 2.89, with 244 complete games of the 457 that he started. He hurled 3,509.1 innings, struck out 2,303 batters and had 52 shutouts.

The last game he pitched was on April 16, 1975. He allowed four runs on six hits in 2⅔ innings, but he was not the pitcher of record in the game won by the Dodgers, 7–6, against Cincinnati.

**QUESTION: Did Marv Throneberry begin his major league career as a second baseman for the Baltimore Orioles? How many games did he play at various positions? What were his career statistics?**

Throneberry, the "Marvelous Marv" of the early and dismal New York Mets, never played second base. He began his career with the New York Yankees in 1955, playing one game at first base. He returned to the

Yankees in 1958 and 1959, playing 94 games at first and 18 in the out-field. In 1960, he played 71 games at first base for Kansas City. In 1961, he was with K.C. and with Baltimore, playing 41 games at first and 25 in the outfield. In 1962, he was with Baltimore and the Mets, playing 97 games at first and two in the outfield. He played three games at first base for the Mets in 1963, his last in the majors. Throneberry finished his career with a batting average of .237 on 281 hits in 1,186 appearances at the plate. He drove in 170 runs.

**QUESTION: In what years did Tom Winsett, Joe Stripp and Gibby Brack play for the old Brooklyn Dodgers at Ebbets Field? Wasn't it true that Winsett had a reputation as a home-run hitter in the minors, but never delivered in the majors?**

Winsett played for the Dodgers from 1936 through 1938, Stripp from 1932 through 1937 and Brack in 1937 and part of 1938. Winsett, known as Long Tom, was a home-run hitter in the minors, but hit only eight, seven with Brooklyn, in his seven years in the majors.

**QUESTION: Which major league teams did Gene Hermanski play for and what were his career statistics?**

Hermanski, an outfielder, played with the Brooklyn Dodgers from 1943 through the beginning of the 1951 season, when he was traded to the Chicago Cubs. He stayed with the Cubs until the beginning of the 1953 season and finished his career that year with the Pittsburgh Pirates. He appeared in 739 games, was at bat 1,960 times, had 533 hits, including 46 home runs, and batted in 259 runs. He finished with a career batting average of .272.

**QUESTION: Could you please tell me whether Jerry Grote, the one-time catcher for the New York Mets, is still playing for the Los Angeles Dodgers? If he is not, what is he doing?**

The Dodgers granted Grote free agency on Nov. 2, 1978. He was a coach with the Mets during spring training in 1979, but was out of base-ball until 1981, when he was signed by the Kansas City Royals.

**QUESTION: In 1946, Hank Greenberg of the Detroit Tigers led the American League in home runs (44) and in runs batted in (127). Despite this, he was traded to the Pittsburgh Pirates. What did the Tigers get for him?**

Greenberg had expressed a desire to finish his career in New York City, where he was born. The Tigers were reluctant to send him to the New York Yankees, a league rival, so Greenberg was waived out of the American League and was sent to the Pirates on Jan. 18, 1947, for "an undisclosed but sizable sum" of money. The 1947 season was his last as an active player.

**QUESTION: How did Stan Musial get the nickname "Stan the Man?" What were his career statistics and some of the honors he won?**

Fans of the old Brooklyn Dodgers, who used to despair each time Musial came to bat in Ebbets Field, pinned the nickname on him in 1946. (His career batting average in that park was .356.) In 22 years, Musial appeared in 3,026 games, was at bat 10,972 times, had 3,630 hits, 475 home runs, 1,951 runs batted in, and an average of .331. He was the league batting champion seven times, won the Most Valuable Player award in 1942, 1946 and 1948. Only Ty Cobb, Hank Aaron and Pete Rose have amassed more career hits than Musial.

**QUESTION: When Lefty Grove won 31 games and lost 4 for the old Philadelphia Athletics in 1931, how many of those victories were in relief?**

Grove won four games and lost one in relief; he also had five saves that year.

**QUESTION: New Year's Eve, 1982, will be the tenth anniversary of Roberto Clemente's death, and I know he finished his career with 3,000 hits, one of the few players who reached that pinnacle. When and where did he get that last hit, off what pitcher, and did he play after he reached the 3,000-mark?**

Clemente got the last hit of his career on Sept. 30, 1972, in Pittsburgh. It was a long double to left-center field off Jon Matlock, then with the New York Mets, in a game the Pirates won, 3–0. The season was not over, but Clemente did not have an official time at bat in the remaining games, so that his 3,000th hit was his last, before his death in a plane crash that New Year's Eve. He was the 11th player to reach that pinnacle, but since then he has been passed by Al Kaline, Pete Rose, Lou Brock and Carl Yastrzemski, and now ranks 15th.

**QUESTION: Nellie Fox received 168 votes in the 1981 balloting for the Baseball Hall of Fame. I never thought he was that great a second baseman. What were his career statistics? Did he establish any records?**

Fox, who has been a candidate since 1971, received even more votes (174) in 1979. He played for 19 years, from 1947 to 1965, mostly with the Chicago White Sox and briefly with the Philadelphia Athletics and the Houston Astros. He had a lifetime batting average of .288, with 790 runs batted in, but only 35 home runs.

Fox holds a number of American League fielding records for second basemen: highest average, 10 or more years, .984; most years leading in putouts, 10; most years leading in chances accepted, 9; most double plays, 1,568.

In addition, Fox and Jimmy Dykes of the Athletics are tied for most chances accepted in a nine-inning game, 17, and Fox is tied with four other players for most years leading the league in double plays, 5.

Fox's durability is exemplified in two other records he holds: most consecutive games played by a second baseman, 798, and most years leading in games played, 8.

Fox died in 1975.

**QUESTION: Bob Elliott of the Boston Braves was listed as the winner of the National League's Most Valuable Player award in 1947, and I couldn't remember him. Could you please tell me something about him and his statistics?**

Elliott started as an outfielder with the Pittsburgh Pirates in 1939. Frankie Frisch, then manager of the Pirates, converted Elliott to a third baseman. In his first infield practice, Elliott supposedly was knocked out by a ground ball, but he persisted and became an acceptable third base-man. He was more known for his hitting, however, than for his fielding. In his 15 years in the major leagues, he batted .289, with 2,061 hits, including 170 home runs, and 1,195 runs batted in. In his m.v.p. year, Elliot batted .317, getting 176 hits, including 22 home runs, and driving in 113 runs. He managed Kansas City to an eighth place finish in 1960. He died at the age of 49 on May 4, 1966.

QUESTION: Did Ernie Banks of the Chicago Cubs ever win the Most Valuable Player award in the National League? What was his career batting average? How many home runs did he hit, and how many were hit in Wrigley Field? What was his best year for hitting home runs, and how many grand slams did he have in his career?

Banks was the m.v.p. in 1958 and 1959. His career batting average was .274 and he had a total of 512 home runs, of which 284 were hit in Wrigley Field. His best year for homers was 1958, when he had 47. He had a total of 12 grand slams, of which five came in 1955 and set a record for one season that was tied by Jim Gentile of Baltimore in 1962.

QUESTION: Monte Weaver was a graduate at the University of Virginia when I was in medical school, and he went on to pitch in the major leagues with the Washington Senators. What was his career record, and what is he doing now?

Weaver pitched in the American League for nine seasons, from 1931 to 1939, eight with Washington and the last with the Boston Red Sox. He won 71 games (22 of them in 1932), lost 50 and had a career earned-run average of 4.36. He also pitched the fourth game of the 1933 World Series, and lost it in the 11th inning, 2–1, to the New York Giants, who went on to win the Series, four games to one. Weaver lives in Orlando, Fla., and grows oranges and grapefruit on a 200-acre farm.

QUESTION: How many home runs did Jimmie Foxx have washed out by rain in 1932, when he finished with 58, two behind Babe Ruth's record of 60 in 1927? What were his career statistics?

Foxx lost two home runs because two games were called by rain before the fifth inning. Foxx, primarily a first baseman, began playing in 1925 with the Philadelphia Athletics as a 17-year-old and ended his career in 1945 with the Philadelphia Phillies. He appeared in 2,317 games, was at bat 8,134 times, had 2,646 hits, including 534 home runs, and a batting average of .325. He drove in 1,922 runs and struck out 1,-311 times. He won the triple crown (batting, home runs and runs batted in) in 1933, and the Most Valuable Player award three times, twice with the Athletics (1931–32) and once with the Boston Red Sox (1938). He also holds the record for the most consecutive years hitting 30 or more home runs—12. He was elected to the Hall of Fame in 1951 and died at the age of 59 on July 21, 1967.

QUESTION: There once were two famous pitcher-catcher brother combinations, Wes and Rick Ferrell and Mort and Walker Cooper. How do the career earned-run averages of the two pitchers and the career batting averages of the two catchers compare?

Mort Cooper had a 2.97 e.r.a. and Wes Ferrell a 4.04. Walker Cooper's batting average was .285 and Rick Ferrell's was .281. Incidentally, Wes Ferrell was also a good batter, with 38 home runs and a career average of .280.

QUESTION: A 1980 article in The New Yorker by Roger Angell mentioned that Bob Gibson's fastball compared with those thrown by Sandy Koufax and Jim Maloney. I know all about Koufax, but who was Maloney? What were his career statistics?

Maloney pitched for the Cincinnati Reds from 1960 through 1970, and finished his career with the California Angels in 1971. He won 134 games and lost 84. He had 1,605 strikeouts, 30 shutouts and an earned-run average of 3.19. He completed 74 games of the 302 that he started. He ranks among the top 10 in career strikeouts per nine innings with 7.81.

QUESTION: When did the Pittsburgh Pirates trade Arky Vaughan, their great shortstop and third baseman, to the Brooklyn Dodgers, and what players did they get for him?

Vaughan was traded on Dec. 12, 1941, for Luke Hamlin, a pitcher; Babe Phelps, a catcher; Pete Coscarart, an infielder; and Jim Wasdell, an outfielder.

QUESTION: Some years ago there was an excellent pitcher with the Pittsburgh Pirates by the name of Bob Friend. What was his career record, where is he now, and what is he doing for a living?

Friend pitched in the major leagues for 16 seasons and ended his baseball career in 1966 with the New York Yankees and the New York Mets. He won 197 games and lost 230, and his earned-run average was 3.58. His best year, in terms of won-lost percentage, was 1958, when he won 22 and dropped 14, though his earned-run average that season was 3.68.

Friend is now a vice-president of Babb Inc., an insurance brokerage in Pittsburgh that he joined in 1976. Earlier he served two terms of four years each as Comptroller of Allegheny County, of which Pittsburgh is part.

QUESTION: After Bill Lee, the Montreal pitcher, grew a beard, Tom LaSorda, the Los Angeles manager, said, "He should play for the House of David." What was the House of David? When did its baseball team play, and did all the players wear beards?

The House of David, a religious sect, was founded in 1903, and is still based in Benton Harbor, Mich. During the 1920's and 1930's, House of David baseball teams toured the country, facing the best of the local semi-professionals. As required by the sect, the players all wore beards with the exception of ringers such as Grover Cleveland Alexander, who by then had retired from major league baseball. Alexander, signed mainly as a drawing card, would pitch two or three innings and then be replaced.

The House of David, whose followers reportedly now have dwindled to about 100, stopped sending its baseball teams around the country in the early 1940's.

QUESTION: During the spring of 1953, my brother had his picture taken with Art Houtteman at the Detroit Tiger training camp. Soon afterward, Houtteman, a pitcher who we thought was a rookie at the time, disappeared from the Tiger roster. On June 14, 1980, he showed up at a game between members of the World Series teams of 1945, the Tigers and the Chicago Cubs. Was that the same Houtteman we thought was a rookie in 1953? And, if so, what is he doing now?

Houtteman was a rookie with the Tigers in 1945 and stayed with them until the beginning of the 1953 season, when he was traded to Cleveland. He stayed with the Indians until he was sent to the Baltimore Orioles after the start of the 1957 season, his last in the majors. He has been working for a number of years as a salesman for the Paragon Steel Company of Detroit.

QUESTION: Did Rocky Colavito, the slugging outfielder, ever pitch in the major leagues? If so, what was his record?

Colavito pitched 3 innings in 1958, when he was with the Cleveland Indians, and 2⅔ innings in 1968, with the New York Yankees. In those 5⅔ innings, all in relief, he allowed one hit and five bases on balls, struck out two, won one game, lost none and gained no saves. His earned-run average was 0.00.

QUESTION: How many major league clubs has Dave Kingman played for? How many home runs has he hit?

Kingman played with the San Francisco Giants from 1971 through 1974. He was sold to the New York Mets in 1975 and played with them until June 15, 1977. He was then traded to the San Diego Padres, sold by the Padres on waivers to the California Angels on Sept. 6, 1977, and was sold to the New York Yankees nine days later. He became a free agent in November of that year, and signed with the Chicago Cubs, who traded him back to the Mets on Feb. 28, 1981, for Steve Henderson. Kingman had 270 home runs at the end of the 1980 season.

QUESTION: How long did Jim Piersall play in the majors, what were his career batting statistics and what is he doing now?

Piersall played from 1950 to 1967, with the Boston Red Sox, the Cleveland Indians, the Washington Senators, the New York Mets and the Los Angeles and California Angels. His career batting average was .272, and he drove in 591 runs and hit 104 homers. He is now a broadcaster for the Chicago White Sox.

QUESTION: How long was Solly Hemus in the major leagues, what was his career record and when did he retire?

Hemus, who was primarily a second baseman and shortstop, played for the St. Louis Cardinals from 1949 to 1956. He then was traded in midseason to the Philadelphia Phillies and stayed with them through 1958. He returned to the Cardinals in 1959 as a player and then as a manager, piloting the club through part of the 1961 season. As a player, he appeared in 969 games, was at bat 2,694 times and had 736 hits for a .273 batting average.

QUESTION: During my high school days in Stockton, Calif., I had a good friend, Bobby Adams, who later became a professional baseball player. How long did he play in the major leagues, what was his career record and what is he doing now?

Adams was in the major leagues for 14 years, beginning in 1946 and ending in 1959. He played with the Cincinnati Reds and the Chicago Cubs in the National League and briefly with the Baltimore Orioles and the Chicago White Sox in the American League. Primarily a second baseman and a third baseman, he was at bat 4,019 times, had 1,082 hits and a batting average of .269. Adams, who lives in Scottsdale, Ariz., is an infield instructor for the Chicago Cubs, working mainly with minor league teams. His son, Mike Adams, also an infielder, is with the Oakland Athletics.

QUESTION: Is Ed Ott of the Pittsburgh Pirates a son of Mel Ott, who is in the Hall of Fame? How many fathers and sons have played in the major leagues? Did any play at the same time?

The Otts are not related. According to the record books, there have been about 100 father-son combinations in the majors, but none have played at the same time. Jim Hegan ended his playing career in 1960 and his son, Mike, began his career in 1964, and this is apparently the closest time span for any father-son playing combination. Connie Mack, while managing the Philadelphia Athletics, had his son, Earle, on the roster of the club for three seasons—1910, 1911 and 1914. Earle Mack appeared in only five games during those years.

QUESTION: Did Clarence Podbielan ever pitch in the major leagues? I remember such a name, but my friends insist there was no such pitcher.

Bud Podbielan pitched nine years with three teams: the Brooklyn Dodgers, from 1949 through part of 1952; the Cincinnati Reds, from 1952 through 1955, and also 1957, and the Cleveland Indians, in 1959. He won 25 games, lost 42 and had an earned-run average of 4.49.

**QUESTION:** Please list Marty Marion's career statistics and which teams he played for.

Marion was with the St. Louis Cardinals from 1940 through 1950 and with the St. Louis Browns in 1952–53. He was a far-ranging short-stop who appeared in 1,572 games (his last two at third base), was at bat 5,506 times, had 1,448 hits for an average of .263. He had 36 home runs, scored 602 times and had 624 runs batted in.

Marion also managed the Cardinals in 1951, the Browns in 1952–53 and the Chicago White Sox in 1954–56. As a manager he compiled a record of 356 games won, 371 lost for a .490 average.

**QUESTION:** When did Sam Mele, an outstanding baseball player for New York University, play in the major leagues and what were his career statistics? What was his record as a manager?

Mele lasted 10 years in the majors, as an outfielder and first base-man. He began with the Boston Red Sox in 1947 and ended with the Cleveland Indians in 1956. In between, he also played with the Washington Senators, the Chicago White Sox, the Baltimore Orioles, the Red Sox again, and then with the Cincinnati Reds. He was at bat 3,437 times, getting 916 hits, and finished with a .267 batting average. He smashed 80 home runs, drove in 544 runs and had a slugging average of .408.

As the manager of the Minnesota Twins from 1961 through 1967, Mele's teams won 518 games and lost 427 for .548. In 1965, the Twins won the A.L. pennant but lost the World Series to the Los Angeles Dodgers, 4–3.

**QUESTION:** How many career grand-slam homers did George Kelly, John Mize and Ernie Lombardi each have?

Kelly had eight, Mize and Lombardi each had six.

**QUESTION:** As a Chicago Cubs fan, I noticed that they sent Miguel Dilone to the Cleveland Indians at the beginning of the 1980 season and that he had a great year. What did the Cubs get for him and what were his 1980 statistics?

The Cubs sent Dilone to a farm club, Wichita in the American Asso-ciation, on April 9, 1980. He was sold to the Indians on May 7 in a cash transaction. Dilone batted .341 with 180 hits in 528 at bats and drove in 40 runs. He had the third best average in the American League and he was also third in stolen bases with 61.

# Football

---

## Rules of the Game

QUESTION: A fair catch is signaled in a National Football League game. Before the ball is caught, time expires. Is the game over?

If a fair catch is signaled, the receiver who signaled must catch the ball. He may then elect to have the game extended by one free kick down. If he successfully drop-kicks the ball or has a placement without a tee, it is three points. The reason he would want to extend the period for the kick, regardless of the score, would be that the points might be a deciding factor in the tie-breaking procedure for winning divisional championships.

QUESTION: A quarterback in the National Football League throws a pass to Player A, who is in the air but lands out of bounds after he tips the ball. The tipped ball is caught inbounds by a teammate before it touches the ground. Is the pass complete? Would it make any difference if the play occurred in the end zone or if Player A was a defensive back, not an offensive player?

If a legal receiver tips the ball while he is inbounds, all players on both teams are eligible to catch the ball. However, a receiver cannot be out of bounds, come back in, and tip the pass.

QUESTION: On first and 10 in a National Football League game, the quarterback hands off to a running back, who gains 16 yards. Just as the runner is about to be tackled, he throws a backward pass to the quarterback, still behind the line of scrimmage, and sprints away. The quarterback then throws him a long pass for a touchdown. Is this legal?

No. Once the ball has been carried past the line of scrimmage, it cannot be thrown back across it. The ball would be ruled dead, there would be a loss of a down and play would resume at the line of scrimmage.

**QUESTION: A punt is blocked in a National League Football game, and the kicker recovers the ball. Is he permitted to throw a forward pass?**

As long as the blocked ball does not cross the scrimmage line, the kicker may pass, or run with the ball as well. If on the block the ball passes the line of scrimmage, however, he may only recover it, not advance it.

**QUESTION: A few weeks ago, you affirmed the legality of a pass by a kicker who had picked up a blocked punt behind the line of scrimmage. What happens in such a situation if there is an ineligible receiver downfield when the pass is caught?**

The pass would not be legal and the offensive team would be penalized 10 yards.

**QUESTION: In professional football, how is pass interference treated in the statistics for the game? Is any credit given for a pass completion or a reception? What happens to the penalty yardage?**

No credit is given for a completion or a reception. The yardage involved in the play is added to the penalty totals of the defensive team.

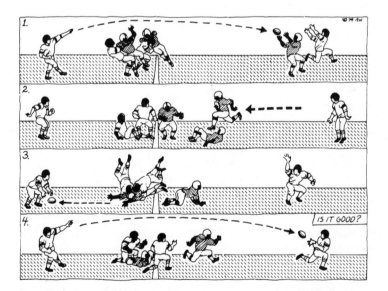

**QUESTION: A long forward pass in a National Football League game is intercepted by the opposing safety, who runs the ball back and is tackled after he crosses the original line of scrimmage. He fumbles the ball, and it is recovered by the quarterback who first threw the ball. Can the quarterback, since he is still behind his line of scrimmage, throw another pass to the original receiver, who is still down the field?**

No. He can run with the fumble, but an offensive team may make only one forward pass during each play from scrimmage.

QUESTION: How long may a National Football League player, on the injured-reserve list but now healthy, practice and engage in workouts with his team and still not be activated? Does a player on the injured-reserve list for the entire season still earn credit toward his pension?

A player with an injury that lasted four weeks or more could practice with his team for the entire season. A player with an injury that lasted for fewer than four weeks would have to be taken off the injured-reserve list.

A player on the injured-reserve list all season earns credit toward his pension.

QUESTION: If a National Football League game ends in a tie, how is it determined who receives at the start of the sudden-death overtime? Does the coin toss at the beginning of the game automatically decide this?

No. At the end of regulation time, the referee tosses a coin at the center of the field, as is done before the game begins. The captain of the visiting team calls the toss. The winner, most likely, chooses to receive.

QUESTION: How does the National Football League rate passers, and when was the system instituted?

The current system was instituted in 1973, and is the ninth such system since 1932. It is a complex one, based on four categories: percentage of touchdown passes per attempt, percentage of completions per attempt, percentage of interceptions per attempt and average yards gained per attempt.

Individual passers are then rated against a standard, starting with .000 and ranging to a maximum of 2.375 in each category. The point rating is then converted into a scale of 100. In exceptional cases, if statistical performance has been outstanding, it is possible for a passer to get a mark higher than 100—as if he had earned an A-plus.

QUESTION: Under the rating of passers in the N.F.L., it is possible for a quarterback to be rated higher than 100, or A-plus. Have any quarterbacks received such a rating?

Yes. Milt Plum of Cleveland was rated at 110.4 in 1960, and that is the highest to date. More recent examples among the other A-plus passers were Ken Stabler of Oakland, with 103.7 in 1976, and Bert Jones of Baltimore, with 102.6 in the same year.

QUESTION: If a punt, kickoff or pass interception is caught beyond the end zone in a National Football League game and then carried into the end zone and downed, would it be ruled a safety or a touchback?

It would be a touchback. Only if the ball were caught in the field of play and carried back into the end zone would it be a safety.

QUESTION: A forward pass is batted by a defensive player in a National Football League game. It is caught by the quarterback who threw the pass, and he throws a second pass down field. A defensive player intercepts the pass and runs for a touchdown. Is it legal?

Yes. While the second pass was illegal, and could not be caught by an offensive player, such passes may be intercepted by the defensive team.

QUESTION: When a team in the National Football League makes a first down, and the markers have to be moved, is there an automatic timeout? What is the rule in college football?

When a team clearly makes a first down in the N.F.L., there is no automatic timeout. When there is any possibility of a measurement for a first down, however, or of consulting a captain about a measurement, there is an automatic timeout. In college football, the official declares a timeout when any first down is made.

QUESTION: Is a defensive player in the National Football League permitted to step out of bounds to knock a pass out of the hands of a receiver? Is he permitted to intercept a pass in this fashion?

The defensive player has a legal right, while out of bounds, to make a play on the receiver or the ball. He cannot intercept the pass, however, unless both feet are inbounds prior to the interception.

QUESTION: If, for any reason, a player in a National Football League game physically attacked one of his own teammates on the field, could an official penalize him?

There would be no penalty, but the officials would do their best to stop the fight and then let the team's coach handle the situation.

QUESTION: If a quarterback in a National Football League game throws a pass that deflects off an official and is caught by an eligible receiver before the ball strikes the ground, what is the ruling?

The catch is legal.

QUESTION: If a ball carrier in pro football fumbles the ball as he is being tackled inside the opponents' 5-yard line, and the ball rolls into the end zone, what is the ruling?

It is a touchback, and the defensive team gets the ball on its own 20 yard line.

QUESTION: In professional football, if a defensive player drives a ball carrier out of bounds, thus ending the play, is he credited with a tackle?

Yes.

**QUESTION:** It is first and goal to go from the 4-yard line in a National Football League game. The offensive team scores on the second down on a rushing play. Is the team credited with a first down, in addition to the touchdown?

Yes. A first down is credited on each scoring play resulting from a rush or a forward pass, regardless of the distance covered.

**QUESTION:** Team A punts on fourth down in an N.F.L. game. Before the ball hits the ground or is touched by the receiving team, a member of Team A catches the ball. Who gets possession of the ball?

The catch is illegal because the ball was not first touched by the receiving team, which gets the ball at the spot of illegal touching or possession.

**QUESTION:** In a National Football League game, a punt returner signals for a fair catch, then muffs it. May he pick up the ball and run with it?

Yes, the run is allowed as long as the ball has touched the ground. If the kicking team recovers, however, the ball is dead at the point of recovery.

**QUESTION:** An offensive player in his own end zone is caught holding a defensive lineman, and the defensive team is awarded a safety. Why? Does this apply to other infractions in the end zone?

According to N.F.L. rules, a safety is awarded when an offensive player commits a foul behind his own goal line. The rules define a foul as any violation of playing rules, so that the awarding of the safety applies to all other infractions by the offense behind its goal line.

**QUESTION:** A quarterback throws a pass over the line of scrimmage, the receiver unintentionally tips the ball into the air, and it sails back over the line of scrimmage to the quarterback, who catches it. Is the ball dead, with an incomplete pass, or may the play continue?

In both college and professional football the pass is considered complete, and so the play continues. Once an eligible receiver has touched the ball first, it may be caught by any other player before it touches the ground.

**QUESTION: On a punt or a kickoff in the National Football League, does the receiving team take possession if the ball rolls dead—untouched by either team—or if the ball is first touched by the kicking team? Is there a different rule for an onside kick? If not, why doesn't the receiving team fall back and let the ball roll dead?**

A punt is not a kickoff, and the rules are not the same. The punt-receiving team is permitted to let the ball roll dead and take possession at that spot. The situation is different on a kickoff, regardless of whether this kick is of the short onside variety. Once the ball has traveled 10 yards or more on a kickoff, either team may recover it, although the kicking team may not advance with it.

**QUESTION: The offensive team comes out of the huddle and the linemen, except one of the tackles, assume three-point stances. The tackle rests his elbows on his knees in a crouched position. After a second, the tackle begins to assume the three-point stance, and a defensive lineman charges across the line and makes contact with him. Who should be penalized?**

The defensive lineman is guilty of encroachment, because the tackle's move was legal. The defense is penalized five yards.

**QUESTION: For a touchdown to be legal in the National Football League, is it the player or the ball that has to break the plane of the end zone? Is there any difference in this regard between a pass and a run?**

A touchdown is scored when the ball, in the possession of a player, breaks the plane of the end zone. There is no difference here between the pass and the run.

**QUESTION: If a back gains 10 yards in an N.F.L. game and then fumbles the ball, which is recovered by the defense, is he credited with 10 yards of rushing?**

The rules state that when a fumble is recovered by the opposing team beyond the line of scrimmage, the runner is credited with yardage gained to the point of his advance or to the point of recovery, whichever is less.

**QUESTION: What constitutes an intentional grounding of a forward pass in the National Football League, and what is the penalty for it?**

When a passer throws, tosses, or lobs the ball to prevent a loss of yards, and the ball strikes the ground, it is intentional grounding. The offending team is penalized with the loss of a down and 10 yards from the line of scrimmage if the passer is in the field of play, or with a safety if the passer is in his own end zone when the ball is released.

**QUESTION: In professional football, are only the end men, as eligible receivers on the line of scrimmage at the time of a snap, permitted to go beyond the line before a ball is punted, drop-kicked or place-kicked?**

Rule 9, Article 3, of the Official Rules for Professional Football lists an exception: "An eligible receiver who, at the snap, is aligned or in motion behind the line and more than one yard outside the end man on his side of the line, clearly making him the outside receiver, *replaces* (emphasis from rule book) that man as the player eligible to go downfield after the snap. All other members of the kicking team must remain at the line of scrimmage until the ball has been kicked."

**QUESTION: A runner in the National Football League breaks through the line of scrimmage and, as he is about to be tackled, tosses a backward pass toward one of his teammates. The ball bounces before that player manages to pick it up. Is he permitted to advance? Is a defensive player, if he recovers the ball, permitted to advance?**

An offensive player may advance if he recovers the ball after it touches the ground. No defensive player may advance in such a situation, as the ball is dead where it is recovered. That player's team next snaps the ball at the point of the turnover.

ROUGHING THE KICKER ?

**QUESTION: Two defensive players rush the kicker in a National Football League game. The first player runs into the kicker, but misses the football. The second player blocks the punt. Is there a roughing penalty?**

According to N.F.L. rules, if the first player runs into the kicker "after the kick has left the kicker's foot at the same instant the second player blocks the kick, the foul for running into the kicker shall not be enforced, unless in the judgement of the referee, the player running into the kicker was clearly the direct cause of the kick being blocked."

**QUESTION: In a National Football League game, a kick returner signals for a fair catch on a punt. Another player on the receiving team catches the ball and runs for a touchdown. What is the ruling?**

The ball is dead at the point of the catch, thus nullifying the touchdown. Such a play occurred at the New York Jets–Baltimore Colts game in 1980, and the Colts lost a touchdown. If the ball had touched the ground, however, or touched a member of the kicking team, the touchdown would have been legal.

**QUESTION: In professional football, Team A's kick for an extra point is blocked, but one of its players recovers the ball behind the line of scrimmage and runs into the end zone with it. How many points does Team A get? What happens if the player who recovers the ball attempts a pass and the ball is intercepted? Can the ball be run back for a touchdown?**

As soon as the kick is blocked, the ball is dead and no points can be scored. The defensive team can never score on a conversion attempt, so the ball would also be dead as soon as the pass was intercepted.

QUESTION: Were National Football League teams ever penalized for two incomplete passes over the goal line in a series of downs? For a fourth-down incompletion in the end zone?

In 1934 a rule was instituted that two incomplete passes in a series of downs or a fourth-down incompletion would result in a touchback. Previously any incomplete pass over the goal line was a touchback. In 1935 the rule was changed to bring the ball back to the point where it was put in play, except when the previous play originated inside the opponent's 20-yard line. In 1975 the rule was again changed, bringing the ball back to the line of scrimmage, even if the fourth-down pass was attempted inside the 20.

QUESTION: May a defensive player in a football game step out of bounds and then step back in to tackle the ball carrier?

Yes, at any time.

QUESTION: When was the two-minute warning rule at the end of each half put into effect in the N.F.L.?

The two-minute warning first appeared in the rules in 1949.

QUESTION: In a National Football League game, an attempt at a field goal falls short, with the kicking team recovering the ball in the field of play beyond the yardage needed for a first down. The defensive team did not touch the ball. Is it a first down? Can the player who recovered the ball continue to advance? If a defensive player recovers the short attempt, is he permitted to run with the ball?

The defensive team gains possession of the ball on missed attempts at field goals. If the kick was attempted beyond the opponent's 20-yard line, possession is at the scrimmage line; if inside the 20-yard line, possession is at that line. A defending player may advance all kicks from scrimmage, including an unsuccessful field goal. One further note: The kicking team may never advance its own kick.

## For the Record

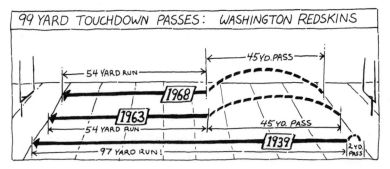

99 YARD TOUCHDOWN PASSES: WASHINGTON REDSKINS

QUESTION: What is the longest touchdown pass play in the history of the National Football League?

Ninety-nine yards, accomplished four times. The first was in 1939, against the Pittsburgh Steelers, when Frankie Filchock of the Washington Redskins tossed a 2-yard pass to Andy Farkas, who then ran 97 yards.

Two of the three other passes were also thrown by Redskins. In 1963 George Izo threw a 45-yard pass to Bobby Mitchell, who ran 54 yards, in a game against the Cleveland Browns. In 1968, against the Chicago Bears, Sonny Jurgensen also threw a 45-yard pass, which Jerry Allen caught and ran with 54 yards.

The only other 99-yard touchdown pass play, from Karl Sweetan of the Detroit Lions to Pat Studstill in a game against the Baltimore Colts in 1966, was never broken down, for some reason, as to the length of the pass and the length of the run.

QUESTION: Who was the first player in the National Football League to rush for 1,000 yards or more in a season? How many games did the season comprise then? Until the number of games in a season was increased, who held the record for the most yards rushed?

Beattie Feathers of the Chicago Bears, in 1934, which was his first year in the league, rushed for 1,004 yards. The Bears played 13 games, although not all the teams in the league did. Until 1946, a season comprised either 12, 11 or 10 games (during the war years). From 1947 through 1960, the season stabilized at 12 games, and in 1961 it went up to 14 games. Jim Brown of Cleveland, in a 12-game season in 1958, rushed for 1,527 yards. That record lasted until 1963, a 14-game season, when Brown gained 1,863 yards. O. J. Simpson, in 1973, another 14-game season, rushed for 2,003 yards, a record that still stands despite the increase to 16 games a season.

QUESTION: When was the New York Giants football franchise founded, what did it cost, and who was the owner? Did one of the first games involve Red Grange and the Chicago Bears?

The Giants were founded in 1925 by Tim Mara, father of Wellington Mara, the Giants' current president, for a franchise fee of $2,500. Grange and the Bears played the Giants at the Polo Grounds on Dec. 6, 1925, before 73,000 fans. The Bears won, 19–7, but the sellout saved Mara from a financially losing season. In a return match in Chicago later in the season, the Giants won, 9–0. They finished their first year with nine victories and four losses.

QUESTION: The New York Giants last made the National Football League playoffs in 1963, which means they have been out for 17 seasons. Is this a record?

No. The Pittsburgh Steelers went 24 seasons, from 1948 through 1971, without making the playoffs. That is the longest stretch since the league began playoffs in 1933.

QUESTION: I've heard a lot about Frank Gifford and his career with New York's football Giants, but never much about his statistics. Can you list some of them?

Gifford was a running back, a flanker and, early in his professional career, a defensive back. He played with the Giants from 1952 through 1964, except for 1961, when he was out of football. He rushed 840 times for 3,609 yards—an average of 4.3 yards an attempt—and 34 touchdowns. As a receiver, he caught 367 passes for 5,434 yards—an average of 14.8—and 43 touchdowns. He passed 63 times, with 29 completions for a gain of 823 yards; 14 of the passes were good for touchdowns. He also kicked two field goals and 10 points after touchdowns. His best year was 1956, when he rushed for 819 yards and caught 51 passes for 603 yards. He was all-pro in 1955, 1956, 1957, and 1959, and was inducted into the Hall of Fame in 1977.

**QUESTION: Who was the quarterback for the New York Giants before Charlie Conerly?**
Conerly came to the Giants in 1948. In 1947, Paul Governali was the quarterback. Governali, a Columbia graduate, was also with the Giants in 1948. Until Conerly arrived and took over the post until 1961, the Giants had had a succession of quarterbacks.

**QUESTION: What happened to John Hicks, the Ohio State guard who was the first draft pick of the New York Giants in 1974?**
Hicks was traded to the Pittsburgh Steelers on April 17, 1978, for Jim Clack, a center, and Ernie Pough, a wide receiver. Hicks played during the 1978 exhibition season, with his last game being against the Giants, but he was injured, placed on the injured-reserve list and never played a regular-season game. He received a Super Bowl ring, but was released by the Steelers and dropped out of the league.

**QUESTION: The first N.F.L. game I ever saw was the championship game between the New York Giants and the Chicago Bears in 1963. I know the Bears won, but I cannot recall the score or the name of the Bear who intercepted Y.A. Tittle's desperation pass in the final seconds. Can you please provide the information?**
The Bears overcame the Giants, 14–10. Tittle was intercepted five times during the contest, but the most damaging one, by Rich Petitbon, came with 2 seconds to play.

**QUESTION: When the New York Giants defeated the Chicago Bears for the National Football League championship in 1956, what was the date of the game, the temperature that day, and who scored for the Giants?**
The Giants trounced the Bears, 47–7, on Dec. 30, with the temperature at 20 degrees. Alex Webster scored two touchdowns, Mel Triplett, Henry Moore, Kyle Rote and Frank Gifford each scored one touchdown, and Ben Agajanian kicked two field goals and five of six extra points.

**QUESTION: I recall in the early 1970's a game between the Jets and the Baltimore Colts in which Joe Namath and Johnny Unitas both completed a lot of passes. What were the passing statistics for that game and were any records set?**
On Sept. 24, 1972, the Jets defeated the Colts, 44–34, at Baltimore. Namath completed 15 of 28 passes for 496 yards and six touchdowns. Unitas completed 26 of 44 passes for 376 yards and two touchdowns. There was only one interception, by the Colts, but no records were set. Namath's 496 passing yards in one game, however, is third in the record book, behind the 554 of Norm Van Brocklin of Los Angeles (1951) and the 505 of Y. A. Tittle of the Giants (1962).

QUESTION: Why does the emblem of the Pittsburgh Steelers appear on only one side of their helmets? Has it always been that way? Are there other teams in the National Football League that follow this practice?

The Steelers are the only team that wears one-emblem helmets, though the Cleveland Browns go them one better: The Browns wear no emblems at all. The Steelers say that there was no particular reason for the decision to have one emblem, that officials of the team simply liked the look of it.

This emblem, by the way, is the logo of the steel industry, which sought to have the team adopt it and approached the Steelers with the idea in the early 1960's. It was first worn by the Steelers in 1962. Before then, they wore a plain black helmet with a yellow stripe in the middle.

QUESTION: Did the Pittsburgh Steelers and the Philadelphia Eagles of the National Football League ever merge? If so, how long did the merger last, what was the team called, and what was its record?

In 1943, because of World War II, the two teams merged for one season, under the name Phil-Pitt, and the home schedule was divided between the two cities. The team finished third in the Eastern Division with a won-lost-tied record of 5–4–1. In 1944, the Chicago Cardinals and Pittsburgh merged under the name Card-Pitt. That team lost all 10 games and finished last in the Western Division. The merger was dissolved the last day of the season.

QUESTION: When did Steve Van Buren play for the Philadelphia Eagles in the National Football League? What were his career statistics?

Van Buren played for the Eagles his entire N.F.L. career, from 1944 through 1951. He rushed 1,320 times for 5,860 yards, an average of 4.4 yards, and scored 69 touchdowns. He helped the Eagles to three consecutive conference titles, from 1947 to 1949, and, in the last two of those three years, to the league championship as well.

QUESTION: Harold Carmichael of the Philadelphia Eagles had his streak of catching passes in consecutive games stopped at 127 in 1980. Which players are closest to him in that category?

Mel Gray of the St. Louis Cardinals, 105 games; Dan Abramowicz of the New Orleans Saints and the San Francisco 49ers, also 105 games; and Lance Alworth of the San Diego Chargers, 96 games. Of the three, only Gray was active in 1980.

QUESTION: Which three teams in the National Football League have the best won-lost records in regular-season play from 1970 through 1979?

Dallas, with 105 victories and 39 defeats is tops. Right behind are Miami, with 104 victories, 39 losses and 1 tie, and Oakland (100–38–6); Minnesota is 99–43–2 and Pittsburgh is 99–44–1.

QUESTION: What are the career ratings of the top 10 passers in National Football League history?

The top 10, with 1,500 or more passing attempts, are (not including 1980): Roger Staubach (83.5); Sonny Jurgensen (82.8); Len Dawson (82.6); Fran Tarkenton (80.5); Bert Jones (80.3); Bart Starr (80.3); Ken Stabler (79.9); Ken Anderson (79.1); Johnny Unitas (78.2); Otto Graham (78.1).

QUESTION: It seems to me that since the first two Super Bowls the American Football Conference has dominated the National Football Conference in regular-season play. What is the yearly record?

In 1970, the first year of interconference competition, the A.F.C. won 12, lost 27 and tied 1; 1971, 15–23–2; 1972, 20–19–1; 1973, 19–19–2; 1974, 23–17; 1975, 23–17; 1976, 16–12; 1977, 19–9; 1978, 31–21; 1979, 36–16; and 1980, 33–19.

The 1980 season was the seventh straight that the A.F.C. had captured the series. The overall record: 247 victories for the A.F.C., 199 for the N.F.C. and six ties.

QUESTION: Before the 1980 season, it seemed to me that most teams in the National Football League wore their dark uniforms at home games. This season, it appears as if half the teams are wearing their light "away" jerseys at home. How is it decided which uniforms are worn?

Each home club must inform the league office by July 1 which color uniforms it intends to wear at all home exhibition and regular season games. The visiting team must then wear a contrasting uniform. A similar rule applies for playoff games.

QUESTION: Has there ever been a National Football League game that ended in a 4–4 tie, with both teams only scoring safeties?

No. The closest thing to it in safeties are two games between Green Bay and Chicago, each of which ended in 2–0 scores, with the Packers winning in 1932 and the Bears in 1938.

QUESTION: Which N.F.L. teams hold the records for the most penalties—total and yardage—in a season? The fewest? Which teams hold the game records in the same categories?

Most penalties (season): the Baltimore Colts, 137, in 1979. Fewest: The Detroit Lions, 19, in 1937.

Most yards: the Oakland Raiders, 1,274 in 1969. Fewest: Detroit, 139 in 1937.

Most penalties (game): the Brooklyn Dodgers and the Chicago Bears, 22, both in 1944. Fewest: 0, by many teams.

Most yards: the Cleveland Browns, 209, in 1951. Fewest: 0, by many teams.

**QUESTION: How many teams in the N.F.L. have not won a game during a season?**

Since 1933, when the league was divided into two divisions, it has happened seven times: 1934, Cincinnati Reds, 0–8; 1942, Detroit Lions, 0–11; 1943, Chicago Cardinals, 0–10; 1944, Brooklyn Tigers and Card-Pitt, each with 0–10; 1960, Dallas Cowboys, 0–11–1; 1976, Tampa Bay Buccaneers, 0–14. No team in the now-defunct American Football League ever went a season without winning at least one game.

**QUESTION: Which players in the National Football League hold the records for the most fumbles in a career, in a season and in a game?**

Career: Roman Gabriel of the Los Angeles Rams and the Philadelphia Eagles, 105; season: Dan Pastorini, then with the Houston Oilers, 17, in 1973; game: Len Dawson of the Kansas City Chiefs, seven, in 1964.

**QUESTION: Who holds the record for the longest punt and the longest field goal in the N.F.L.?**

Punt: 98 yards, by Steve O'Neal of the New York Jets against the Denver Broncos on Sept. 21, 1969.

Field goal: 63 yards, by Tom Dempsey of the New Orleans Saints against the Detroit Lions on Nov. 8, 1970.

**QUESTION: Which quarterback in the National Football League has been intercepted the fewest times in a season? The most times? Who holds the career record for the most passes intercepted?**

In 1976, Joe Ferguson of Buffalo was intercepted only once in passing 151 times for an 0.66 percentage. In 1962, George Blanda, then with Houston, was intercepted 42 times. Blanda also holds the career record of 277 interceptions.

**QUESTION: Which five running backs have scored the most touchdowns in one National Football League season?**

O.J. Simpson is the leader with 23 touchdowns for Buffalo in 1975. Chuck Foreman of Minnesota tallied 22 in the same year and Gale Sayers of Chicago also scored 22 in 1965, his first season in the league. Lenny Moore of Baltimore in 1964 and Leroy Kelly of Cleveland in 1968 each scored 20 touchdowns.

**QUESTION: Who are the top five touchdown scorers in the history of the National Football League?**

Jim Brown of the Cleveland Browns, with 126; Lenny Moore of the Baltimore Colts, 113; Don Hutson of the Green Bay Packers, 105; Jim Taylor of the Packers and the New Orleans Saints, 93, and Bobby Mitchell of the Browns and the Washington Redskins, 91.

QUESTION: Which players in the National Football League have rushed for 1,000 or more yards in their first three seasons? In their first four?

Three players, John Brockington of the Green Bay Packers, Tony Dorsett of the Dallas Cowboys and Earl Campbell of the Houston Oilers, have gained that many yards in their first three seasons. Brockington's totals in his first three years—1971, 1972 and 1973—were 1,105, 1,027 and 1,144. Dorsett's totals in 1977, 1978 and 1979 were 1,007, 1,325 and 1,107. Campbell's totals in 1978, 1979 and 1980 were 1,450, 1,697 and 1,934.

Only Dorsett, who rushed for 1,185 in 1980, has topped the 1,000-yard mark four years in a row.

QUESTION: As a follow-up to the question regarding the rushing records of National Football League backs: How many rushers, inactive and active, among the top 10 in total yardage have averaged 1,000 yards or more a season?

Only four: Jim Brown, who gained 12,312 yards (the most in the league's history) in nine seasons for the Cleveland Browns; O.J. Simpson, who had 11,236 in 11 seasons with the Buffalo Bills and the San Francisco 49ers and who is second on the career list; Franco Harris, who has 9,352 in nine seasons with the Pittsburgh Steelers and who is third on the list; and Walter Payton of the Chicago Bears, who has 8,386 in six years with the Chicago Bears and who is now fifth on the list.

Payton captured his fifth straight National Football Conference rushing title in 1980 with 1,460 yards, and, at the rate he is going, might well surpass Brown's record before his career ends.

QUESTION: Since the inception of professional football's sudden-death-overtime rule for regular-season games, how many times has the team that won the coin toss before the overtime gone on to win the game?

The rule was instituted in 1974, and since then 58 games, as of the end of the 1980 season, have been tied at the end of regulation time. The team that won the toss drove, on 19 occasions, for the winning score, without its opponent touching the ball. In 29 games, the team that won the toss won the game. In 25 games, the team that lost the toss won the game. There have been four overtime ties. Incidentally, 37 of those games have been decided by a field goal and 17 by a touchdown.

QUESTION: What are the career pass-catching statistics of Lynn Swann of the Pittsburgh Steelers?

Swann has played seven seasons in the N.F.L., and by the end of regular play in 1980 he had caught 284 passes for 4,692 yards and an average of 16.5 yards per reception. He has scored 46 touchdowns on passes, one on rushing and one on a punt return.

QUESTION: Since 1946, when Cleveland was in the All-American Football Conference and was known as the Rams, has the team had any place-kickers other than Lou Groza and Don Cockroft?

In 1960, Sam Baker was the place-kicker. Groza started with Cleveland in 1946 and stayed with the team when it switched to the National

Football League in 1950 and became the Browns. He was not on the team in 1960, but returned the next season and continued playing through 1967. Cockroft took over in 1968 and still holds the job. Incidentally, Cleveland fielded a team in 1919, in the American Professional Football Association, and was in and out of that league until it first joined N.F.L. in 1937. With the exception of 1943, it stayed in the N.F.L. until it switched in 1946 to the A.A.F.C.

**QUESTION: Since 1950, what is the won-and-lost record of the Cleveland Browns of the National Football League, and where has the team finished each year?**

Including the 1980 season, the Browns have won 270 games, lost 158 and tied 9 regular-season and playoff games. The number of teams and the names of the division in which the Browns have played have changed over the years, but they have finished first 14 times, tied for first once, finished second four times, tied for second twice, finished third six times and fourth four times. The Browns also won the N.F.L. championship in 1950, 1954, 1955 and 1964.

**QUESTION: Are Greg Pruitt and Mike Pruitt of the Cleveland Browns related? What are the career statistics of these two backs, how old are they, and where did they go to college?**

The Pruitts are not related. Greg Pruitt was born on Aug. 18, 1951, and starred at the University of Oklahoma. He was out with injuries for a good part of the 1979 season, and had only 40 rushes in 1980. His career statistics since joining the Browns in 1973: 1,127 rushing attempts, 5,372 yards gained for a 4.7 average and 25 touchdowns. He scored no touchdowns in 1980 and gained only 117 yards.

Mike Pruitt was born on April 3, 1954, and attended Purdue University. He has been with the Browns since 1976 and in 1980 gained 1,034 yards, his second straight 1,000-yard year, and scored six touchdowns. His career statistics: 747 rushing attempts, 3,231 yards gained for a 4.3 average and 21 touchdowns.

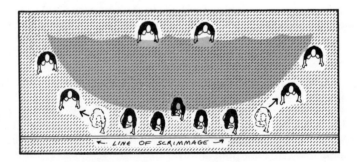

**QUESTION: In the early 1950's, Tom Landry, now coach of the Dallas Cowboys, was part of the New York Giants' "umbrella defense." What was that defense, and who were the three other backs involved?**

The "umbrella defense" was designed by Steve Owen, the Giant coach, to contain the passing attack of the Cleveland Browns. The formation began with six linemen and a middle linebacker just behind the line, two backs playing outside of and behind the ends, and two other backs playing deep in the middle. The defensive ends would retreat to help out the four backs, Landry, Emlen Tunnell, Harmon Rowe and Otto Schnellbacher. All together, the arrangement of defenders resembled an upside-down umbrella.

**QUESTION: Why do the Dallas Cowboys use the "shotgun" formation on offense, and what advantages does it offer?**

Tom Landry, the Dallas coach, employs the shotgun formation because he feels it gives his quarterback more time to read the defense, and offers more protection. Not all coaches agree with this philosophy, obviously, since the shotgun means that the play in all probability will be a pass.

**QUESTION: What is the flex defense used by the Dallas Cowboys? Do any other teams in the National Football League use it?**

The flex defense was conceived by Tom Landry, the Cowboys' coach, and has been used since the early 1960's. In the defense one (and sometimes two) of the four defensive linemen is stationed one yard behind the scrimmage line. In various combinations, there can be three Dallas linemen "up" and one "back." In most cases, a tackle is the flex lineman. The purpose is to confuse the blocking of the offensive line. The flex lineman "reads" the offensive play and then commits himself to the movement of the ball. The flex is used only in down-and-yard situations where a running play is anticipated. The only other coach to use such an alignment has been Dick Nolan, a Landry protégé and the former head coach at San Francisco and New Orleans.

**QUESTION: A deflected Oakland Raider pass that resulted in a touchdown against the San Diego Chargers in the 1980 American Football Conference championship game brought up mention of the "Immaculate Reception" pass caught by Franco Harris of the Pittsburgh Steelers. When did that catch take place and which other players were involved?**

The pass took place on Dec. 23, 1972, at Three Rivers Stadium, with the Steelers, in their first playoff game since 1947, facing the Raiders. The Steelers, with 22 seconds remaining in the game and trailing, 7–6, had a fourth-and-10 on their own 40-yard line. Terry Bradshaw threw a long pass to John Fuqua that was deflected by Jack Tatum, the Raider safety. Harris caught the deflected ball and raced for a touchdown. The Steelers won, 13–7, but lost the title game to the Miami Dolphins, 21–17.

**QUESTION: In a 1979 San Diego-Oakland game in the National Football League, San Diego attempted an onside kick. The ball failed to go the necessary 10 yards, but a Raider player touched it first and a Charger player recovered it. Since the ball did not go across the Raider free-kick line, why were the Chargers awarded possession of the ball?**

A short free kick usually calls for a 5-yard penalty for the kicking team and the setting of new free-kick lines, unless the penalty is refused by the receivers. In the instance you cite, however, a member of the receiving team touched the ball first and the Chargers were entitled to retain possession since they recovered the ball.

QUESTION: When did Tony Canadeo, the Gray Ghost, play for the Green Bay Packers, how big was he, what were his playing statistics, and where is he now?

Canadeo, a halfback, was 5 feet 11 inches, and his listed weight, when he began with the Packers in 1941 and when he finished in 1952, was 190 pounds. He rushed 1,025 times, gained 4,197 yards (for an average of 4.1) and scored 186 points in 10 seasons. He was in military service in 1944 and 1945. He was elected to the Pro Football Hall of Fame in 1974 and is still associated with the Packers, as a member of the executive committee and the board of directors.

QUESTION: During one N.F.L. season, Tom Matte, a running back, had to play quarterback for the Baltimore Colts because of injuries to Johnny Unitas and Gary Cuozzo. What year was that, how many games were involved, and how did Matte fare?

Matte, in 1965, appeared in four games at quarterback. On Dec. 12, he replaced Cuozzo, the replacement for Unitas, in a game won by the Green Bay Packers, 42–27. Matte started the last game of the season against the Los Angeles Rams, and the Colts won, 20–17. In the Western Conference playoff the Colts, with Matte at quarterback, lost a sudden-death game to the Packers, 13–10. In his final game as a quarterback, in the Playoff Bowl, Matte led the Colts to a 35–3 victory over the Dallas Cowboys.

QUESTION: How did Roger Staubach of the Dallas Cowboys and Terry Bradshaw of the Pittsburgh Steelers rate as quarterbacks in the 1979 season?

According to National Football League statistics, Staubach had 84.9 rating points and Bradshaw 84.8, which is as close as you can get. Staubach had 413 passing attempts, and completed 231 for a completion percentage of 55.9. He gained 3,190 yards and had 25 touchdown passes. Bradshaw had 368 attempts, 207 completions and a 56.3 percentage. He gained 2,915 yards and had 28 touchdown passes.

QUESTION: What are the National Football League career coaching records of Vince Lombardi, Don Shula and Tom Landry?

Lombardi ended his career, including playoff games, with 105 victories, 35 defeats and 6 ties. Including the 1980 season, Shula's record is 120–53–1 and Landry's record is 201–120–6.

QUESTION: When the Miami Dolphins beat the Washington Redskins, 14-7, in the Super Bowl on Jan. 14, 1973, to finish with a perfect 17-0 season record, which players were on the starting offensive team?

Backfield: Bob Griese, Larry Csonka and Jim Kiick; receivers: Howard Twilley, Paul Warfield and Marv Fleming; linemen: Wayne Moore, Norm Evans, Bob Kuechenberg, Jim Langer and Larry Little.

QUESTION: In a 1980 game between the Miami Dolphins and the Cincinnati Bengals, Miami executed a successful onside punt. I've heard of an onside kick, but what is an onside punt?

The play described took place after a safety. Miami, putting the ball in play as required on its 20-yard line, elected to punt, rather than kick off. The ball traveled 12 yards, making it legal, under the free-kick rules, for either team to recover it. The Cincinnati players, not expecting Miami to execute such a maneuver deep in its territory, had dropped back as soon as the ball was punted to protect the receiver. The Dolphins thus were able to recover the ball.

QUESTION: Please list the players who scored points in the famous 73–0 defeat of the Washington Redskins by the Chicago Bears in the 1940 National Football League championship game.

Ten players scored a total of 11 touchdowns: Harry Clark (2), Ken Kavanaugh, Clyde (Bulldog) Turner, Hamp Pool, Ray Nolting, George McAfee, Gary Famiglietti, Joe Maniaci, Bill Osmanski and Sid Luckman.

Six players scored the 7 points after touchdowns: Bob Snyder (2), Jack Manders, Phil Martinovich, Dick Plasman, Joe Stydahar and Maniaci.

QUESTION: George Blanda had a magnificent record for longevity in the National Football League, but isn't it true that Pudge Heffelfinger played professional football longer than Blanda?

Yes. Blanda, who was born on Sept. 17, 1927, played 26 seasons, from 1949 through 1975, an N.F.L. record, retiring when he was 48 years of age. Heffelfinger, who was born on Dec. 20, 1867, reputedly played football for 50 years, of which at least 41 were professional. A three-time all-American at Yale, he is listed as the first professional player in history, receiving $500 to play a game in Pittsburgh in 1892. He retired a few days short of his 66th birthday in 1933. He supposedly was the first guard to pull out of the line and lead interference for the ball carrier.

QUESTION: Who were the original members of the defensive Fearsome Foursome of the Los Angeles Rams?

Merlin Olsen, David (Deacon) Jones, Roosevelt Grier and Lamar Lundy, who first played together in 1963.

QUESTION: How many graduates of Southern California and Penn State were on National Football League rosters in the 1978 season? Which college leads in producing the most players for the league?

Thirty-eight Southern California graduates were on N.F.L. rosters, and 25 Penn State graduates. Southern California is the leader in this category, not only for 1978 but also for the entire history of the league.

QUESTION: Is a dome stadium being built for the Minnesota Vikings and the Minnesota Twins, and, if so, when will it be ready?

Yes. It is scheduled to be completed in 1983.

QUESTION: What do the initials in O.A. (Bum) Phillips's name stand for, and how did the New Orleans Saints' coach get his nickname?

The initials stand for Oail Andrew. When Phillips was a boy, his sister, trying to call him "brother," would pronounce it "bumble." This later became "Bum."

**QUESTION:** In 1949, when the New York Yankees and the Brooklyn Dodgers merged in the All-American Football Conference, where did the merged team play its home games, who was the coach, and what was its won-lost record?

The Brooklyn-New York team played six games at Yankee Stadium and six away, winning eight and losing four to finish third in the league. The coach was Red Strader. That was the fourth and final season for the league.

**QUESTION:** Paul (Bear) Bryant has coached at Maryland, Kentucky, Texas A & M and Alabama. How many of his quarterbacks have played in the National Football League?

Babe Parilli and George Blanda (Kentucky) and Joe Namath, Kenny Stabler, Scott Hunter, Richard Todd and Jeff Rutledge (Alabama).

**QUESTION:** What was the average salary of a player in the National Football League for each of the last three seasons?

1980: $78,657; 1979: $68,893; 1978: $62,000

**QUESTION:** What is the average length of a player's career in the National Football League?

According to the N.F.L. Players' Association, four and a half years.

**QUESTION:** Which teams made up the American Football League right before it merged with the National Football League? Which of those teams since the merger have the best and the worst records in the league?

The leagues were merged in 1966, but played separate schedules until the 1970 season. The A.F.L. teams that merged with the older league were the New York Jets, Houston, Boston (now New England), Buffalo, Miami, Oakland, Kansas City, San Diego, Denver and Cincinnati.

The Oakland Raiders since 1970 have won 111 games, lost 43 and tied six, for the best record, although Miami, with a 112–47–1 record, has won one more game. The Jets, at 57–103, have the worst record.

**QUESTION:** It is common knowledge that Jackie Robinson was the first black player in major league baseball. Are there any records on the first black player in the National Football League?

There were four black professional players in the pre-N.F.L. years, according to the Pro Football Hall of Fame in Canton, Ohio. They were Charles W. Follis, a halfback for the Shelby Athletic Club (1902–04); Charles (Doc) Baker, a halfback for the Akron Indians (1906–08 and 1911); Henry McDonald, a halfback for the Rochester Jeffersons (1911–17); and Gideon (Charlie) Smith, a tackle for the Canton Bulldogs (one game in 1915).

The first two blacks in the N.F.L. were Fritz Pollard, the great Brown University back who played for Akron (1919–21 and 1925–26), Milwaukee (1922), Hammond (1923–25) and Providence (1925), and Robert (Rube) Marshall, an end for Rock Island (1919 and 1921) and Cleveland (1920).

No statistics were kept by the N.F.L. until 1933.

**QUESTION: In what years was Frank (Pop) Ivy a professional football coach in the United States and for which teams? What was his record?**

Ivy coached the Chicago Cardinals of the National Football League in 1958 (winning 2 games, losing 9 and tying 1) and in 1959 (2–10); the St. Louis Cardinals in 1960 (6–5–1) and in 1961 (7–7). He also coached the Houston Oilers of the American Football League in 1962 (11–3) and in 1963 (6–8).

**QUESTION: What were Jim Brown's career scoring and rushing statistics in the National Football League?**

Brown, who played nine seasons, leads the league in both categories. He scored 106 touchdowns on rushing and 20 on pass receptions, for a total of 126. In 2,359 rushing attempts, Brown gained 12,312 yards for an average of 5.2 yards a carry.

**QUESTION: When was Chris Bahr of the Oakland Raiders born? How many field-goal attempts did he miss against the Denver Broncos in the 1980 game won by the Raiders 9-3?**

Bahr was born on Feb. 3, 1953. He missed four attempts at field goals and one attempt at a point after touchdown in that Monday night game on Dec. 1.

**QUESTION: What teams did Ahmad Rashad play for before he joined the Minnesota Vikings? What are his career statistics?**

Rashad, who formerly played under the name of Bobby Moore, was a wide receiver for the St. Louis Cardinals in 1972 and 1973 and for the Buffalo Bills in 1974. He played out his option with the Bills and was signed as a free agent by the Seattle Seahawks in 1975, but missed the entire season because of a knee injury. He was traded to the Vikings on Sept. 7, 1976. Rashad, in eight playing seasons ending with 1980, caught 414 passes for 5,714 yards, an average of 13.8 yards a reception. Included were 37 touchdown passes.

# Hockey

## Rules of the Game

GOALIE REMOVED...

AND DEFENSE FOULS = AUTOMATIC GOAL.

**QUESTION: In the National Hockey League, is there any circumstance in which a team can be credited with a goal without actually putting the puck into the net, or without the opposing teams's putting the puck into its own net accidentally?**

Yes. Rule 83 (c) of the league's Official Rule Book says:

"If, when the opposing goalkeeper has been removed from the ice, a player in control of the puck is tripped or otherwise fouled with no opposition between him and the opposing goal, thus preventing a reasonable scoring opportunity, the Referee shall immediately stop the play and award a goal to the attacking team."

**QUESTION: Is there a rule that goalies must wear face masks in the National Hockey League?**

There is no rule that goaltenders must wear masks, just as there is none that skaters must wear helmets.

**QUESTION: Is offside called in the National Hockey league if a player on Team A directs the puck backward across his own blue line, into the attacking zone of Team B, while a Team B player is still within that zone?**

No. Rule 71(d) of the N.H.L.'s Official Rule Book states:

"If a player legally carries or passes the puck back into his own defending zone while a player of the opposing team is in such defending zone, the 'offside' shall be ignored and play permitted to continue."

**QUESTION:** Did the National Hockey League ever have major and minor penalty shots? If so, what was the difference?

The penalty shot, which is awarded when a player in possession of the puck is tripped or otherwise fouled and thus kept from having a clear shot on goal, was of two types—major and minor—from the 1941–42 season through 1945–46. The differences were in both definition and execution.

A minor penalty shot resulted from such an infraction by the goaltender. Any player on the team that had been fouled, regardless of whether he was on ice at the time of the infraction, was permitted to take the shot. The puck was placed at center ice, and the player, moving one-on-one against the goalie, had to shoot before he crossed the penalty line, a two-inch-wide red strip 28 feet from and parallel to the goal line.

A major penalty shot resulted from such a foul by any player other than the goalie. Only the fouled player was permitted to take the shot. He took the puck from the opposing team's blue line and let fly from wherever he chose. This, of course, is the procedure familiar to today's N.H.L. fans. The current penalty shot applies to such infractions by all players—goalies and skaters.

**QUESTION:** A player on a breakaway is tripped from behind, and so is entitled to a penalty shot. The opposing goalie has been removed previously in favor of a sixth skater, however. What is the ruling?

Rule 31(d) of the official N.H.L. Rule Book contains this paragraph:

"If, at the time a penalty shot is awarded, the goalkeeper of the penalized team has been removed from the ice to substitute another player, the goalkeeper shall be permitted to return to the ice before the penalty shot is taken."

**QUESTION:** Is the goalie or any other player on defense in the National Hockey League permitted to throw his stick at the puck?

The rules definitely prohibit throwing or shooting a stick at a puck. When this occurs, the referee allows the play to be completed, and if a goal is not scored the offensive team is awarded a penalty shot. In a second example, if the defending goalie has been removed, and a stick is thrown at an attacking player who has a chance at an open-net goal, thus preventing the shot, the referee must award a goal to the attacking team.

**QUESTION:** Icing (shooting the puck beyond the goal line of the opposing team) is about to be called, but a player from the offending team reaches the puck first. Does this now become a two-line pass offside? What happens if he touches the puck before it goes over the goal line?

If the player was onside, that is, he was not over the center line (which applies to icing calls) before the puck crossed it, it is not an offside or icing and play continues. This applies to both situations.

**QUESTION:** If a player stickhandles the puck so that his body crosses the blue line before the puck, is this offside?

A player is offside when both skates are completely over the edge of the blue line. In this case, if his skates are behind the line, even if his body is not, it is not an offside.

**QUESTION: What is the exact definition of a "shot on goal?"**

A shot on goal is any deliberate action taken by an attacking player to shoot or deflect the puck with his stick onto the opposing goal, and which actually enters the goal or which, except for the interference of the goalkeeper or any other player, would have entered the net. This does not include shots that hit the post, clearing shots from a player at his own end, unless deliberate, or deflection off a defender, unless the puck goes into the net.

**QUESTION: In an N.H.L. game, Player A loses the puck to Player B. Player A grabs the sweater of Player B, who immediately starts to punch him. Player A does not retaliate. What is the ruling?**

Since Player A did not retaliate to the punch, he would be assessed a minor penalty for holding. Player B would, if he kept punching away at his opponent, be assessed a major penalty for fighting. However, if it was only a one-punch incident and then a shove, he could be assessed a minor penalty for roughing. The referee would have to decide at the time of the incident.

**QUESTION: Why don't officials in the National Hockey League stop a fight as quickly as possible rather than let the two combatants slug each other for several minutes?**

From long experience officials have learned that if two players evenly matched in size are allowed to mix it up for a few minutes without interference, they are apt to stop fighting by themselves much quicker than if someone tries to interfere at once. By waiting a few minutes, too, the officials can keep an eye on the other players and make sure the fight is not spreading.

If the fighting players are unevenly matched in size, however, or if one falls or is knocked to the ice, the officials will attempt to stop the fight immediately, to prevent injury.

**QUESTION: Is it permissible for any player, either attacker or defender, to enter the goalkeeper's crease area?**

N.H.L. rules specifically bar any attacking player from entering the crease, unless the puck is there or unless the physical interference of a defending player has put the attacker there.

The only restriction against a defending skater in the crease is that he may not fall on or hold the puck when it is there. To do so results in a penalty shot for the attacking side.

**QUESTION: In an N.H.L. game, an attacking team is in its offensive zone. One of the attacking players breaks his stick and drops it, as the rules require. One of the defensive players kicks the broken stick into the play. What is the ruling?**

The defensive player would receive a minor penalty of two minutes for interference.

**QUESTION: What is the ruling if a player in the N.H.L. leaves the penalty box before his penalty has expired?**

It does not matter if play is in progress or not, he incurs a minor penalty, which he must serve after his unexpired penalty.

**QUESTION: Are open-net goals recorded against the goalie who has just left the net?**

No. All open-net goals are recorded against the team, not the goalie. It does not matter if he is still on the ice trying to reach the bench.

**QUESTION: Does a player's salary decrease if he is sent down to a farm club by a National Hockey League team?**

Most of the older players have a stipulation in their contracts that prevent any reduction in their salaries. Some of the younger and less experienced players do not, and their salaries are adjusted when they are sent to a farm club.

**QUESTION: If an attacking player in the National Hockey League takes a shot on goal and the puck deflects off a teammate's skate and into the net, is the goal given to the player who took the shot?**

No. Rule 55 (d) of the Official Rule Book states: "If the puck shall have been deflected into the goal from the shot of an attacking player by striking any part of the person of a player on the same side, a goal shall be allowed. The player who deflected the puck shall be credited with the goal."

**QUESTION: Can there be an icing call on a power play in the National Hockey League? Also, exactly how does the league's rule book define icing?**

Icing is called on a power play, though of course only against the team with numerical superiority. As for definition, the rule is No. 61 (a) of the N.H.L.'s Official Rule Book. It states in part: "For the purpose of this rule, the center line will divide the ice into halves. Should any player of a team, equal or superior in numerical strength to the opposing team, shoot, bat, or deflect the puck from his own half of the ice beyond the goal line of the opposing team, play shall be stopped and the puck faced off at the end of the face-off spot of the offending team."

**QUESTION: Is there a limit to the number of men a National Hockey League team can play short-handed?**

No fewer than four players, including the goalie, can be on the ice for any one team. If two penalties have reduced the total to four, and if a third player then incurs a penalty before the expiration of either of the first two, his penalty time does not begin until one of the two others has elapsed. However, the third player must go immediately to the penalty box, and a substitute replaces him on the ice until the penalty time begins.

**QUESTION:** When an offensive team in the National Hockey League has the puck behind its own goal, how long is it allowed to fiddle with the puck and wait before passing it or bringing it up the ice?

The rule book is explicit on this. A team is allowed to carry the puck once behind its own goal on a given play, but it then must always advance the puck toward the opposite goal, except if opposing players prevent this. If the puck is not advanced quickly, play is stopped and a faceoff is made at either end spot adjacent to the goal of the team violating the rule. A second infraction results in a minor penalty to the player delaying the game.

**QUESTION:** In the National Hockey League, who selects the captain of each team and what are his duties?

Captains are appointed by each team, and no playing coach is permitted to act as one. The captain is the only player permitted to discuss with the referee any questions relating to interpretations of rules that may arise during a game. The captain must wear the letter "C" on the front of his sweater, and the letter must be about three inches in height.

**QUESTION:** When a goaltender has been pulled late in a National Hockey League game, is a player on his team allowed to block a shot in the crease with his glove?

Yes, the player may block a shot in the crease with his glove, but he may not fall on the puck as a goaltender is permitted to do.

**QUESTION:** What happens if a goalie or another player breaks his stick during a game?

A goaltender may continue to play with a broken stick until action is stopped or until he has been legally provided with a stick by a teammate. He may not go to his team's bench for a replacement.

A player other than a goalie must drop the broken portion of his stick to be able to continue play. He must obtain a new stick at his bench, and may not receive a stick thrown on the ice from any part of the rink.

**QUESTION:** Announcers of a National Hockey League game will often say that a penalty called near the end of a period can be carried over to the next period. What penalties, if any, cannot be carried over? Also, when there is a false faceoff, why isn't the clock turned back to make up for the wasted time?

All penalties in the N.H.L. are carried over into the next period, and announcers are apparently trying to clarify the point for their listeners. False faceoffs, which waste only a second or so, are considered part of the game.

# For the Record

**QUESTION: What was the Stanley Cup "fog final"?**

That was the series played in the spring of 1975, in which the Philadelphia Flyers beat the Buffalo Sabres, four games to two. In the third game of the series, on May 20, the Sabres defeated the Flyers, 5–4, at 18 minutes 29 seconds of overtime, after Referee Lloyd Gilmour had stopped the action 12 times in the last 33 minutes because high temperature and humidity inside the Memorial Auditorium in Buffalo were causing an ice-surface "fog." Each time Gilmour stopped the play he asked the players to skate around the rink in an effort to make the steam rise away. The temperature was 76 degrees outside the arena but reportedly 90 degrees on the ice.

**QUESTION: Has any team in the National Hockey League won the Stanley Cup without having a winning percentage during the regular season?**

It has happened twice. In 1937–38, the Chicago Black Hawks won 14 games, lost 25, tied nine and finished third in the American Division. In 1948–49, the Toronto Maple Leafs had a 22–25–13 record and finished fourth in what was then a six-team league.

**QUESTION: The New York Islanders won the 1980 Stanley Cup on an overtime goal, but has a Cup playoff game ever been decided by a penalty shot in overtime? How many penalty shots have there been during all the N.H.L. playoffs, and how many were successful?**

No playoff games have been decided by a penalty shot in overtime. There have been only six penalty shots in all the playoffs, none in overtime, and only one was successful. That was taken by Wayne Connelly of Minnesota against Terry Sawchuk of Los Angeles on April 9, 1968, in a game won by Minnesota, 7–5.

QUESTION: Frequent mention is made of the "hat trick" in hockey (three or more goals in a game by one player). Why is it called the hat trick?

The term hat trick apparently originated in cricket in 1882. It was used to describe the feat of a bowler taking three wickets on successive balls. The bowler's reward was a new hat from his cricket club. The expression first cropped up in hockey in the early 1900's, and there is some confusion as to its actual meaning. The most accepted definition of a hat trick, according to the National Hockey League Guide, is three successive goals by one player without another player from either team scoring in between. Nevertheless, three or more non-consecutive goals by a player in a game are often called a hat trick, and fans continue to throw their hats onto the ice when this happens.

QUESTION: How many players in the National Hockey League have achieved a double "hat trick" (six or more goals) in a game?

Eight, with one player, Joe Malone of Quebec, scoring seven goals on Jan. 31, 1920. The six-goal scorers: Newsy Lalonde of the Montreal Canadiens, on Jan. 10, 1920; Malone, March 10, 1920; Corb Denneny of the Toronto St. Pats, Jan. 26, 1921; Cy Denneny of Ottawa, March 7, 1921; Syd Howe of Detroit, Feb. 3, 1944; Red Berenson of St. Louis, Nov. 7, 1968, and Darryl Sittler of the Toronto Maple Leafs, Feb. 7, 1976.

QUESTION: Now that Mike Bossy of the New York Islanders has tied Maurice Richard's record of 50 goals in 50 games, how many empty-net goals did he score? How many did Richard score? How many did Phil Esposito have when he set the record of 76 goals for a season?

Bossy scored three empty-net goals in that 1980–81 streak. No such records were kept when Richard set the record in 1944–45. Esposito, who set his mark in 1970–71, had no empty-net goals.

QUESTION: In what season did the now defunct World Hockey Association begin operating, and who were the charter members?

The W.H.A. began operations in 1972–73, with 12 teams. The teams in the Eastern division were: Quebec Nordiques, New England Whalers, New York Raiders, Ottawa Nationals, Cleveland Crusaders and Philadelphia Blazers. The teams in the Western division were: Los Angeles Sharks, Alberta Oilers, Houston Aeros, Minnesota Fighting Saints, Chicago Cougars and Winnipeg Jets.

QUESTION: Has the National Hockey League's Stanley Cup ever been won in an overtime of the seventh game? Have there been such overtime victories in the National Basketball Association? Has a World Series seventh game ever been decided in extra innings? Have there ever been any overtime decisions in the National Football League title games?

Yes, in all four sports.

Hockey: 1949–50, the Detroit Red Wings over the New York Rangers, 4–3, at 8 minutes 31 seconds of the second overtime; 1953–54, Detroit over the Montreal Canadiens, 2–1, at 4:29.

Basketball: 1961–62, the Boston Celtics 110, the Los Angeles Lakers 107.

Baseball: 1912, the Boston Red Sox 3, the New York Giants 2, in 10 innings; 1924, the Washington Senators 4, the Giants 3, in 12 innings.

Football: 1958, the Baltimore Colts 23, the New York Giants 17, for the N.F.L. title. In addition, in 1962 the Dallas Texans captured the American Football League title by beating the Houston Oilers in overtime, 20–17.

**QUESTION: Now that the National Hockey League has expanded again, from 17 teams to 21, I would like to know the years the previous expansion teams joined the original six cities in the league.**

In 1967, Los Angeles, Minnesota, Philadelphia, Pittsburgh, St. Louis and California, which later that season became Oakland. In 1970, Buffalo and Vancouver. In 1972, Atlanta and the New York Islanders. In 1974, Washington and Kansas City, which franchise became Colorado in 1976. Oakland moved to Cleveland in 1976 and two years later merged with Minnesota.

**QUESTION: When did the N.H.L. begin the tradition of playing both the Canadian and American national anthems before games between teams from both countries?**

The Detroit Red Wings say they have been doing it for at least 30 years. According to the N.H.L. office, it was first discussed for all teams after the major expansion in 1967, and approved in 1969.

**QUESTION: Has there ever been a National Hockey League game that ended in a scoreless tie without a penalty being called? Also, who was the tallest goaltender in N.H.L. history?**

On Feb. 20, 1944, the Chicago Black Hawks and the Toronto Maple Leafs played the only such tie. The game lasted only one hour and 55 minutes.

Ken Dryden of the Montreal Canadiens and Gary Smith, who played on a number of N.H.L. teams, were the tallest goalies, at 6 feet 4 inches.

**QUESTION: Which goalie, at the end of the 1979–80 season, held the N.H.L. record for most shutouts in one season, and which goalie was the career leader?**

The single-season record was set by George Hainsworth of Montreal, who achieved 22 shutouts in a 44-game season in 1928–29. Terry

Sawchuk, who played from 1949 to 1970 with Detroit, Boston, Toronto, Los Angeles and the New York Rangers, is the career leader, with 103 shutouts in 971 games. Hainsworth's career, with Montreal and Toronto, lasted from 1926 to 1937, and he ended with 94 shutouts in 464 games. That was only nine fewer shutouts than amassed by Sawchuk, who played in 507 more games.

**QUESTION: How old was Terry Sawchuk when he died, and what did he die of? What were his career statistics as a goalie in the National Hockey League?**

Sawchuk died in May 1970 at the age of 40 after having been hospitalized a month because of internal injuries suffered in an off-the-ice scuffle with a New York Ranger teammate, Ron Stewart. A Nassau County grand jury ruled that the death was accidental, clearing Stewart of responsibility.

Sawchuk played from the 1949–50 season through 1969–70, mostly with the Detroit Red Wings. He appeared in 971 games and allowed 2,401 goals, for a goals-against average of 2.50. He registered 103 shutouts—the only goalie who has ever reached 100—and four times either won outright or shared the Vezina Trophy, which goes annually to regular goalies of the team with the fewest scores yielded.

**QUESTION: Have two players on the same team ever scored as many as four goals each in a National Hockey League game?**

Twice. On March 3, 1920, Newsy Lalonde and Harry Cameron of the Montreal Canadiens scored four each against the Quebec Bulldogs, in a game Montreal won, 16–3. On Jan. 14, 1922, Brothers Sprague and Odie Cleghorn, also of the Canadiens, duplicated the feat in a 10–6 victory over the Hamilton Tigers.

**QUESTION: Which team in the N.H.L. has scored the most points during a season? Which team has had the fewest losses during a season?**

The Montreal Canadiens, in an 80-game schedule in 1976–77, scored 132 points on 60 victories, eight defeats and 12 ties. Three teams, the Ottawa Senators (1919–20 in 24 games), the Boston Bruins (1929–30 in 44 games) and the Canadiens (1943–44 in 50 games) each lost only five times. In a minimum 70-game schedule, however, the Canadiens lead with their eight defeats in 1976–77.

**QUESTION: In the National Hockey League, which team has scored the most goals in one game and which team has scored the most consecutive goals in one game?**

The Montreal Canadiens bombarded the Quebec City Bulldogs, 16–3, on March 31, 1920. The Detroit Red Wings, on Jan. 23, 1944, shut out the New York Rangers, 15–0.

**QUESTION: How many players in the National Hockey League have scored 50 goals in one season? Who are the leaders in this statistic, and who was the first player to accomplish this feat?**

A total of 28 players—eight in 1980–81 season alone—have scored 50 or more goals, for a total of 54 times. Guy Lafleur has reached that peak six times, and Bobby Hull and Phil Esposito each five times. Maurice Richard of the Montreal Canadiens, in 1944–45, was the first; he tallied 50 goals in 50 games, the first 50-goal scorer to average a goal a game.

**QUESTION: Who are the three top N.H.L. career goal scorers and what are the statistics for each?**
Gordie Howe, 26 seasons, 1,767 games, 801 goals and 1,049 assists for 1,850 points; Phil Esposito, 18 seasons, 1,282 games, 717 goals, 873 assists for 1,590 points; Bobby Hull, 16 seasons, 1,063 games, 610 goals, 560 assists for 1,170 points.

**QUESTION: Which player in the National Hockey League holds the record for the most points in one season?**
Phil Esposito amassed 152 points in 78 regular-season games in 1970–71, when he was with the Boston Bruins. His total of 76 goals that season is also a record. Esposito added three goals and seven assists in seven playoff games, but this 162-point all-games total was tied when Guy Lafleur of the Montreal Canadiens scored 136 points in 80 regular-season games and 26 points in 14 playoff games during the 1976–77 season.

**QUESTION: Who are the top career leaders in the National Hockey League in scoring three or more goals a game?**
Phil Esposito, 32 times (27 three-goal games and five four-goal games); Bobby Hull, 28 times (24 three-goal games and four four-goal games); and Cy Denneny and Maurice Richard, each 26 times. Denneny had 20 three-goal games, five four-goal games and a six-goal game; Richard had 23 three-goal games, two four-goal games and a five-goal game.

**QUESTION: Which team had the most shots on goal in a National Hockey League game and won? Which team had the most and lost?**
The Boston Bruins, on March 4, 1941, took 83 shots in defeating the Chicago Black Hawks, 3–2.
The Pittsburgh Pirates, on Dec. 26, 1925, took 68 but lost to the New York Americans, 3–1. The Americans took 73 shots in that game, and the combined total of 141 is a league record.

**QUESTION: When did the now-defunct New York Americans and the New York Rangers join the National Hockey League? What was the starting lineup for each team in its first season?**
The Americans began play in the 1925–26 season in the newly opened third Madison Square Garden at 50th Street and Eighth Avenue; the Rangers joined the league for the 1926–27 season.
The starting lineup for the Americans: Vernon (Jake) Forbes, goalie; Kenneth Randall and Joseph (Bullet Joe) Simpson, defensemen; and William (Billy) Burch, Wilfred (Shorty) Green and Alexander McKinnon, forwards; for the Rangers: Lorne Chabot, goalie; Clarence (Taffy) Abel and Ivan (Ching) Johnson, defensemen; and Frank Boucher, William (Bill) Cook and Frederick (Bun) Cook, forwards.

QUESTION: For the 1978–79 season, the New York Rangers went back to their old-style uniforms, with "Rangers" printed diagonally across the front, instead of using the uniforms with the emblems on the front. Why?

After Fred Shero took over as the Ranger general manager and coach on June 2, 1978, he decided to emphasize the traditional uniform in an attempt to motivate the team. The emblem uniform had been introduced by his predecessor, John Ferguson. Shero, no longer with the Rangers, may have had the right idea; the Rangers, after all, made it to the Stanley Cup finals in 1979.

QUESTION: The New York Rangers' unusual feat of scoring two open-net goals in the final game of their playoff series against the Philadelphia Flyers in 1979 did not draw much comment. Had it ever been done before?

Yes, often. The Chicago Black Hawks hold the National Hockey League record for a single game. They scored five empty-net goals against the Montreal Canadiens on the final day of the 1969–70 regular season. In order to gain the playoffs that season, the Canadiens needed to win, tie or score at least five goals in the last game. They pulled the goalie early in an attempt to do this but nonetheless failed at all three tasks, losing to Chicago, 10–2.

QUESTION: In what year did the New York Rangers edge out the Montreal Canadiens for the playoffs on the last day of the season? How did it happen?

On April 15, 1970, the Rangers stopped the Detroit Red Wings, 9–5, at Madison Square Garden, while Montreal was being walloped by the Chicago Black Hawks, 10–2, in Chicago. This enabled the Rangers to tie the Canadiens in points, each having 92, and to outscore them in goals, 246–244, thus qualifying for the playoffs instead of the Canadiens. In their game, the Rangers set a club record of 65 shots on goal. It was also the only year since 1948–49 that Montreal failed to make the playoffs.

**QUESTION: What is the New York Rangers' cumulative record, through the 1980-81 season, against the five other teams that were in the National Hockey League the year the Rangers joined?**

There were more than five. When the Rangers began playing, in the 1926–27 season, there were 10 teams in the N.H.L., which was split into two divisions. The Rangers were in the American Division with Detroit and Chicago (two other new franchises), Boston, and the Pittsburgh Pirates. The five teams in the Canadian Division were Ottawa, Toronto, the Montreal Maroons, the Montreal Canadiens and the New York Americans, who had begun playing in Madison Square Garden the previous seasons.

The Rangers had a losing record through the 1980–81 season against each of the five other teams that survive from those days:

Versus Boston—195 victories, 239 defeats, 86 ties.
Versus Chicago—212–217–91.
Versus Detroit—189–230–98.
Versus Toronto—170–241–88.
Versus Montreal Canadiens—153–266–80.

**QUESTION: Who were the players involved in the trade that brought Phil Esposito to the New York Rangers from the Boston Bruins, and what were the career statistics of each at the time of the trade?**

Esposito came to the Rangers, along with Carol Vadnais, on Nov. 7, 1975, in exchange for Brad Park, Jean Ratelle and Joe Zanussi. The career statistics of each then were:

Esposito: 533 goals, 653 assists, 1,186 points; Vadnais: 111–221—332; Park: 95–283—378; Ratelle: 336–481—817; and Zanussi: 0–2—2.

**QUESTION: Dave and Don Maloney, brothers with the New York Rangers, played as juniors with the Kitchener Rangers of the Ontario Hockey Association. Please list their career statistics with Kitchener.**

Dave Maloney, who played 119 games with Kitchener from 1971–72 to 1973–74, scored 23 goals and had 74 assists for 97 points, and was assessed 210 penalty minutes. Don Maloney played 156 games from 1974–75 to 1977–78 and had 80 goals, 52 assists and 232 penalty minutes.

**QUESTION: How many of the top 25 goal-scorers in N.H.L. history have played for the New York Rangers?**

Six. They are, with goal totals up until the start of the 1980–81 season: Phil Esposito (710); Jean Ratelle (480); Rod Gilbert (406); Bernie Geoffrion (394); Dean Prentice (391) and Andy Bathgate (349).

**QUESTION: Since the New York Rangers were formed, how many goals have they scored and how many were scored against them?**

Including the 1980–81 season, 10,355 goals for and 10,633 against.

**QUESTION: How did the New York Rangers come by their name?**
The first owner of the club was Tex Rickard, the noted fight promoter. The team was called Tex's Rangers at first.

**QUESTION: How many power-play goals did the New York Rangers and the New York Islanders score during the 1979–80 season? How many were scored against them? How many shorthanded goals were scored by each team and against each team?**
The Rangers scored 79 power-play goals, the Islanders 63; 54 were scored against the Rangers, 71 against the Islanders. The Rangers scored eight short-handed goals, the Islanders seven; eight were scored against the Rangers, four against the Islanders.

**QUESTION: The Rangers and the Colorado Rockies once scored four goals in 1 minute and 1 second, a record for two teams, and much better than the single-team mark. However, which single teams in the National Hockey League hold the records for scoring the fastest five, four and three goals?**
Five: Pittsburgh Penguins, 2 minutes, 7 seconds, in defeating the St. Louis Blues, 10–4, on Nov. 22, 1972.
Four: Boston Bruins, 1 minute, 20 seconds, in stopping the Rangers, 14–3, on Jan. 21, 1945.
Three: Boston, 20 seconds, in trouncing Vancouver, 8–3, on Feb. 25, 1971.

**QUESTION: The current rivalry between the New York Rangers and the New York Islanders recalls the competition between the Rangers and the now-defunct New York Americans when both played in the old Madison Square Garden. How long did that series last, and how well did the Rangers do?**
The series started in the 1926–27 season, when the Rangers joined the National Hockey League, and ended with the 1940–41 season, after which the Americans dropped out. The Rangers won 57 games, lost 23 and tied 14, and scored 299 goals, to 189 for the Americans.

**QUESTION: Which National Hockey League teams did Al Arbour, the coach of the New York Islanders, play for, and when? What were his career statistics? Did any of his teams win the Stanley Cup?**
Arbour played for the Detroit Red Wings (1953–54, 1956–58), the Chicago Black Hawks (1958–61), the Toronto Maple Leafs (1961–66) and the St. Louis Blues (1967–71). As a defenseman, he appeared in 626 regular-season games, scored 12 goals and had 68 assists. He was on five teams that won the Stanley Cup: Detroit (1954), Chicago (1961) and Toronto (1962–63–64).

**QUESTION: How many players were drafted ahead of Bryan Trottier before the New York Islanders selected him in 1974? How many made it to the National Hockey League?**
Of the 21 players drafted ahead of Trottier, all but one played at least one game in the league. Don Larway, drafted 18th, did not.

QUESTION: Denis Potvin of the New York Islanders scored two short-handed goals against the Toronto Maple Leafs on March 15, 1980. Was that a record?

Potvin's feat tied a record that had been achieved by a number of other players.

QUESTION: What are Mike Bossy's career statistics for the four seasons he has been with the New York Islanders? Has any other player ever scored 50 or more goals in his first four years? Who is the career leader in scoring 50 or more goals in a season?

Bossy has 241 goals, 187 assists and 428 points for his first four seasons, ending with 1980–81. No other player has scored 50 or more goals in each of his first four seasons in the National Hockey League. Guy Lafleur of the Montreal Canadiens, who failed to score 50 goals in 1980–81, turned the trick six years in a row, but he began his streak in his fourth season in the league. Lafleur broke Phil Esposito's record of five straight seasons, 1970–71 through 1974–75. Esposito was playing for the Boston Bruins when he set his record, and he had been in the league four years when he started his scoring streak.

QUESTION: Who was the first black to play in the National Hockey League?

The first black in the league was Willie O'Ree, a Boston Bruin forward. He played two games in the 1957–58 season and 43 in 1960–61, scoring four goals and making 10 assists.

# Basketball

## Rules of the Game

INBOUNDS PASS...

BUZZ!

TIP!

IT'S GOOD!

RN

**QUESTION: Team A has just scored and taken the lead by 1 point in a National Basketball Association game that has three or four seconds left. A player for Team B, inbounding the ball, throws it the length of the court, straight for the hoop. Such a basket will be disallowed unless another player first touches the ball, of course, but will goaltending be called if either a defensive or an offensive player interferes with the course of the ball while it is directly over or on the rim of the hoop?**

No, for the very reason you cite: The ball is not live on an inbounds pass until another player touches it.

A defensive player would be unlikely to touch the ball, because he would be taking the risk of turning an illegal basket into a legal one, but if he did touch it, and if it went through the hoop, the goal would count. It would count as well if the ball were touched by an offensive player.

**QUESTION: As a result of injuries and players' fouling out, a basketball team may find itself with fewer than five eligible players during a game. What does the team do?**

The rules are different for professional and collegiate basketball.

In the National Basketball Association, Rule 3, Section I states: "No team may be reduced to less than five players. If and when a player in the game receives his sixth personal foul and all substitutes have already been disqualified, said player remains in the game and is charged with a personal and team foul. All subsequent personal fouls shall be treated similarly. All players who have six or more personal fouls and remain in the game shall be treated similarly."

In college basketball, if a team is down to four players, it continues playing with only them. If it is down to three, the same. However, finishing a game with fewer than five players rarely occurs.

**QUESTION: Which team receives the ball after a technical foul in the National Basketball Association? Has the rule been changed recently?**

Rule 12, Section VI, Note 4 of the Official Rules of the N.B.A. states, "On technical foul attempts, whether the attempt has been successful or not, the ball shall be returned to the team having possession at the time the foul was called, and play shall be resumed from a point out of bounds where the play ended." The rule has not been changed recently.

**QUESTION: I know that both players and coaches in the National Basketball Association can draw technical fouls for misconduct, but do the fines differ?**

No. The first misconduct technical in a game costs a player or a coach $75, and the second $150 more and automatic ejection from the game. If ejection occurs on the first technical, the fine is $225. A further automatic fine of $500 will be imposed on an ejected player or coach who does not immediately leave the playing area. Finally, upon review, the commissioner may levy a subsequent fine of as much as $10,000 for any act of misconduct.

**QUESTION: Are doubleheaders during the regular season barred by the National Basketball Association?**

No, but they are not often scheduled. One such doubleheader, at the Houston Astrodome on Feb. 4, 1969, drew 41,163 fans. The attraction was Elvin Hayes, then in his rookie year with San Diego. Hayes had been a great college star at the University of Houston, and he did not disappoint his fans, scoring 36 points as San Diego beat Boston, 135–126. In the other game, Cincinnati defeated Detroit, 125–114. Less than a year later, on Jan. 22, 1970, 21,619 fans attended another doubleheader involving Hayes at the Astrodome.

**QUESTION: There is a scramble under the backboard in a National Basketball Association game, and a player on Team A finds himself with both feet out of bounds as he catches a ball on the fly that was sent out of bounds by a player on Team B. Whose ball is it?**

It is Team B's ball. The N.B.A. rule covering this situation states: "If the ball is out of bounds because of touching a player who is on or outside a boundary, such player caused it to go out."

The National Collegiate Athletic Association has a similar rule.

**QUESTION: It seems to me that there has been a greater emphasis on assists in the N.B.A. in recent years. Has there been a change in the way assists are credited to players? Who are the career leaders? Who holds the season record?**

There has been no change in the way assists are credited, but there are more assists because the season is longer.

The top five assist leaders are: Oscar Robertson, 9,887; Lenny Wilkens, 7,211; Bob Cousy, 6,995; Guy Rodgers, 6,917; and Jerry West, 6,238. Kevin Porter, in 1978–79, set the season record with 1,099, an average of 13.4 a game.

**QUESTION: If a player in the National Basketball Association breaks the rim in dunking the ball, does the basket count? Does the game end there because of the broken basket?**

As long as the ball goes through the basket, it counts for 2 points. The home team is required to have a spare board on hand for just such emergencies, so the game would continue.

**QUESTION: On an attempted shot in the National Basketball Association, the ball rebounds off the rim and rolls along the top edges of the backboard. Is the ball still in play?**

Yes. All the edges of the backboard sides, top and bottom, are considered inbounds.

**QUESTION: A player in the National Basketball Association has his arms clamped by an opponent as he is about to attempt a shot. Because the ball has not been released, how many free throws are awarded?**

Two. Although the ball was not released, the player is considered to have been fouled in the act of shooting because he had already started the motion that preceded his attempt to score.

**QUESTION: In the National Basketball Association, what is the difference between a backcourt foul and a loose-ball foul?**

A backcourt foul is a personal foul committed against a team in control of the ball behind the midcourt line as it is attempting to advance toward its opponent's basket. Two foul shots are awarded for this violation; if the offending team is in the penalty situation, the offended team gets three shots to make two.

A loose-ball foul is a personal foul committed while the ball is in the air for a shot or during rebounding, and where the ball is not in possession of any player. The offending team will be charged with a team foul, the offending player with a personal foul, no foul try will be taken, and the team fouled will retain possession. In a penalty situation, all free throws that apply on the personal foul will be attempted.

Another variation occurs when a loose-ball foul is called against the defensive team as a field goal or foul shot is being successfully attempted. In that instance, and it does not matter which offensive player is fouled, the free throw will be attempted.

## For the Record

**QUESTION: How many players in the National Basketball Association have scored more than 10,000 points and have had more than 10,000 rebounds, not including playoff games?**

Fifteen, as of the end of the 1979–80 season. They are: Wilt Chamberlain, 31,419 points and 23,924 rebounds; Elgin Baylor, 23,149 and 11,463; Kareem Abdul-Jabbar, 24,175 and 12,346; Elvin Hayes, 23,008 and 13,867; Walt Bellamy, 20,941 and 14,241; Bob Pettit, 20,880 and 12,848; Dolph Schayes, 19,249 and 11,256; Bill Russell, 14,522 and 21,620; Nate Thurmond, 14,437 and 14,464; Jerry Lucas, 14,053 and 12,942; Dave Cowens, 13,192 and 10,170, John Kerr, 12,480 and 10,092; Paul Silas, 11,782 and 12,357; Bill Bridges, 11,012 and 11,054, and Wes Unseld, 10,117 and 13,096.

**QUESTION:** Since the inception of the 24-second clock in the National Basketball Association, what has been the lowest score by one team?

On Feb. 27, 1955, Milwaukee scored 57 points, to Boston's 62. Milwaukee's total in that game still stands as the lowest since the inception of the 24-second clock, at the start of the 1954–55 season, and the total by the two teams is also the lowest.

**QUESTION:** Has anyone who was not on the championship team ever been selected as the most valuable player in the National Basketball Association playoffs?

In 1969, the first year of the award, Jerry West of the Los Angeles Lakers was chosen though his team was beaten by the Boston Celtics in the final round, four games to three. No other such player has ever been selected.

**QUESTION:** How many players in the National Basketball Association have been the scoring leader and have had the best field-goal percentage in the same season?

Four players have been leaders in both categories, and one of them, Wilt Chamberlain, accomplished it four times. Here are the statistics:

1951–52: Paul Arizin of Philadelphia, 1,674 points and a .448 average.

1952–53: Neil Johnston, also of Philadelphia, 1,564 and .452.

1960–61: Chamberlain, with Philadelphia, 3,033 and .509.

1962–63: Chamberlain, with San Francisco, 3,586 and .528.

1964–65: Chamberlain, with San Francisco and Philadelphia, 2,534 and .510.

1965–66: Chamberlain, with Philadelphia, 2,649 and .540.

1973–74: Bob McAdoo of Buffalo, 2,261 for a 30.6 average (in 1969–70, average points per game became the determining factor in scoring) and .547.

**QUESTION:** Did Wilt Chamberlain ever play in the American Basketball Association when he was coaching the San Diego Conquistadors? What were his statistics as a player and as a coach? When did the team fold?

Chamberlain coached San Diego only for the 1973–74 season, and he did not play. The team won 37 games and lost 47, then won two games and lost four in the playoffs. The Conquistadors became the Sails for the 1975–76 season; the team was not absorbed into the National Basketball Association for the 1976–77 season. A new team was established in San Diego for the 1978–79 season.

**QUESTION:** Was Wilt Chamberlain's reputation as a poor free-throw shooter deserved? What were his career statistics? When he scored 100 points against the Knicks, how did his free-throw average in that game compare with his career average?

During his career, Chamberlain made 6,057 free throws out of 11,862 attempts, a .511 average, which speaks for itself. In the historic game against the Knicks, on March 2, 1962, at Hershey, Pa., he sank 28 of 32 free throws, for .875. He also made 36 field goals as Philadelphia trounced the Knicks, 169–147.

QUESTION: When a player in the National Basketball Association is fouled in the act of shooting, and the ball misses the basket, is the attempt counted in calculating his field-goal shooting statistics?

No.

QUESTION: I've heard the expression, "The opera isn't over until the fat lady sings," a number of times. I know that it has the same meaning as "the game isn't over until the last man is out." It has been attributed to a number of people, including Dick Motta, now coach of the Dallas Mavericks of the N.B.A. Who did originate it?

The expression has been used for a number of years by Dan Cook, a sportscaster with a CBS affiliate in San Antonio, in reference to the Spurs. Motta heard it in that city and began to use it, as have other coaches, commentators and writers.

QUESTION: In the last 10 years, how many rookies in the National Basketball Association averaged 20 or more points a game for a season?

Eight. In 1970–71: Geoff Petrie of Portland, 24.8, and Pete Maravich of Atlanta, 23.2; 1971–72: Sidney Wicks of Portland, 24.5; 1976–77: Adrian Dantley of Buffalo, 20.3; 1977–78: Walter Davis of Phoenix and Bernard King of New Jersey, each with 24.2; 1979–80: Bill Cartwright of the Knicks, 21.7, and Larry Bird of Boston, 21.3.

QUESTION: Among the guards in the National Basketball Association who have career averages of at least 18 points a game and have scored at least 10,000 points, who are the top five in field-goal percentage?

As of the end of the 1979–80 season, the five leading guards, inactive and active, were: Walt Frazier, .490 for 13 seasons, with 15,581 points and an average of 18.9; Calvin Murphy, .486 for 10 seasons, 15,212 and 19.1; Oscar Robertson, .485 for 14 seasons, 26,710 and 25.7; Jerry West, .474 for 14 seasons, 25,192 and 27.0, and Nate Archibald, .466 for nine seasons, 13,482 and 21.9.

QUESTION: Some time ago I saw a list of all the National Basketball Association players who have scored 20,000 or more points in their careers. Only one was an active player, Kareem Abdul-Jabbar. Are there any other active players now on that list? How many active players are among the top 30 career scorers?

As of the end of the 1979–80 season, only Elvin Hayes, with 23,108 points had joined Jabbar, who had 24,175, and was fifth on the list, with Hayes seventh. Bob Lanier was 23d with 15,896; Bob McAdoo was 25th with 15,627; Bob Dandridge was 29th with 15,248 and Calvin Murphy was 30th with 15,212.

QUESTION: Who are the top five career scorers in the National Basketball Association playoffs?

Jerry West, 4,457 points; John Havlicek, 3,776; Elgin Baylor, 3,623; Wilt Chamberlain, 3,607, and Sam Jones, 2,909.

QUESTION: Which teams hold the records for the longest winning and losing streaks in the National Basketball Association?

The Los Angeles Lakers won 33 straight games in the 1971–72 season. The Detroit Pistons lost 21 straight games, 14 in 1979–80 and seven in 1980–81. Both streaks are N.B.A. records.

QUESTION: Since the inception of the 3-point goal in the National Basketball Association in the 1979–80 season, have any players been fouled while making the shot, thus turning it into a possible 4-point play?

Yes, a number of times. The first of these players to make 4 points on a field-goal shot was Stan Smith of Chicago against Milwaukee on Oct. 21, 1979. Despite the 4 points, and another 3-point goal by Smith, the Bucks defeated the Bulls, 113–111.

QUESTION: What individual made the most 3-point goals during the 1979–80 N.B.A. season? Who had the highest percentage of such shots made?

Brian Taylor of San Diego led the league with 90. Based on a minimum of 25 successful attempts, Fred Brown of Seattle was the percentage leader with 39 of 88 attempts for .443.

QUESTION: Three alumni of one college—St. Joseph's of Philadelphia—were coaching in the N.B.A. in 1980–81: Jack Ramsay (Portland Trail Blazers), Jack McKinney (Indiana Pacers) and Paul Westhead (Los Angeles Lakers). Has this happened before?

Yes, as recently as the 1978–79 season. Larry Brown (Denver Nuggets), Doug Moe (San Antonio Spurs) and Billy Cunningham (Philadelphia 76ers) were alumni of the University of North Carolina.

QUESTION: What were the lowest and highest scoring quarters in the National Basketball Association in the 1979–80 regular season? What is the record in those categories?

Detroit scored 50 points against Chicago on Jan. 22, for the highest quarter. Houston scored only 10 against Utah on Feb. 22, and Golden State did the same against Milwaukee on March 8, for the lowest quarter.

Buffalo holds the record for the most—58—against Boston on Oct. 20, 1972. The least amount of points ever scored in one quarter is 1, by Minneapolis against Fort Wayne on Nov. 22, 1950. That game ended in a 19–18 victory for Fort Wayne, which tallied only 3 points in each of two quarters. The game was played before the 24-second clock went into effect.

QUESTION: Can you please tell me the origin of the term "barn-burner," referring to extremely close games, especially basketball?

According to The New Columbia Encyclopedia, the word derives from the fabled Dutchman who burned his barn to rid it of rats. It was also the name of the radical elements of the Democratic party in New York State from 1842 to 1848. Webster's Sports Dictionary defines barn-burner as "an unusually close or exciting contest," but does not say who first used the word in relation to sports.

**QUESTION: In what year were the New York Knicks formed? What is their best record for a season? Their worst record? Which numbers have the Knicks retired?**

The Knicks' first season was 1946–47, when the league was called the Basketball Association of America. (It became the National Basketball Association for the 1949–50 season.) The Knicks' best year was 1969–70, when they won 60 games, lost 22 and went on to capture their first league championship. The worst season was 1962–63, when they finished 21–59. Three numbers have been retired: Walt Frazier's 10, Willis Reed's 19, and Dave DeBusschere's 22. The three players were members of the championship team.

**QUESTION: How many years has Red Holzman been a coach in the National Basketball Association? What is his career record, and what is his record with the Knicks?**

Holzman is in his 18th season of coaching. He started with the Milwaukee Hawks (later the St. Louis Hawks) in 1953–54, and became the Knick coach in 1967–68. Including 1980–81, he has 663 career victories and 555 losses; his Knick record is 580–435. Only Red Auerbach, with 938 victories, has won more games than Holzman.

**QUESTION: Who are the Knicks career leaders in games played, scoring, field goals made and rebounds?**

Games: Walt Frazier, 759 (10 seasons); scoring: Frazier, 14,617 points; field goals: Frazier, 5,736; rebounds: Willis Reed, 8,414 (10 seasons).

**QUESTION: Whom did the New York Knicks play in their first game, where was it played, and who was the leading scorer, Leo Gottlieb or Sonny Hertzberg?**

The Knickerbockers defeated the Toronto Huskies, 68–66, on Nov. 1, 1946, at Toronto. Gottlieb was the top New York scorer, with 14 points; Hertzberg had 2. The top scorers for Toronto were Ed Sadowsky (18) and George Nostrand (16). The 24-second rule was not yet in effect; thus the low score.

**QUESTION:** When did Leo Gottlieb play for the New York Knicks, who was the coach, and who were some of his teammates?

Gottlieb played in 1946–47 and 1947–48. Neil Cohalan coached the first season, and Joe Lapchick the second. Some of the other Knick players in those two seasons were Ossie Schectman, Stan Stutz, Tommy Byrnes, Sonny Hertzberg, Ralph Kaplowitz, Bill van Breda Kolff, Bud Palmer and Carl Braun.

**QUESTION:** Who was the first authentic jump shooter in professional basketball, Paul Arizin or Bob Pettit?

Neither. Joe Fulks, who was called Jumpin' Joe, is usually credited with being the first jump shooter in professional basketball. He starred for Philadelphia in the late 1940's and the early 1950's. Arizin played pro ball from 1951 to 1962, and Pettit from 1955 to 1965, so obviously Arizin was ahead of Pettit.

But the player who truly revolutionized basketball shooting styles was not a pro. In December 1936 Hank Luisetti and his Stanford University team came to New York and overwhelmed a good squad from Long Island University, 45–31, ending an L.I.U. winning streak of 43 games. Luisetti's running, one-handed, off-the-ear shot, a forerunner of the jump shots you see today in the National Basketball Association, stunned the fans at the Madison Square Garden game. Basketball, until then almost exclusively a game of the set shot, was never the same again.

**QUESTION:** My father keeps telling me that Max Zaslofsky was a great professional basketball player who scored from 40 feet out. What teams did he play for and what were his career statistics?

Zaslofsky played for the Chicago Stags of the Basketball Association of America from 1946–47 through 1949–50, the season the league merged with the established National Basketball League to become the National Basketball Association. He then played with the New York Knicks from 1950–51 through 1952–53, with Baltimore, Milwaukee and Fort Wayne in 1953–54, and with Fort Wayne for two more seasons.

He played in 540 games, scored 2,854 goals and 2,282 fouls for a total of 7,990 points, a game average of 14.8. He led the B.A.A. in scoring in 1947–48 with 1,007 points, a 21-point average. Zaslofsky was not a jump shooter, but was noted for his two-handed set shot from more than 30 feet out, and, probably, from 40 feet out at times.

**QUESTION:** A few years ago the Chicago Bulls drafted John Laskowski, a guard for Indiana University. How long did he last in the National Basketball Association, what were his statistics and where is he now?

Laskowski played two seasons with Chicago, 1975–76 and 1976–77, appearing in 118 games and scoring 832 points for a 7.1 average. He is now working for a real estate concern in Indianapolis.

**QUESTION:** What ever happened to Terry Dischinger, who was the National Basketball Association's rookie of the year in 1962–63, when he was with Chicago? How long did he play in the league and where is he now?

Dischinger was in the league nine seasons. He played with Baltimore in 1963–64, and with Detroit from 1964–65 through 1971–72, taking time out for military service in 1965–66 and 1966–67. He was traded to Portland on July 31, 1972, for Fred Foster, and finished his career there the next season. He is practicing dentistry now in Portland.

**QUESTION: Where did Darrall Imhoff play basketball in college? What were his career statistics in the National Basketball Association?**

Imhoff played for the University of California and helped the Golden Bears win the National Collegiate Athletic Association title in 1959, scoring 10 points in the 71–70 victory over West Virginia. California again reached the championship game in 1960, but lost to Ohio State, 75–55, with Imhoff scoring 8 points.

The Knicks made Imhoff their first pick in the 1960 draft, but he only stayed with them for two seasons. He then played with Detroit, Los Angeles, Philadelphia, Cincinnati and Portland, retiring after the 1971–72 season. He appeared in 801 games, scoring 5,759 points on 2,299 field goals and 1,161 free throws. He averaged 7.2 points a game.

**QUESTION: What happened to Bill Willoughby, the young basketball player signed in 1975 out of Dwight Morrow High School in Englewood, N.J.?**

Willoughby was drafted by the Atlanta Hawks and played with them for two seasons, then was traded to the Buffalo Braves on Sept. 13, 1977, for a future draft choice. He stayed with Buffalo (now the San Diego Clippers) through the season but was placed on waivers before the 1978–79 season opened and was not picked up. In his first three years in the league he scored 861 points, for an average of 5.5 a game. Eventually, after an unproductive stint with the Cleveland Cavaliers, he was signed, on Nov. 28, 1980, by the Houston Rockets, and helped them gain the N.B.A. finals, which they lost to Boston, 4–2. Willoughby appeared in 55 games as a Rocket during the regular season and scored 349 points for a 6.3 average.

**QUESTION: To me, George Gervin, the Iceman of the National Basketball Association, is something of a mystery man as well. How long has he been with the San Antonio Spurs? With whom did he play before? What are his scoring statistics as a professional?**

Gervin played his college ball at Eastern Michigan University, then left school to join the American Basketball Association. He spent four seasons in the A.B.A. (1972–76), with the Virginia Squires and San Antonio. For those four years, he averaged 21.9 points per game. He shot .491 percent on his 2-point field-goal attempts, .234 on 3-point field goals and .831 on free throws.

He joined the N.B.A. with the Spurs in 1976–77, averaging 23.1 points. His field-goal percentage was .544 and his free-throw percentage .833. His figures in 1977–78 were 27.2, .536 and .830. For 1978–79, they were 29.6, .541 and .826. For 1979–80, they were 33.1, .528 and .852. For 1980–81, they were 27.1, .492 and .826. He became the fifth player in N.B.A. history to win three or more consecutive scoring titles (1977–78, 1978–79, 1979–80). The four others were George Mikan, Neil Johnston,

Bob McAdoo and Wilt Chamberlain, who holds the record with seven straight titles.

**QUESTION: Were there any men's minor leagues in professional basketball in operation in the 1979–80 season? If so, which cities were involved?**

The Continental Basketball Association, with headquarters in Lafayette Hill, Pa., was the only league in operation. The Western Basketball Association, which was supposed to have merged with the C.B.A., folded in September of 1979. There were eight teams in the surviving league: Rochester; Utica, N.Y.; Lancaster, Pa.; Lehigh Valley, Pa.; the Pennsylvania Barons of Scranton and Wilkes-Barre; Maine, which played in Bangor; Anchorage, and Hawaii.

**QUESTION: Texas Western captured the National Collegiate Athletic Association basketball championship in 1966. Did any member of that team make it to the National Basketball Association?**

One, Dave Lattin, who played with San Francisco in 1967–68 and with Phoenix in 1968–69. He also played the next three seasons in the American Basketball Association.

**QUESTION: What was Dave DeBusschere's record as a coach of the Detroit Pistons? When was he traded to the Knicks and which players were involved?**

DeBusschere was a player-coach of the Pistons for part of the 1964–65 season, all of 1965–66 and part of 1966–67 before becoming a full-time player again. As a coach, he won 79 games and lost 143. He was traded to the Knicks on Dec. 19, 1968 for Walt Bellamy, a center, and Howie Komives, a guard. The Knicks retired DeBusschere's "22" on March 24, 1981.

**QUESTION: Now that it appears as if Bill Walton may never play again in the National Basketball Association, what are his career statistics?**

Walton, who was still on the injured-reserve list of the San Diego Clippers at the end of the 1980–81 season, has appeared in 223 games, 14 with San Diego and the rest with Portland, which he joined in 1974–75. He has scored 1,594 field goals in 3,050 attempts, 664 free throws in 992 attempts, for 3,772 points and an average of 16.9 a game. He grabbed 581 offensive rebounds and 2,367 defensive rebounds for a total of 2,948.

# Boxing

## Rules of the Game

**QUESTION: Were six-ounce gloves ever used in boxing matches in New York State?**

From the time gloves were first used in boxing in 1818, the weight of the gloves has varied in different periods, ranging from 10 ounces to two ounces. On June 8, 1963, the New York State Commission ordered the use of eight-ounce gloves in all matches, but prior to that, from 1951 on, six-ounce gloves were compulsory in all championship matches, while eight-ounce gloves were used in other bouts.

**QUESTION: What is the required size of a boxing ring and why do they vary for different fights?**

The Marquis of Queensberry rules, in 1867, specified that a ring should be 24 feet square, or as near that size as practicable. Today, most rings are not less than 18 feet nor more than 20 feet square. However, because some states do not have boxing commissions, and because many arenas where boxing matches are held vary in size, the rings are sometimes smaller than that standard. Until there is a national boxing commission that will set a standard size for all rings, this condition will prevail.

**QUESTION: Are professional prize fighters insured in the ring? If so, who pays the premium?**

Different states have their own requirements, but in New York State a fighter is insured for $10,000 in death benefits and for $750 in medical treatment. The promoter must pay to the New York State Athletic Commission, which oversees the insurance, $15 for each fighter for each bout on a card. In addition, promoters are required to carry Workmen's Compensation, and the fighters are also insured under that program.

**QUESTION: Red Smith and others use the term "sweet science" (sometimes the first letters are capitalized) as a synonym for pugilism. What is the origin of the phrase?**

A.J. Liebling, in the introduction to his book "The Sweet Science," attributes the phrase "sweet science of bruising" to a column written by Pierce Egan of England in 1824. The column is contained in "Boxiana," a collection of articles by Mr. Egan, who began writing in 1812.

# For the Record

**QUESTION: How many fights did Sam Langford win and lose? Did he ever win a championship? How long did he fight?**

Langford began fighting as a featherweight in 1902 and ended his career as a heavyweight in 1924. He fought 252 times, winning 99 bouts by knockouts, 37 by decisions and one by a foul. He lost 19 decisions and was knocked out four times. Thirty-one bouts ended in draws, 59 in no-decision and two were declared no-contest. He never fought for a title and never held one. He became blind after his retirement, was elected to the Boxing Hall of Fame in 1955 and died at the age of 75 on Jan. 12, 1956.

**QUESTION: How old was Abe Attell when he won boxing's featherweight championship, when he lost it and when he died? What was his career record?**

Attell, who was born on Feb. 22, 1884, won the vacated featherweight title at the age of 17, on a decision over George Dixon on Oct. 28, 1901. (This was a 15-round bout, and it took place only eight days after Attell and Dixon, meeting initially for the championship, had fought to a 20-round draw.) He lost the crown on his 28th birthday, Feb. 22, 1912, to Johnny Kilbane in 20 rounds. Attell fought 168 bouts, won 91 (47 by knockout), lost 10 (three by knockout) and drew 17. There were 50 no-decisions. He died on Feb. 7, 1970, two weeks before he was to turn 86.

**QUESTION: How many heavyweight boxers retired without losing a fight after they won the championship? Which heavyweight champion weighed the least? Which weighed the most?**

James J. Jeffries in 1905, Gene Tunney in 1928, Joe Louis in 1949, Rocky Marciano in 1956 and Muhammad Ali in 1970 (the first time) all retired undefeated. However, Jeffries, Louis and Ali all returned to the ring again and were beaten.

Bob Fitzsimmons, who won the crown in 1897 and also, at different times, the middleweight and light-heavyweight championships, weighed 167 pounds, the least of any heavyweight titleholder. Primo Carnera, who held the crown for less than a year from 1933 to 1934, weighed 260½ pounds and was the heaviest champion.

**QUESTION: Which fighter held the heavyweight title for the longest period of time, and who took the championship away from him? Who held the crown for the shortest period?**

Joe Louis won the title on June 22, 1937. He held it until he retired on March 1, 1949, as undefeated champion, after a reign of 11 years and eight months and eight days.

Leon Spinks, who took the crown from Muhammad Ali on Feb. 15, 1978, and lost it back to him on Sept. 15, 1978, held the title for seven months, the shortest period on record.

**QUESTION: Has there ever been a draw in a world championship heavyweight bout?**

There have been four draws: 1860, John Heenan and Tom Sayers, 42 rounds; 1888, John L. Sullivan and Charley Mitchell, 39 rounds; 1906, Tommy Burns and Jack O'Brien, 20 rounds, and 1913, Jack Johnson and Battling Jim Johnson, 10 rounds.

**QUESTION: When did Max Schmeling win the world heavyweight title, and when did he lose it? When was his last fight and what were his careeer statistics? Did he ever hold any European titles?**

Schmeling won the vacant world heavyweight crown—Gene Tunney had retired as champion—on a foul by Jack Sharkey in the fourth round on June 12, 1930. He successfully defended the title once, by knocking out Young Stribling a year later, before losing it to Sharkey on a decision after 15 rounds June 21, 1932. His last fight, at the age of 43, was against Richard Vogt, to whom he lost a decision in a 10-round match in Berlin on Oct. 31, 1948.

In all, Schmeling fought 70 bouts, winning 39 on knockouts, 14 on decisions and three on fouls. He lost five bouts on decisions and five by knockouts, and fought four draws. He held the European heavyweight and light-heavyweight titles at different times.

**QUESTION: Where and when did Rocky Marciano fight Roland LaStarza and what were the results?**

Marciano won a split decision from LaStarza in a 10-round bout on March 24, 1950, at Madison Square Garden. Then, after Marciano had won the heavyweight championship, he knocked out LaStarza in the 11th round on Sept. 24, 1953, at the Polo Grounds.

**QUESTION: Rocky Marciano was undefeated as a professional fighter, but did he ever lose a bout as an amateur? Also, how old was he when he retired from the ring?**

Marciano, who was 32 years old when he retired, lost one bout as an amateur, to Coley Wallace. Wallace turned professional in 1950, and ended his career in 1956 with a record of 20 victories and 7 losses. Wallace was perhaps better known for playing the role of Joe Louis in the 1953 movie, "The Joe Louis Story."

**QUESTION: How many fighters did Rocky Marciano fail to knock out and who were they?**

Marciano, unbeaten in 49 bouts, won six on decisions from Don Mogard, Ted Lowry (twice), Roland LaStarza, Red Applegate and Ezzard Charles.

**QUESTION: How many fighters lasted 15 rounds with Joe Louis and what were the results?**

There were four such bouts, in the first three of which Louis successfully defended his heavyweight title—defeating Tommy Farr on Aug. 30, 1937, Arturo Godoy on Feb. 9, 1940, and Jersey Joe Walcott on Dec. 5, 1947. After Louis retired as undefeated champion in 1949, he tried a comeback, but on Sept. 27, 1950, he was beaten by Ezzard Charles, who had become his successor, in a title fight that lasted 15 rounds.

**QUESTION: What were Battling Levinsky's career statistics? How long did he hold the light-heavyweight boxing title? What was his real name and when did he die?**

Levinsky began boxing in 1906, but his record until 1910 is not available. From 1910 until he retired in 1929, he had 274 bouts, winning 25 on knockouts, 41 by decisions and one on a foul. He had 13 draws. He lost 13 on decisions, two on fouls, four by knockouts and 175 ended in no decisions. Levinsky's real name was Barney Lebrowitz and he fought under the name of Barney Williams until 1913. He won the light-heavyweight title from Jack Dillon on a 12-round decision on Oct. 24, 1916, and lost it on a knockout in the fourth round to Georges Carpentier on Oct. 12, 1920.

On Jan. 1, 1915, Levinsky fought three 10-round no-decision bouts—in the morning with Bartley Madden, in the afternoon with Soldier Kearns and in the evening with Gunboat Smith.

Levinsky died on Feb. 12, 1949, a few months short of his 59th birthday.

**QUESTION: How many fights did Tommy Loughran have, when did he win the light-heavyweight title and when did he lose it?**

Loughran had 171 bouts in his 18-year boxing career. He won 95, lost 23, drew eight and was involved in 45 no-decisions. After Jack Delaney vacated the light-heavyweight title, Loughran met Mike McTigue for the crown on Oct. 7, 1927, and won a 15-round decision. He never lost the title but instead gave it up in 1929, after six successful defenses, to campaign as a heavyweight.

**QUESTION: How old was Battling Siki, who won and lost the light-heavyweight championship of the world, when he was murdered in New York City? What were Siki's career statistics and how many of those bouts were in the United States?**

Siki, whose real name was Louis Phal, was born in Senegal, French West Africa, on Sept. 16, 1897. He was found shot to death on West 41st Street and Ninth Avenue on Dec. 15, 1925, at the age of 28. He had been intoxicated and involved in a drunken brawl before being slain.

Siki fought 74 times, winning 29 bouts on knockouts and 25 on decisions. He lost 10 fights on decisions, one on a foul and one on a knockout. His record also included one draw, six no-decision bouts and one fight that ended in no-contest. Twenty-four of his fights were in the United States.

QUESTION: How many times did Harry Greb fight Jackie Clark, and what were the results? Did Greb ever win the world light-heavyweight title?

Greb fought Clark three times: On Oct. 16, 1916, he earned a 10-round decision; on Nov. 14, 1916, he knocked out Clark in the third round; on May 5, 1917, he and Clark drew after 20 rounds. Greb never won the world light-heavyweight crown, only the American championship, beating Gene Tunney on May 23, 1922, for the vacant title. That loss was the only one in Tunney's career. Greb then lost the championship to Tunney on Feb. 23, 1923. Greb won the world middleweight title on Aug. 31, 1923, defeating Johnny Wilson in 15 rounds. Greb lost that title on a 15-round decision to Tiger Flowers on Aug. 19, 1926.

QUESTION: Did Marcel Cerdan, the French middleweight, ever fight Sugar Ray Robinson? What was Cerdan's career record, and did he ever win the world middleweight title? If so, where was the title fight held and how long did he retain the crown?

Cerdan, who never fought Robinson, had 113 bouts and won 109—66 on knockouts and 43 on decisions. He lost one by a decision, two because of fouls and one by a knockout. He won the middleweight title Sept. 21, 1948, at Roosevelt Stadium in Jersey City by stopping Tony Zale, who was unable to come out for the 12th round. The next June 16, at Briggs Stadium in Detroit, Jake LaMotta took the title away when Cerdan, having injured his shoulder, was unable to come out for the 10th. This was Cerdan's last bout. Four months later he was killed in an airplane crash in the Azores.

QUESTION: In the 1950's, I think, there was a nationally ranked boxer who was deaf. Who was he, what was his record and how did he know when a round was over?

The boxer was Eugene Hairston, a middleweight from the Bronx. He fought between 1947 and 1952. In 63 bouts, he won 24 on knockouts and 21 on decisions; he lost three on knockouts and 10 on decisions. Five bouts ended in draws. Three of his losses were to Kid Gavilan, Johnny Bratton and Jake LaMotta. The red light in each corner signified the end of the round to Hairston. In addition, the referee, at the sound of the bell, would raise both arms in the air.

QUESTION: Did Al (Bummy) Davis ever fight Bob Montgomery? If he did, who won?

Davis knocked out Montgomery in the first round on Feb. 18, 1944. But only two weeks later, on March 3, Montgomery defeated Beau Jack in 15 rounds, regaining the lightweight title recognized by the New York State Boxing Commission.

**QUESTION: Did Sid Terris ever win the lightweight title? What were his career statistics? How many times did Jess Willard defend the heavyweight title?**

Terris, an outstanding fighter from the East Side of Manhattan in the 1920's, never won a title. He had 107 bouts and won 70 by decision, 12 by knockout and three by fouls. He lost seven bouts by decision, one by a foul and four by knockout. Four bouts ended in draws, and six with no decision.

Willard, who won the title by knocking out Jack Johnson in 26 rounds on April 5, 1915, defended the crown twice. He fought Frank Moran in a bout that ended with no decision after 10 rounds and was knocked out by Jack Dempsey in three rounds on July 4, 1919.

**QUESTION: What was the boxer Kid Chocolate's real name? How many championships did he hold and what was his lifetime record? When did he fight Petey Hayes and was the bout filmed?**

Chocolate was born Eligio Sadinias at Cerro, Cuba, on Jan. 6, 1910. At one point in his career he held the world junior lightweight title and the New York State featherweight crown. Chocolate fought 161 times, winning 64 bouts by knockouts and 81 by decision. He lost eight decisions, was knocked out twice and fought six draws. Chocolate met Hayes once, on July 11, 1934, losing a 10-round decision. In those days, because it was so expensive to film fights, non-title bouts were rarely filmed, and the Hayes fight was not.

**QUESTION: How many times did Ike Williams, then the lightweight champion, fight Kid Gavilan, who later won the welterweight title? How long did each hold his title?**

Williams fought Gavilan three times, winning a 10-round decision on Feb. 27, 1948, and losing a pair of 10-round decisions on Jan. 28, 1949, and April 1, 1949.

Williams won his crown on Aug. 4, 1947, knocking out Bob Montgomery in the sixth round. He lost the title on a knockout in the 14th round by James Carter on May 25, 1951.

Gavilan defeated Johnny Bratton in 15 rounds on May 18, 1951. Bratton had won the welterweight title in an elimination tournament after the retirement of Sugar Ray Robinson. Gavilan, however, was not universally recognized as champion until he beat Billy Graham in 15 rounds on Aug. 29, 1951. He lost the title to Johnny Saxton, also in 15 rounds, on Oct. 20, 1954.

**QUESTION: Did Lew Feldman ever fight Tommy Paul for the featherweight title? Did he ever fight Kid Chocolate for the crown?**

Feldman, on Aug. 25, 1932, won a 10-round decision from Paul, who was the champion, but the bout was not sanctioned by the National Boxing Association. Feldman then met Chocolate three times. He lost a 10-round decision on Nov. 2, 1931, lost a 15-round decision on June 1, 1932, and was knocked out in the 12th round on Oct. 13, 1932, a bout in which Chocolate won the New York State featherweight title.

**QUESTION:** Victor McLaglen, the late noted actor, also had a reputation in boxing. What did he accomplish in that sport?

McLaglen was a big man, 6 feet 3 inches and 220 pounds. As a youth, before becoming an actor, he did a lot of boxing and wrestling. He once estimated that he had had nearly 1,000 bouts, most of them with a traveling show in which he offered $15 to any man who could stay in the ring with him for three minutes. His most notable feat in the ring was a six-round exhibition with Jack Johnson, then the heavyweight champion, on March 10, 1909, in Vancouver, for which McLaglen earned $900.

**QUESTION:** What was Steve Belloise's record as a middleweight fighter? Did he ever face Sugar Ray Robinson or Jake LaMotta? I recall that Belloise had a brother who was also a fighter. What was his record?

Belloise, a New York City fighter, never fought LaMotta, but was knocked out by Robinson in the seventh round on Aug. 24, 1949. He began fighting in 1938, and his career, interrupted by Navy service during World War II, ended in 1950. He had 110 bouts, winning 59 on knockouts and 35 on decisions. He lost eight decisions and was kayoed five times. He won one bout when his opponent was disqualified and fought two draws.

Mike Belloise, his older brother, was a featherweight who boxed from 1932 until 1947. He had 126 bouts, won 19 on knockouts and 65 on decisions. He lost 14 on knockouts and 15 on decisions. He fought 13 draws. Mike Belloise died on June 2, 1969.

**QUESTION:** I have an autographed picture of a middleweight fighter, Walter (Popeye) Woods, and I would like to know more about him. When did he fight, what was his overall record and did he ever fight for a title?

Woods, a popular East Side boxer, had 70 bouts between 1936 and 1946. He won 28 by knockouts, 29 by decisions and two on fouls; he was knocked out six times, lost two decisions and fought three draws. He never did fight for a title, but he opposed some top middleweights—Solly Kreiger, with whom he split two bouts, Ken Overlin, whom he defeated, and Ceferino Garcia and Jake LaMotta, both of whom knocked him out.

**QUESTION:** What was Gunboat Smith's ring record? Is he still a runner for a Wall Street firm?

Smith, whose name was Edward J., was a heavyweight who fought from 1906 to 1921. He faced a number of prominent fighters, including Georges Carpentier, Battling Levinsky, Jack Dempsey, Luis Firpo and Harry Wills. He had 131 bouts, winning 40 by knockouts, 15 by decisions and one on a foul. He lost 11 by knockouts, eight by decisions and one on a foul. In addition, six bouts ended in draws and 49 in no-decisions. Smith died on Aug. 6, 1974 at the age of 87.

**QUESTION:** Billy Petrolle, who was known as the "Fargo Express," was a good lightweight boxer who never won a title. What was his ring record, how many fights did he have with boxers who were champions or who became champions?

Petrolle fought 157 times, winning 63 bouts on knockouts, 22 on decisions and four on fouls. He was knocked out three times, lost 17 decisions and fought 10 draws. Thirty-seven bouts ended in no-decision and one was ruled no-contest.

Of those fights, which took place between 1924 and 1934, thirteen were against six men who were champions or who became champions— Sammy Mandell, Jack Kid Berg, Tony Canzoneri, Jimmy McLarnin, Barney Ross and Battling Battalino. Of those fights, he won five, lost six; two ended in a draw and no-contest.

**QUESTION: What was Carmen Basilio's lifetime ring record and how did he fare against Sugar Ray Robinson?**

Basilio fought as a welterweight and a middleweight, winning world titles in each division. He had 79 bouts between 1948 and 1961, winning 27 by knockouts and 29 by decisions. He lost 14 decisions and was knocked out twice. He also had seven draws.

Basilio met Robinson twice. On Sept. 23, 1957, he won the world middleweight crown in 15 rounds; on March 25, 1958, he lost the title to Robinson, again in 15 rounds.

# Memorable Bouts

**QUESTION: Contrary to popular belief, was not Joe Louis, who died in 1981, actually ahead before he knocked out Billy Conn in their first fight, on June 18, 1941? How did the judges and the referee score the fight before the knockout?**

Louis was definitely losing before he stopped Conn at 2 minutes 58 seconds of the 13th round, according to the officials and press accounts. Here is how the officials rated the fight:

| Round | Referee Eddie Josephs | Judge Bill Healy | Judge Marty Monroe |
|---|---|---|---|
| 1 | Louis | Louis | Louis |
| 2 | Louis | Louis | Louis |
| 3 | Conn | Conn | Conn |
| 4 | Conn | Conn | Conn |
| 5 | Louis | Louis | Louis |
| 6 | Louis | Louis | Louis |
| 7 | Conn | Louis | Conn |
| 8 | Conn | Conn | Conn |
| 9 | Conn | Conn | Conn |
| 10 | Louis | Louis | even |
| 11 | Conn | Conn | Conn |
| 12 | Conn | Conn | Conn |

Conn was ahead on Josephs' card, 7–5, and on Monroe's, 7–4, one round even, while Healy had scored six rounds for each fighter.

**QUESTION: A 1978 tribute to Joe Louis in Las Vegas, Nev., mentioned, in relation to his financial troubles, that he had donated his purses for two fights to charity. Which fights were they, and when did they occur?**

Louis knocked out Buddy Baer in the first round on Jan. 9, 1942, in New York and gave his purse to the Naval Relief Fund. On March 27 of the same year he stopped Abe Simon in the sixth round in New York and, to equalize his generosity, gave that purse to the Army Relief Fund.

**QUESTION: On Sept. 27, 1950, when he attempted to regain his heavyweight crown, Joe Louis lost a 15-round decision to Ezzard Charles. Who were the officials and how did they vote?**

The three officials were Referee Mark Conn and Judges Frank Forbes and Joe Agnello, all of whom voted Charles the winner. Conn gave Charles 10 rounds and Louis 5; Forbes scored the bout 13–2, and Agnello 12–3.

**QUESTION: When did Jack Dempsey knock out Jess Willard, Georges Carpentier and Luis Angel Firpo, where were the bouts fought and how many knockdowns were there in each fight?**

Dempsey fought Willard on July 4, 1919, in the Bay View Park Arena in Toledo, Ohio. He won the heavyweight title when Willard refused to come out for the fourth round. Willard had been knocked down six times, all in the first round.

Dempsey knocked Carpentier down in the fourth round and knocked him out later in the same round. The bout was fought at Boyle's Thirty Acres in Jersey City on July 2, 1921.

The Firpo fight, held at the Polo Grounds in New York on Sept. 14, 1923, ended with a knockout in the second round. Firpo was floored eight times before the knockout, and Dempsey twice.

**QUESTION: Was Jack Dempsey ever knocked out during his boxing career? What was his record?**

Dempsey was knocked out only once, in the first round, by Fireman Jim Flynn on Feb. 13, 1917. Dempsey had 80 bouts, winning 49 by knockouts, 10 by decision and one on a foul. In addition to his loss to Flynn, he lost six times by decision and fought seven draws. Five bouts ended without a decision and one was ruled no-contest.

**QUESTION: Gene Tunney's 1978 death revived talk of the "long count." What happened exactly?**

The place was Soldier Field in Chicago, the date Sept. 22, 1927. In his heavyweight championship rematch with Jack Dempsey, from whom he had taken the title a year earlier, Tunney was battered to the floor in the seventh round. The knockdown timekeeper, Paul Beeler, started the count as Referee Dave Barry motioned Dempsey to a neutral corner. Dempsey did not go there until Beeler's count reached 4, after which Barry began his count at 1. Tunney struggled to his feet at 9, having enjoyed the benefit of a 13-second rest. He avoided Dempsey's punches the rest of the round and went on to win a 10-round decision.

**QUESTION: On the morning of May 20, 1927, Charles A. Lindbergh took off for Paris on the first successful solo flight across the Atlantic. That night, a friend of mine insists, Jack Sharkey fought Tom Heeney. Is he correct?**

No. Sharkey fought Jim Maloney that night, knocking him out in the fifth round. He fought Heeney to a 12-round draw on Jan. 13, 1928.

**QUESTION: Did Jack Sharkey win the heavyweight boxing championship on a foul call against Max Schmeling?**

No. Sharkey won the title from Schmeling on a 15-round decision. That was on June 21, 1932, in the Long Island City Bowl. The foul that you recall occurred two years earlier, on June 12, 1930, at Yankee Stadium. That bout, the first between Schmeling and Sharkey, was for the title vacated in 1928, when Gene Tunney retired. Schmeling won on a foul, a low blow, in the fourth round.

**QUESTION: Who was the first American, in the days of bare-knuckle fights, to hold the world heavyweight championship? When was the last such heavyweight title fight and who was involved?**

On May 30, 1880, Paddy Ryan knocked out Joe Goss, an Englishman, in the 87th round near Collier's Station, W. Va., and became the first American to win the world crown. In those days, a woozy fighter could slip to the ground, without being hit, and the round automatically ended. He could do this over and over again, at the start of a new round, until he had fully recovered. This practice resulted in bouts of extraordinary length.

The last title fight with bare knuckles took place on July 8, 1889, at Richburg, Miss., when John L. Sullivan defeated Jake Kilrain in 75 rounds.

**QUESTION: What were the dates and the results of Jake LaMotta's six bouts with Sugar Ray Robinson? Did he ever fight Rocky Graziano or Tony Zale? What was LaMotta's lifetime ring record?**

Oct. 2, 1942: LaMotta lost to Robinson in 10 rounds; Feb. 5, 1943: won, 10 rounds; Feb. 26, 1943: lost, 10 rounds; Feb. 23, 1945, lost, 10 rounds; Sept. 26, 1945: lost, 12 rounds; Feb. 14, 1951, lost his world middleweight crown by a knockout in the 13th round.

LaMotta never fought Graziano or Zale. His career record: in 106 bouts, he won 30 by knockouts and 53 by decisions. He lost 15 by decisions, four by knockouts and fought four draws.

**QUESTION: Was Jake LaMotta ever knocked off his feet during his career?**

Once, against Danny Nardico on Dec. 31, 1952. LaMotta was beaten badly in the seventh round and went down. He managed to last out the round, but the fight was stopped before the start of the eighth round and it was ruled an eight-round technical knockout. The fight took place near the end of his career.

# Golf

## Rules of the Game

**QUESTION: In a golf tournament, Smith hits his second shot onto the edge of the green. Jones's second shot strikes Smith's ball and causes it to roll off the green and come to rest just under the lip of a sand trap, while Jones's ball remains on the green. From where does Smith play his third shot, the original lie or the bunker?**

Smith may, according to The Rules of Golf, "either play his ball as it lies or, before another stroke is played by either side, . . . replace the ball." In this instance, he will undoubtedly choose to play his ball from the original lie.

Since only one ball was on the green initially, there is no penalty for Jones. If both balls had been on the green, however, Jones would have been penalized two strokes, and Smith would have had to return his ball to the original lie.

**QUESTION: Two golfers playing together dump their shots into the same sand trap, one a couple of inches behind the other. The player who has to hit first obviously will disturb the lie of the other ball. What is the correct procedure?**

The player who shoots first asks to have the other ball lifted when he considers that it may interfere with his play (Rule 24, Rules of Golf). The ball so lifted "shall be replaced after the player has played his stroke."

Just how the ball is to be replaced is defined in Rule 22, 3B. If the original lie of the second ball is altered, as it probably will be by the first player's explosion shot, "the ball shall be placed in the nearest lie most similar to that which it originally occupied, not more than two club lengths from the original lie and not nearer the hole."

**QUESTION: Two golf balls come to rest on the fairway touching each other. What is the ruling?**

According to The Rules of Golf, a competitor may have a ball lifted if it interferes with his play. The lifted ball must be replaced after the shot. If a ball is accidentally moved in doing this, there is no penalty and the ball that is moved is returned to its original position.

**QUESTION: A golfer in an amateur stroke-play tournament hits a ball from a bunker. The ball strikes the top of the bunker, bounces back and rolls against his shoe. When the player moves his foot, the ball rolls into his footprint in the sand. What is the penalty, two strokes or more?**

The movement of the player's foot is considered part of the action in which he stopped his own ball. There is a two-stroke penalty for stopping the ball, but no additional penalty.

**QUESTION: In stroke play, a player's putt stops on the lip of the cup, overhanging the hole. The player purposely casts his shadow over the hole for about 20 seconds, and the ball falls into the hole. Is this permissible?**

Casting a shadow is an old wives' tale; to do so does not enhance the chances of the ball's dropping into the hole, although the ball did in this instance. The rules permit a player to wait about four or five seconds, but not 20, before taking his shot. The player would not be penalized for shadowing the hole, but he would be penalized two strokes for delaying play.

**QUESTION: Three golf players are on the green, and the fourth is on the fringe of the green. Does the player on the fringe putt first even if one of those on the green is farther from the hole?**

No. According to the rules, the ball farthest from the hole must be played first.

**QUESTION: While swinging at a ball that is outside a bunker, a golfer touches the sand in the bunker on his backswing. Is there a penalty?**

No. The player is not considered in the hazard.

**QUESTION: My usual golfing opponent drove his tee shot off the fairway and under a wheelbarrow that had inadvertently been left there by a groundskeeper. He picked up the ball and dropped it, saying it was permissible under the obstruction rule. I said no, and insisted that he should have been penalized. Who is right?**

You are. Since the obstruction was movable, your opponent was required to move the wheelbarrow, not his ball. He should have been penalized a stroke for lifting the ball and two strokes for playing the ball from the wrong place.

**QUESTION: In golf, where is the proper place to leave a rake: inside the sand trap, where it may affect the lie of the golf ball, or outside, where it may prevent the ball from rolling into the trap or possibly causing the ball to ricochet?**

The United States Golf Association recommends that the rake be placed outside the bunker, as far away as is practical, and at a spot where it would be least likely to deflect the ball.

**QUESTION: Two amateur golfers hit their approach shots to a green that is behind a high bunker. When they near the green, they find that the two balls are on the far side and that one is in a trap. The balls are of the same make and number, and cannot be distinguished from each other. Both players claim the ball that is not in the trap. What is the ruling?**

Because neither player can positively identify his ball, both balls have to be considered lost. According to Rule 29 1-a of the United States

Golf Association, each player "shall play his next stroke as nearly as possible at the spot from which the original ball was played or moved by him, adding a penalty stroke to his score for the hole."

**QUESTION: During stroke play, my opponent's golf ball stopped near a fence that marked out-of-bounds. The fence interfered with his subsequent swing, and he termed it an obstruction because it was man-made. He then dropped away without taking a penalty and played toward the green. Was he correct?**

No. An out-of-bounds fence is not an obstruction. Your opponent should have incurred a three-stroke penalty, one for lifting the ball and two for not replacing it.

**QUESTION: Did a round of golf always consist of 18 holes?**

No. In the early years, the length of the golf courses in Great Britain and Scotland varied, some with 6 holes, others 7, 13, 15 and so on. A match at a course with seven holes, for example, may have consisted of three rounds, or 21 holes. At the Royal and Ancient Golf Club of St. Andrews, in Scotland, the game for generations was played nine holes out and the same nine for playing home. Because of the dominant role St. Andrews played in the development of golf, 18 became the accepted total.

**QUESTION: I keep reading about "rabbits" on the professional golf tour. What does it mean?**

Rabbits, or "non-exempt players," as the Professional Golf Association prefers to call them, are those players who must compete each Monday to qualify for that week's tournament. The places open for non-exempt players vary each week, depending on the popularity of the tournament, but there usually are about 25 spots available. Even to compete in the qualifying rounds, the players must pay a $25 fee, but if they make the tournament, they do not have to pay the $25 fee for that competition.

According to the P.G.A. officials, there are about 85 non-exempt players seeking tournament places each Monday. This is a drop from the 130 to 150 in previous years.

DON'T TOUCH THAT BALL!

**QUESTION:** The wind moves a golfer's ball before he can address it. He replaces it, in its original position, and holes out. Is this permissible?

No, since under the rules the wind is not an outside agency. In medal play, the golfer would incur a penalty of three strokes, one for lifting his ball and two for playing it from the wrong place. In match play, he would lose the hole.

**QUESTION:** A golfer hits a high drive, and the ball half-buries itself in the fairway in clay-like soil. On the next shot, with a wedge, the ball sticks to the club along with a glob of soil. What is the ruling?

On the assumption that the player has completed his stroke, he is considered, under Rule 26-2a, to have stopped his ball and to have incurred a penalty of the loss of the hole in match play, and, under Rule 26-3a, to have incurred a penalty of two strokes in stroke play.

**QUESTION:** Am I allowed to add or replace a golf club during a round of play?

If a player has started the round with fewer than 14 clubs, he may add as many as needed to reach the maximum of 14. If a player has started with 14 clubs, he may replace a club that becomes unfit in the normal course of play. In both instances, the addition or replacement of clubs may not be made by borrowing from any other person playing on the course.

**QUESTION:** A golfer on a fairway hits a ball that comes to rest on a bridge over a water hazard. The entire bridge is within the confines of the hazard. Does the player get relief under Rule 31, which covers obstructions?

The player can, if he wishes, play the ball from the bridge. If he does not wish to do so, Rule 31 states that the ball in a hazard must be dropped in the hazard. In this case, the ball, depending on the size of the bridge, might well drop in the water rather than roll off the bridge to firm ground. He therefore can resort to Rule 33, which covers hazards, and drop a ball under penalty of one stroke, "behind the water hazard, keeping the spot at which the ball last crossed the margin of the water hazard between himself and the hole, and with no limit to how far behind the water hazard the ball may be dropped." He may also drop a ball as near as possible to the spot from which the original ball was played.

**QUESTION:** If a golfer's ball lands on the green of another hole, is there an allowance for a lift or does he hit from that green?

The golfer is permitted to lift the ball and, at a point nearest to where the ball lies but which is not nearer the hole he is playing and which is not in a hazard or on the green, drop the ball without penalty within one club length.

**QUESTION:** Please explain how a golfer's handicap is determined.

The handicap depends on a player's average strokes and the rating (degree of difficulty) of the course he plays. Let us assume that his course is rated at 72. After playing 20 rounds of 18 holes each, he then totals the scores for his 10 best rounds and divides by 10 to determine an average. Then he subtracts the course rating for the differential, which he multiplies by 96 percent for his handicap. An example: a player's 10 best rounds are 80, 84, 83, 80, 85, 79, 80, 78, 82 and 85. The sum is 816 and the average is 81.6. Subtracting the course rating of 72 leaves 9.6. Multiply by .96 and you arrive at 9.216. The player's handicap, rounded to the nearest whole number, is 9.

QUESTION: What is the usual pay for a caddie if a professional golfer wins a major tournament? If he finishes out of the money?

According to Tom Place, Public Information Director of the P.G.A. Tour, many of the leading golfers have caddies on retainers of about $200 a week. In addition, those caddies will receive about 4 or 5 percent of any tournament winnings. The lesser known golfers will hire caddies at tournaments, and pay them about $200 for their services. If players finish in the money, they will augment that fee with a tip, the size of which depends on how much help they have received from their caddies.

QUESTION: What is a professional golfer allowed to discuss with his caddie during tournament play?

A player may discuss anything with his caddie. He may also, except on the putting green, have his caddie indicate the line of play to him, although the caddie may not stand on or close to the line while the shot is being made.

QUESTION: When you watch professional golfers on television, you never see them taking practice swings on the fairways. Are they illegal?

No. The pros practice their full swings so frequently they are almost always in a groove. They do practice difficult half-swing chip shots or when they are in the rough or under a tree, and sometimes they take warm-up swings on the tee.

# For the Record

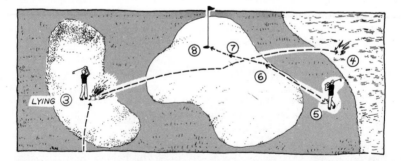

QUESTION: In the Memorial Tournament at the Muirfield Village Golf Club in Ohio in May 1980, which I was watching on television, John Fought hit a ball from a bunker that bounced over the green and into a water hazard. The cameras then shifted to another player. The commentators never explained from what position Fought played the next ball, though later it was announced that he had carded an 8 on the hole. Please explain where he dropped the ball and how the 8 came about.

Fought had started the hole with a tee shot that landed in a creek. He dropped out, which added a penalty stroke. His next shot landed in the bunker to the left of the green. It was his fourth shot that bounced into the water hazard. As is required by the rules, he dropped out of the hazard at a point on the embankment that was not nearer to the pin than where the ball had entered the water. Now lying 5, he chipped onto the green with his sixth shot. He then two-putted, making a total of 8 for the hole.

**QUESTION: Was there a playoff between Bob Goalby and Roberto de Vicenzo in the 1968 Masters golf tournament? If not, please explain exactly what happened.**

Goalby won the tournament on a 277 without a playoff, but there would have been one, of 18 holes, if de Vicenzo had not signed an incorrectly marked card. On the 17th hole of the final round, de Vicenzo was paired with Tommy Aaron and shot a 3. Aaron inadvertently marked the score as a 4. When the round was over, de Vicenzo signed the card without noticing the error. The card was accepted, and thus de Vicenzo was deprived of a stroke and a tie with Goalby.

**QUESTION: The United States Open championship in 1980 took place at the Baltusrol Golf Club in Springfield, N.J., and, in 1981, at the Merion Golf Club in Pennsylvania. Those two clubs, along with the Oakmont (Pa.) Country Club, appear to be favorite courses for the Open and the United States Amateur championship. How many times have these tournaments been held at each of the three clubs?**

The Open: at Baltusrol, six times (1903, 1915, 1936, 1954, 1967, 1980); at Merion, four times (1934, 1950, 1971, 1981); at Oakmont, five times (1927, 1935, 1953, 1962, 1973).

The Amateur: at Baltusrol, three times (1904, 1926, 1946); at Merion, four times (1916, 1924, 1930, 1966); at Oakmont, four times (1919, 1925, 1938, 1969).

**QUESTION: How many times did Willie Anderson win the United States Open? Was one of those victories at the Baltusrol Golf Club in New Jersey? Did he win any other major events?**

Anderson won the Open in 1901, 1903, 1904 and 1905, with the 1903 victory being at Baltusrol. He is among four golfers to have won the Open four times, but the only one to have done so in three consecutive years. The other four-time winners are: Bobby Jones (1923, 1926, 1929, 1930); Ben Hogan (1948, 1950, 1951, 1953); and Jack Nicklaus (1962, 1967, 1972, 1980).

Anderson also captured the Western Open—when it was considered to be the second major tournament in the United States—four times (1902, 1904, 1908, 1909). Born in 1880, he was among the first of the Scottish professionals to come to the United States, arriving in the mid-1890's. He died in 1910.

**QUESTION: What is the lowest-scoring round on the tour of the Professional Golfers' Association in the last 30 years? Did the record-holder win the tournament in which the round was shot? Also, has anyone ever shot a double eagle in a P.G.A. tourney?**

Al Geiberger shot a 13-under-par 59 in the second round of the 1977 Memphis Classic, at the Colonial Country Club, and that is the lowest round on record. The previous mark, 60, was held by seven players: Al Brosch, in 1951; Bill Nary, 1952; Ted Kroll, 1954; Wally Ulrich, 1954; Tommy Bolt, 1954; Mike Souchak, 1955, and Sam Snead, 1957. Geiberger, who shot 11 birdies, one eagle and six pars in that round, won the tourney with a 273.

There have been many double eagles (three under par) in P.G.A. play. The most famous was probably Gene Sarazen's 2 on the 15th hole of the fourth round of the 1935 Masters. He holed out a 220-yard shot with a 4-wood, enabling him to tie Craig Wood for first place. Sarazen then went on to beat Wood in a playoff.

**QUESTION: Who played the roles of Ben Hogan and his wife in the movie about his life, what was the title and in what year was it released?**

Glenn Ford played Hogan and Anne Baxter played his wife in "Follow the Sun," which was released in 1951.

**QUESTION: I remember as a young man in the 1930's talk of a mysterious character who was supposed to be the best golfer in the world, although I'm not sure that he ever competed. Who was he, and how much truth was there to the talk about his prowess?**

John Montague, who became famous among the Hollywood movie stars he associated with because of his golfing ability, was regarded very highly by many golf professionals, including George Von Elm, who called him the best golfer in the world. Montague, whose real name was La Verne Moore, was, because of all the publicity he received in Hollywood, identified as an alleged participant earlier in a tavern holdup in upstate New York. He was brought back to New York for trial, but finally acquitted. Montague was famous for his trick shots, but, in one of his rare tournament appearances, shot an 80 in the opening round of the United States Open and dropped out. There is little doubt that the mysterious Montague had ability, but how much is a matter of conjecture.

**QUESTION: How many holes-in-one were made in 1978? Who is the oldest male golfer to make one? The oldest female?**

There were 28,576 holes-in-one last year, a record, according to Golf Digest magazine, which began keeping count of aces in 1952.

Maude Hutton of Sun City Center, Fla., 86 years of age, last year became the oldest woman to score an ace. Bill Diddel of Naples, Fla., 93, scored his seventh ace in 1978—he made his first in 1902—to tie with George Henry Miller of Anaheim, Calif., as the oldest man to make a hole-in-one.

**QUESTION: About this time two years ago, you answered a question on how many holes-in-one had been made in 1978. Can you do the same for 1980?**

According to Golf Digest's Hole-in-One Clearing House, a record 31,559 were made in 1980. Norman L. Manley, 57 years old, of Long Beach, Calif., registered two more holes-in-one and increased his career total to 47. A Jacksonville, Fla., psychiatrist, Dr. Richard Craiger, scored eight aces in 1980. He had not, before 1980, made a single hole-in-one in 17 years he had been playing golf.

**QUESTION: Has anyone ever played a round by throwing a golf ball around a course, and, if so, what is the lowest score for this feat?**

According to the Guinness Sports Record Book, a man named Joe Flynn recorded the lowest such score, 82, for an 18-hole course of more than 6,000 yards. The record was set March 27, 1975, on the 6,228-yard Port Royal Course in Bermuda.

**QUESTION: How many victories in the Ladies Professional Golf Association Tour do the following players have: Shirley Englehorn, Beverly Hanson, Betty Hicks, Ruth Jessen and Marilynn Smith? Are the 17 victories by Nancy Lopez in two years (nine in 1978 and eight in 1979) a record?**

Including the 1980 tour, Miss Smith, who is still active, had 22 victories. Mrs. Englehorn finished her career with 11 victories, Mrs. Hanson with 15, Miss Jessen with 11 and Miss Hicks with none. Mickey Wright, who captured 13 tournaments in 1963 and 11 in 1964, holds the two-year record.

**QUESTION: Some of the pioneers of the Ladies Professional Golf Association Tour were Betty Jameson, Mary Lena Faulk, Fay Crocker, Helen Dettweiler and Peggy Kirk Bell. How many victories did each have in their playing careers? Also, what are the three major tournaments recognized by the LPGA?**

Miss Jameson won nine events: one each in 1948, 1949, 1952, 1953, and 1954, and four in 1955. Miss Faulk won 10: one each in 1956, 1957, 1958 and 1964, two in 1962 and four in 1961. Miss Crocker won 11: three in 1955 and two each in 1956, 1957, 1958 and 1960. Miss Dettweiler, one of the founders and charter members of the L.P.G.A., did not win an event, and neither did Miss Bell.

The three major championships are the L.P.G.A. Championship, the U.S. Women's Open Championship and the Peter Jackson Classic.

**QUESTION: Since the first Masters tournament in 1934, has any golfer ever won the Masters, the United States Open, the British Open and the P.G.A. championship in the same year? If not, who came closest?**

No golfer has won those four events in one year, although Gene Sarazen, Ben Hogan, Jack Nicklaus and Gary Player have captured the four events in different years. Hogan, in 1953, won three and is the only golfer to manage even that.

**QUESTION: Arnold Palmer is still playing on the P.G.A. Tour and winning very little money for a man who used to be No. 1. How much did he win in 1980, where does he stand in the career listing, and why is he still playing?**

Palmer won $16,589 and ranks 133 for 1980, which is about midway in the listing. He finished the year with $1,857,552 in career earnings, fourth behind Jack Nicklaus ($3,581,213), Lee Trevino ($2,473,992) and Tom Watson ($2,202,241).

Palmer has many business interests these days, and his tour winnings are of little consequence to him. He plays for the exposure and because he is a competitor and still hopes to win a tournament here and there.

**QUESTION: Since Tom Watson won more P.G.A. tournaments and more money in 1980 than did Lee Trevino, why did Trevino win the Vardon Trophy?**

The Vardon Trophy, named in honor of Harry Vardon, the British golfer, is awarded each year to a P.G.A. member who maintains the lowest average per round. A minimum of 80 rounds in tournaments considered official by the P.G.A. is needed to qualify for the trophy. Trevino averaged 69.73 strokes per round to Watson's 69.95. Watson's second-place finish kept him from winning the trophy for the fourth straight year.

**QUESTION: What were the 1980 P.G.A. Tour earnings for Calvin Peete, Lee Elder, Jim Dent and Pete Brown and what were their rankings? Which of the four will be exempt from qualifying for tournament play in 1981?**

Peete earned $105,716 and ranked 42d; Elder, $17,692 and 129th; Dent, $16,223 and 136th; Brown, $591.25 and 239th. Peete will not have to qualify because he finished among the top 60 in earnings. Elder is still exempt and does not have to qualify because he played in the Ryder Cup matches in 1979. Dent and Brown will have to qualify until they gain exempt status.

**QUESTION: How many P.G.A. Tour golfers have earned more than $1,000,000 in tournament play? How many reached that peak in 1980?**

There are now 27 golfers on the million-dollar list. Five made it in 1980: George Archer, Charles Coody, Ben Crenshaw, Bob Murphy and Lanny Wadkins.

**QUESTION: Which golfer on the P.G.A. Tour was the first to win $200,000 or more in one year? How many have achieved that mark since? How many in 1980?**

Billy Casper, in 1968, was the first, earning $205,168. Since then, 23 golfers have topped that mark 48 different times. In 1980, nine golfers, exceeding the previous record of six, did it. They were: Tom Watson ($530,808); Lee Trevino ($385,814); Curtis Strange ($271,888); Andy Bean ($269,033); Ben Crenshaw ($237,727); Jerry Pate ($222,976); George Burns ($219,928); Craig Stadler ($206,291), and Mike Reid ($206,097).

**QUESTION: How many first-time winners were there on the 1980 P.G.A. Tour?**

Twelve, tying the record. They were: Craig Stadler (Bob Hope Classic); Jeff Mitchell (Phoenix Open); George Burns (Bing Crosby Pro-Am); Doug Tewell (Heritage Classic and IVB-Philadelphia Classic); Mark Pfeil (Tallahassee Open); Scott Simpson (Western Open); Scott Hoch (Quad Cities Open); Peter Jacobsen (Buick-Goodyear Open); Don Pooley (B.C. Open); Phil Hancock (Hall of Fame); Mike Sullivan (Southern Open); Dan Holldorson (Pensacola Open).

**QUESTION:** Who were the leaders on the 1980 P.G.A. Tour in average scoring per round and average putts per round?

Scoring: Lee Trevino (69.73); Tom Watson (69.95); Jerry Pate (70.72); Andy Bean (70.73), and Keith Fergus (70.75).

Putting: Pate (28.81); Watson and George Burns (each with 28.93); Don January (28.96), and Ray Floyd (29.05).

**QUESTION:** Who were the leaders on the 1980 P.G.A. Tour in birdies (one under par) and eagles (two under par)?

Birdies: Andy Bean (388); Curtis Strange (382); George Burns (374); Mike Reid (358), and Rex Caldwell (353).

Eagles: Dave Eichelberger (16); Buddy Gardner (13); Bruce Lietzke (12), and Bill Kratzert, Bob Murphy, Tom Purtzer and Keith Fergus (each with 11).

**QUESTION:** While there are prominent athletes from the Soviet Union in just about every sport, I have never heard of a golfer from that country. Are there any golf courses in the Soviet Union?

There are none as yet, but Robert Trent Jones, the golf architect, is in the process of laying out the first course at Nachibino, which is about 20 miles west of Moscow.

**QUESTION:** How did the words par, birdie and eagle enter the game of golf?

Par is the evolution of yardage scales to define perfect play. The United States Golf Association so defined it in 1911 to establish handicaps for stroke play. The British, incidentally, employ bogey to indicate par, though Americans use that word to indicate one over par.

According to the U.S.G.A., the word birdie evolved from a remark made by one Ab Smith, while playing in Atlantic City in 1903: "That's a bird of a shot." The Golfers' Handbook says: "Birdie, eagle and albatross are words coined in America to represent respectively holes done in one below par, two below par and three below par."

# Tennis

## Rules of the Game

WHOSE POINT?

**QUESTION: Player A in a singles tennis match hits a soft slice that lands just over the net on Player B's side, but, after bouncing, the ball returns to Player A's side. Is it Player A's point? Also, can Player B run around the net and return the ball to his side of the net, run back and return his own shot?**

It is a legitimate point for Player A, if his opponent cannot get to the ball. However, Player B is entitled to run around the net and, without invading the singles area of the court (he can invade the doubles area), return the ball, but not into his own court. He must hit the ball into Player A's court before it bounces again.

**QUESTION: As a follow-up to your recent answer that a tennis player can run around the net to hit a ball that has already bounced in his court and then returned to his opponent's court: Could that player reach over the net to hit the ball before it bounced again?**

Yes. Once the ball has bounced in his court, he can reach over the net. However, he must not touch the net, the post or the ground in his opponent's court.

**QUESTION: A soft shot by Player A in a tennis match lands just over the net. Player B returns the shot, but his momentum carries him forward diagonally in such a way that he falls down, without touching the net, beyond the net on Player A's side of the court, although outside the court. Does he lose the point?**

No. Any player is entitled to fall beyond the net if his momentum after hitting a ball carries him there.

**QUESTION:** A tennis player anticipates a weak second serve, runs into the service box and is hit by the ball before it strikes the ground. What is the ruling?

When a serve that is not a let touches the receiver or anything that he wears or carries before it hits the ground, the server wins the point.

**QUESTION:** I always understood that a server in tennis had to have one foot on the ground when his racquet met the ball, but today you see servers with both feet in the air at the moment of impact. Has the rule been changed? Is there an advantage in a leaping serve?

In 1959 the United States Tennis Association removed the requirement that one foot had to be in contact with the ground while serving. Whether there is an advantage in a leaping serve is a matter of debate. Many tennis experts question the advantage because the server loses the element of stability.

**QUESTION:** What is the definition of an "unforced error" in tennis and is this an official statistic?

When a player hits a ball that is not a winner—perhaps it is simply a soft shot that lands directly in front of his opponent—then the opponent commits an unforced error if he drives the ball into the net or out of the court. This is not an official statistic, although, because it adds a dimension to news-media coverage, it is usually kept at major tournaments. Coaches, of course, will also keep track of such errors.

**QUESTION:** In tennis, how is it decided which tie breaker is to be used in a tournament?

The International Tennis Federation decreed in 1974 that the 7-of-12 tie breaker was the only one authorized for use in its sanctioned tournaments. However, many other tournaments often use the 5-of-9 tie breaker.

**QUESTION:** How are doubles teams selected for important tennis tournaments? Do players approach each other informally, or what?

Doubles teams, as you surmised, evolve in informal fashion, with players approaching each other. However, if the players find they are compatible on the court, that informal relationship can develop into a permanent one for years. Prime examples of this among the men are: Bob Hewitt and Frew McMillan of South Africa, and Stan Smith and Bob Lutz, who won the Davis Cup doubles for the United States in 1979 (although doubles players for the Cup are selected by the team captain). Among the women: Billie Jean King and Rosemary Casals, and Louise Brough and Mrs. Margaret Osborne duPont, all of the United States, were paired for years.

**QUESTION:** Why were some of the sets in the French Open reported as 9-7 or 10-8? I thought tie breakers had eliminated this type of scoring.

Under International Tennis Federation rules, tie breakers normally would not be used in the third set of a best-of-three match or the fifth set of a best-of-five match, and the French Open followed this procedure. However, any nation has the option of stipulating, in a tournament sanctioned by the federation, that the tie breaker will be in effect in all sets. Since this has been done in some tournaments, it may be the cause of the confusion.

**QUESTION: Is the serve in tennis alternated for the entire match? Which player starts serving if there is a tie breaker? Which player begins serving the set after a tie breaker?**

Service is alternated for the entire match. The important thing to remember is that the player who begins the match serves all odd-numbered games (1,3,5,7) and his opponent serves the even-numbered games (2,4,6). A tiebreaker is considered the seventh game, so the first player would begin serving. Once the tie breaker is over, no matter who served last, his opponent would start the next set.

**QUESTION: Do tennis players change ends of a court when the total number of games played is odd, or when the number of games in that particular set is odd?**

The players change ends at the end of the first, third and every subsequent alternate game of each set, and at the end of each set, unless the total number of games in that set is even. In that case, the change is not made until the end of the first game of the next set.

**QUESTION: How often are new tennis balls put into play in a tennis match?**

The ball-change pattern is specified by the referee before a match begins. The chair umpire, however, may call for a change of tennis balls at other than the prescribed time if, in his opinion, abnormal conditions warrant it.

# For the Record

**QUESTION: How did scoring originate in tennis? Why 15, 30, 40, deuce?**

The scoring survives for the most part from the game's medieval origins—that is, from France, where the sport's ancestor was called *jeu de paume*, game of the palm, because the ball was then hit with the palm of the hand instead of with a racquet. A game went to 60 points and was divided into four parts—15, 30, 45, 60. (Today's "40" is simply an abbreviation of the original "45.") Why 60 points in a game? Because apparently the number was of particular significance then. There were the 60 seconds in a minute and the 60 minutes in an hour, of course, reflecting what was then a familiar number system that had a base of 60.

As for deuce, it is a corruption of the French *à deux*, which meant that a player tied with his opponent at 45 had to win two consecutive points for the game.

**QUESTION: I am curious about the use of the word "seed," when used to rank tennis players in a tournament. What is the origin of the word?**

The word stems from the Old English, *saed*. Its original meaning, in agriculture, meant "to separate or select from a group." Tennis adopted the word in an attempt to separate the better players so that they would not face each other in the early rounds of a tournament. The practice of seeding was instituted at the 1919 Wimbledon championships because of the tremendous number of entries.

QUESTION: In tennis, the word "volley" was often used to denote the warm-up period. In recent years, it has been more or less supplanted by "rally." What is the difference between the two, and what is the derivation of "volley?"

Volley is derived from the French, *volée*, meaning flight, and the Latin *volare*, meaning to fly. In tennis it came to mean to hit a ball before it touched the ground. Rally connotes a series of shots, whether on the fly or after the ball hits the ground.

Rally, technically, is the correct term for a warm-up period, which may include all kinds of shots, but volley is still used in friendly matches.

QUESTION: Why, in tennis, is the word "love" used instead of zero?

Malcolm D. Whitman, a tennis historian, gave the following explanation, one of many such, in his 1921 book, *Tennis Origins and Mysteries:*

"The use of the word 'love' to suggest 'nothing' in tennis is as old as the English language. In the year 971, we find the equivalent of the expression 'neither love nor money.' Similar expressions have been in common use for centuries. Later ... there developed the expression in competitive games 'to play for love,' meaning 'to play for nothing' ... It would seem most natural for the English to have used the word to indicate no score when they first began to play the game."

QUESTION: How did the Wightman Cup tennis series between the United States and Great Britain originate?

The competition began in 1923, when Mrs. George W. Wightman of Boston donated a sterling vase to the United States Lawn Tennis Association for international women's team tennis. Great Britain immediately challenged for the cup, and the match was the first to be contested in the newly opened West Side Tennis Club at Forest Hills. Mrs. Wightman, as Hazel Hotchkiss, was the national women's singles champion in 1909, 1910 and 1911. After her marriage, she again won the title in 1919. She competed in that first Wightman Cup match, playing in the doubles and helping the United States to win, 7–0.

QUESTION: What constitutes a grand slam in tennis? How many men and women have accomplished the feat?

Tennis grand slams, which must be achieved in a calendar year, comprise the championships of the United States, Britain (Wimbledon), France and Australia. Don Budge, in 1938, and Rod Laver, in 1962 and 1969, are the only two men who have achieved it, and Maureen Connolly, in 1953, and Margaret Court Smith, in 1970, are the only two women.

QUESTION: Don Budge, in 1938, was the first player to win the grand slam of tennis (the Australian, French, Wimbledon and United States titles). One of his weapons was an awesome backhand that is still regarded as one of the best ever. What made his backhand so strong?

According to reports of his play at the time, Budge's natural power, rhythm and timing were exceptional. He himself said that the stroke was a natural adaptation from the left-handed swing that he used in baseball, although he threw right-handed. When he first began to play tennis, he used his brother's racquet, and, because it was too heavy for him, he held the handle with two hands. As he grew older and stronger, he still supported that 15-ounce racquet with both hands, but would let go with the left hand as he began the forward movement. As a junior tennis competitor, the shot was a slice, but later on he hit into the ball instead of down.

**QUESTION: Have any ambidextrous tennis players ever been among the winners at Wimbledon? Has a member of a royal family—British or otherwise—ever competed there?**

John Bromwich of Australia was ambidextrous, and he won the doubles title in 1948, with Frank Sedgman as his partner. He won it again in 1950, with Adrian Quist as his partner.

The Duke of York, later King George VI of England, competed in the doubles in 1926 with Wing Commander Louis Greig as his partner. They were eliminated in the first round.

**QUESTION: When did France first win the Davis Cup, breaking the monopoly held by the United States, Britain and Australia? Who were the opposing players, and what were the scores of the matches?**

France first won the Davis Cup in 1927, beating the United States, 3–2, and then held the cup until 1933. In 1927 Rene Lacoste defeated Bill Johnston, 6–3, 6–2, 6–2; Bill Tilden won from Henri Cochet, 6–4, 2–6, 6–2, 8–6; Tilden and Francis Hunter stopped Jean Borotra and Jacques Brugnon, 3–6, 6–3, 6–3, 4–6, 6–0; Lacoste defeated Tilden, 6–3, 4–6, 6–3, 6–2, and Cochet beat Johnston, 6–4, 4–6, 6–2, 6–4.

**QUESTION: Which tennis players in the United States, both men and women, have been ranked in the top 10 the most times? Which have been ranked No. 1 the most?**

W. A. (Bill) Larned was ranked for 19 years, between 1892 and 1911, but his No. 1 ranking for eight years leaves him second to Bill Tilden, who was No. 1 for 10 years out of the 12 that he was ranked between 1918 and 1929.

Billie Jean King, who has been playing since 1960, has been ranked 17 times, up through 1980. Molla Mallory (1915–1928), Helen Wills Moody (1922–1933) and Mrs. King each have been ranked No. 1 seven times.

**QUESTION: How many national tennis titles has Chris Evert Lloyd won in her career? How many such titles did she win in 1980 and to which major players did she lose in that year?**

Mrs. Lloyd has won a total (open, clay court and indoors) of 12 United States women's championships, all in singles. Earlier in her career she took six United States junior titles, three in singles and three in doubles.

Mrs. Lloyd has won 16 national titles of other countries, all but five in singles. In 1980, she won the French Open, the United States Open

Clay Court Championships and the United States Open, all in singles. During that year she lost three times to Tracy Austin, twice to Martina Navratilova and once each to Evonne Goolagong and Hana Mandlikova.

**QUESTION: How many major tennis titles did Maureen Connolly win in her career?**

Miss Connolly's career was cut short by a serious leg injury sustained when a truck hit a horse she was riding. In the few years she played tennis, she captured the United States singles title three times (1951–53), Wimbledon three times (1952–54), the French championship twice (1953–54), the Australian title (1953) and the Italian (1954). She also won the Italian doubles title (1953).

Miss Connolly, in 1953, was the first woman to achieve the Grand Slam with her victories in the United States, Britain, France and Australia. She also won the United States clay court singles championship (1953) and, earlier, in the girls' 18 class, the singles (1949) and doubles crowns (1950).

She married Norman Brinker after retiring and died of cancer at the age of 34 on June 21, 1969.

**QUESTION: When did Anita Lizana win the United States women's singles tennis title, what country was she from and whom did she beat? Did she ever win another major tennis championship?**

Miss Lizana, from Chile, defeated Jadwiga Jedrzejowska of Poland in the 1937 final, 6–4, 6–2. She never won another major title.

**QUESTION: In recent months I have read a great deal about tennis stars of the past, such as Bill Tilden, R. Norris Williams and Maurice McLaughlin. Vinnie Richards has not been mentioned, and I remember him as a great player. Wasn't he a ranking player? Did he win any national titles?**

Richards was ranked among the top 10 players in the United States in five years: 1921 (3d), 1922 (3d), 1923 (4th), 1924 (2d) and 1925 (3d). He won a number of national championships, including five doubles, two mixed doubles, three indoor singles, five indoor doubles and one clay court doubles. He also captured seven titles as a boy (ages 15 and 18) in singles and doubles, and gold medals in the 1924 Olympics in singles and doubles.

Richards, who was born in 1903 and died in 1959, also captured the Wimbledon doubles (1924) and the French doubles (1926). He was one of the first professional tennis players and won a number of championships in that field.

**QUESTION: Now that Czechoslovakia became the first East European nation to win the Davis Cup, in 1980, please list all the previous winners.**

There have been 69 finals since the Davis Cup competition began in 1900. The United States leads with 26 victories, Australia has 24, Britain nine, France six, and South Africa, Sweden and Italy, in addition to Czechoslovakia, each has one.

**QUESTION: Has Bjorn Borg ever been defeated at Wimbledon?**

Yes. In 1974, Borg lost to Ismail el-Shafei, 6–2, 6–3, 6–1, in the fourth round; in 1975, he lost to Arthur Ashe, 2–6, 6–4, 8–6, 6–1, in the quarterfinals. Then, in 1981, he lost to John McEnroe, 4–6, 7–6, 7–6, 6–4, in the finals.

**QUESTION: In Davis Cup competition, the defending champion now has to play its way into the final round, but it wasn't always that way. When were the rules changed?**

The challenge round, which allowed the defending cup champion freedom from play until one survivor was left from the eliminations, was dropped in 1972.

**QUESTION: Jimmy Connors failed to appear at the presentation ceremony of the Wimbledon centennial, in 1977, and so the medal that he was to have received as a former Wimbledon champion was denied him. Has Connors ever received that medal, or are the officials of the world's most prestigious tennis tournament continuing to withhold it?**

As far as the All England Lawn Tennis and Croquet Club is concerned, the incident was closed when Connors declined to appear to receive the medal. According to a club official, there is no present intention to reopen "an incident that is past and finished."

# Other Racquet Sports

THE PHILADELPHIA SHOT

**QUESTION: What is the "Philadelphia shot" in squash racquets?**

It is one of the trickiest shots in the game. The ball is hit high into the front wall at such an angle that it strikes the left side wall and immediately flies diagonally across the court and hits deep on the right side wall. The ball develops a reverse spin as it strikes the first side wall so that when it bounces off the second wall it comes out straight, parallel to the back wall, making it difficult to strike.

**QUESTION: Squash racquets, a sport of growing popularity, was imported from Britain. Is there a difference in the way the game is played there?**

The British court is larger than the American court, and the ball is slower. Consequently the British game is slower and one of attrition. A match can last 2½ hours; an American match of five games, with more kill shots, is usually over in 75 minutes.

QUESTION: When I first began playing squash, American players used a hard ball and a heavy racquet, the British a soft ball and light racquet. Now, the Americans are using lighter racquets and a new type of ball. Why? How different is the new ball from the old? What do the different color dots on the balls mean?

In an attempt to reconcile the British and American versions of squash, the size of the ball used here was reduced from 1¾ inches in diameter to 1⅝ inches, with the weight range reduced from 1.05–1.1 ounces to .68–.73 ounces. The weight of the racquet was reduced from 9¼ ounces to 8½–9 ounces, comparable to the British 8½–8¾.

The blue dot on the ball means it should be used on any court where the temperature is over 60 degrees; the white ball should be used when the temperature is below 60. The yellow-dot ball was experimental. According to Ted Friel, chairman of the Racquets and Ball Committee of the United States Squash Racquets Association, the average player should never use the blue-dot ball. However, despite all the changes instituted, the British are still using their softer ball.

QUESTION: Is there a difference in court sizes between platform tennis and paddle tennis?

Confusion sometimes arises because platform-tennis players often call their sport paddle tennis, but in fact there are several differences.

In platform tennis the overall dimensions are a little more than 30 feet by 60 feet and the elevated deck is surrounded by a 12-foot-high galvanized steel-wire screening. The actual playing lines are 20 feet by 44 feet and the net that bisects the court is 34 inches high at the center and 37 inches high at the end posts.

In paddle tennis, the court is 20 feet by 50 feet, with three feet at each end of the court being a lob area. A ball landing in that area had to have first been hit as high as 10 feet or more to stay in play. The net is 31 inches high with a sag of no more than one inch in the center. Space behind each baseline varies from 10 feet (on the West Coast) to 15 feet (on the East Coast).

QUESTION: Can you tell me if paddleball has more than one set of rules? Also, racquetball? And if so, why?

There is more than one set of rules in each sport because there are organizations that are offshoots of the original groups, the United States Paddleball Association and the United States Racquetball Association. Each of these groups issues its own set of rules.

# Horse Racing

## Thoroughbreds

**QUESTION: Seattle Slew closed out his racing career with earnings of $1,208,726. Where does he rank on the career list? Who is first?**

Seattle Slew ranks 16th. Spectacular Bid is first, having won $1,117,790 in 1980 to make his career total $2,781,607.

**QUESTION: What are the career racing statistics of Angel Cordero Jr. and Laffit Pincay Jr.? How many Triple Crown races have they won?**

At the end of 1980, Cordero had ridden 23,730 mounts, with 4,178 firsts, 3,651 seconds and 3,297 thirds, and amassed purses of $55,157,512; Pincay had been on 19,560 mounts, with 4,326 firsts, 3,279 seconds and 2,786 thirds, and his purses were $55,528,524.

Cordero won the Kentucky Derby in 1974 on Cannonade and in 1976 on Bold Forbes, the Preakness in 1980 on Codex, and the Belmont Stakes in 1976 on Bold Forbes. Pincay has never won a Triple Crown race.

**QUESTION: How many fillies, if any, have won the Kentucky Derby, the Preakness or the Belmont Stakes? How many have placed second? Please name them and the year in which they raced.**

In the Kentucky Derby, Regret won in 1915 and Genuine Risk in 1980. Lady Navarre finished second to Sir Huon in 1906.

In the Preakness, Flocarline won in 1903, Whimsical in 1906, Rhine Maiden in 1915 and Nellie Morse in 1924. Second-place finishers were Sadie S. in 1901 (behind The Parader), Kiamesha in 1905 (behind Cairngorm), Content in 1906 (behind Whimsical), Polly Ann in 1921 (behind Broomspun) and Genuine Risk in 1980 (behind Codex).

In the Belmont Stakes, Ruthless won the first running of the race, in 1867, and Tanya won in 1905. Genuine Risk finished second in 1980 (behind Temperance Hill).

## QUESTION: Has an apprentice jockey ever won the Kentucky Derby, the Preakness or the Belmont? Who was the youngest jockey to win the Derby?

Two apprentices have won the Derby, Ira Hanford on Bold Venture in 1936 and Bill Boland on Middleground in 1950. No records on apprentice victories are kept on the two other stakes races.

Boland, who was born on July 16, 1933, was the youngest jockey to win the Derby, being two months short of his 17th birthday.

## QUESTION: Is there a Triple Crown in racing in England? If so, what are the races and who were the winners?

The Triple Crown in England consists of the Epsom Derby, St. Leger Stakes and the Two Thousand Guineas. There have been 15 such winners:

West Australian (1853); Gladiateur (1865); Lord Lyon (1866); Ormonde (1886); Common (1891); Isinglass (1893); Galtee More (1897); Flying Fox (1899); Diamond Jubilee (1900); Rock Sand (1903); Pommern (1915); Gay Crusader (1917); Gainsborough (1918); Bahram (1935); and Nijinsky II (1970).

## QUESTION: Has any female jockey ever been on a mount in one of the Triple Crown races?

Women have been racing since 1969 at thoroughbred tracks, but only one, Diane Crump, has had a mount in the Triple Crown events. She was aboard Fathom in the 1970 Kentucky Derby and finished 15th in a 17-horse race.

## QUESTION: Please list Bill Shoemaker's career racing earnings, victories and how many times he has won Triple Crown races.

Shoemaker, who was born on Aug. 19, 1931, had, at the end of 1980, 34,215 mounts, 7,923 victories, 5,336 seconds, 4,257 thirds and $79,672,384 in earnings, the most of any jockey in history.

Shoemaker won the Kentucky Derby with Swaps (1955), Tomy Lee (1959) and Lucky Debonair (1965); Preakness: Candy Spots (1963) and Damascus (1967); Belmont Stakes: Gallant Man (1957), Sword Dancer (1959), Jaipur (1962), Damascus (1967), and Avatar (1975).

## QUESTION: Who wrote the famous poem about Earl Sande, the jockey, and when was it written?

Damon Runyon was the author of the poem, the first version of which he wrote in 1922. That poem contained the famous lines:

> *Gimme a handy*
> *Guy like Sande*
> *Ridin' them horses in.*

In 1930, in writing about the Kentucky Derby, Runyon came up with a new version, one that was, perhaps, the best known of his poems. The first stanza follows:

> Say, have they turned back the pages,
> Back to the past once more?
> Back to the racin' ages
> An' a Derby out of the yore?
> Say, don't tell me I'm daffy,
> Ain't that the same ol' grin?
> Why it's that handy
> Guy named Sande
> Bootin' a winner in!

**QUESTION: In thoroughbred racing, which horses were horse of the year from 1950 through 1960?**

1950—Hill Prince; 1951—Counterpoint; 1952—One Count; 1953—Tom Fool; 1954—Native Dancer; 1955—Nashua; 1956—Swaps; 1957—Bold Ruler; 1958—Round Table; 1959—Sword Dancer; 1960—Kelso (his first of five consecutive horse-of-the-year designations).

**QUESTION: Did Noor ever win the Santa Anita Handicap? If so, when, and who finished second and third? Also, at what track did Citation make his comeback after breaking down at the Tanforan Race Track in California?**

Noor won the Santa Anita Handicap in 1950, with Citation finishing second and Two Lea third. Citation broke down in December 1948, and made his comeback earlier at Santa Anita on Jan. 11, 1950, winning a purse of $2,500, far below his usual earnings for a race.

**QUESTION: Has there ever been a stakes race in which one horse was so overwhelming a favorite that all the other entries withdrew, and the favorite thus had a "walkover" to collect the purse? Was Citation ever involved in such a race?**

There have been many walkovers in horse racing. Citation was the beneficiary of such withdrawals in the Pimlico Special on Oct. 29, 1948.

**QUESTION: If a jockey finishes first, second or third in a claiming race or a stakes race, what is he paid? Also, if he finishes out of the money?**

The policy varies in different states, but in New York a jockey gets 10 percent of the winner's purse. If a jockey does not have a specific contract with an owner, he gets $55 for second, $45 for third and $35 for finishing out of the money.

**QUESTION: Jockeys, I understand, ride with one stirrup longer than the other. Which stirrup is longer, and what is the purpose?**

The stirrup on the left side, the side closest to the rail, is usually longer. This practice, called "acey-deucy," is a matter of style or comfort. Racing strategy is not involved.

**QUESTION: What were the locations of three Brooklyn race tracks—Brighton Beach, Gravesend and Sheepshead Bay?**

The Brighton Beach track was situated southeast of the present intersection of Ocean Parkway and Neptune Avenue. Gravesend was southwest of the intersection that now is Ocean Parkway and Kings Highway. Sheepshead Bay, which was run by the Coney Island Jockey Club and was sometimes referred to as the Coney Island track, was northeast of the place that is now Ocean and Jerome Avenues.

**QUESTION: Where was Morris Park situated, and was it a track for thoroughbreds or trotters? How long was it in existence?**

Morris Park, a thoroughbred track, was situated in the Westchester hills about two miles east of the Jerome Park Reservoir in the Borough of the Bronx, New York City. It was built because the reservoir had displaced the old Jerome Park race track. Racing began at Morris Park in 1889 and ended in 1905, when the Westchester Racing Association took possession of the new Belmont Park on Long Island.

**QUESTION: Around 1920, was there a Butler Race Track and, if so, where was it located?**

There was no Butler Race Track; you obviously mean the Empire City Race Track in Yonkers, built by James Butler. Empire City opened in 1898 and was, for a brief period, a harness track. It was then converted for thoroughbred racing. Empire City closed in 1945, and the Yonkers Raceway opened on the same site in 1950, with the track reduced from a mile to a half-mile for harness racing.

**QUESTION: Is is true that Jesse Owens once won a race against a horse? If so, when, where and at what distance? And what was the name of the horse?**

After the 1936 Olympics, Owens became a professional and took on many running challenges. One of those challenges took place in Havana, on Dec. 27, 1936, when he defeated a chestnut gelding named Julio McCaw by 20 yards in a 100-yard race. There was one catch, however: Owens, whose time that day was 9.9 seconds, had the advantage of a 40-yard handicap.

**QUESTION: Newspaper photographs of the recent English Derby showed the horses running counterclockwise, as they do in the United States. I was under the impression that horses ran clockwise in Britain and on the Continent. Will you please explain?**

There is no hard-and-fast rule about horses' running clockwise or counterclockwise. The rules department of the Jockey Club in London, arbiter of the sport, says the answer depends simply on the way the course is built. The International Racing Bureau in London affirms that the same is true on the Continent.

Whether a horse is running clockwise or counterclockwise is an important point, by the way, among keen race followers, because some horses have a preference for one or the other, often to a degree that significantly affects form.

**QUESTION: Were any winners of the Kentucky Derby ever bred in New Jersey?**

Yes, two. Regret, who won the race in 1915 and was the first filly to do so, was bred by Harry Payne Whitney at his Brookdale Farm in Red Bank. Cavalcade, the 1934 victor, was bred by F. Wallace Armstrong at his Meadowview Farms in Moorestown.

**QUESTION: When did Ruffian race against Foolish Pleasure and was there any parimutuel betting?**

Ruffian faced Foolish Pleasure in the Great Match Race Stakes on July 6, 1975. There was parimutuel betting only to win and Foolish Pleasure paid $3.80. Ruffian broke down during the race and was later destroyed.

**QUESTION: Chris McCarron in 1980 was the fourth different jockey to win the most races (405) and the most purses ($7,663,300). Who were the three others?**

Willie Shoemaker accomplished this double four times, in 1953 (485 and $1,784,187), in 1954 (380 and $1,876,760), in 1958 (300 and $2,961,693) and in 1959 (347 and $2,843,133). Laffit Pincay Jr. did it in 1971 (380 and $3,784,377) and Steve Cauthen did it in 1977 (487 and $6,151,750).

**QUESTION: How many times did Eddie Arcaro and Johnny Longden win the Kentucky Derby, the Preakness Stakes and the Belmont Stakes?**

Arcaro won the Derby in 1938 (Lawrin), 1941 (Whirlaway), 1945 (Hoop Jr.), 1948 (Citation) and 1952 (Hill Gail). Preakness: 1941 (Whirlaway), 1948 (Citation), 1950 (Hill Prince), 1951 (Bold), 1955 (Nashua) and 1957 (Bold Ruler). Belmont: 1941 (Whirlaway), 1942 (Shut Out), 1945 (Pavot), 1948 (Citation), 1952 (One Count) and 1955 (Nashua).

Longden captured the Triple Crown in 1943 on Count Fleet, for his only victories in those races.

**QUESTION: How many times did Seabiscuit face War Admiral? Did they ever meet in a match race?**

Seabiscuit defeated the supposedly invincible War Admiral by four lengths at Pimlico on Nov. 1, 1938. The time for the 1 3/16-mile race was one minute 56.3 seconds, with Seabiscuit winning $15,000. There were no other starters in the race, the Pimlico Special, but technically it was not a match race. According to the Thoroughbred Racing Association, it was the only time the two horses raced against each other. Earlier in 1938, on Memorial Day, Seabiscuit withdrew from a race at Belmont Park in which War Admiral was entered. War Admiral was sent to stud early in 1939.

**QUESTION: Was there ever thoroughbred horse racing in Texas during the 1930's? If so, at which tracks?**

Parimutuel betting is barred in Texas, but there was a brief period, from 1933 to 1937, in which it was legal. During that period, there was racing at four tracks: Arlington Downs, between Dallas and Fort Worth; Alamo Downs, near San Antonio; Epsom Downs, near Houston; and the Dallas State Fairgrounds.

QUESTION: Through 1980, who are the 10 leading jockeys in career victories?

1. Bill Shoemaker, 7,923; 2. John Longden, 6,032; 3. Eddie Arcaro, 4,779; 4. Steve Brooks, 4,451; 5. Walter Blum, 4,382; 6. Laffit Pincay Jr., 4,326; 7. Larry Snyder, 4,213; 8. Angel Cordero, 4,178; 9. Sandy Hawley, 4,072; 10. Avelino Gomez, 4,058 (exclusive of victories in Havana and Mexico City).

# Pacers and Trotters

QUESTION: What races constitute the triple crown in trotting and pacing? How many such winners have there been in each?

The Yonkers Trot, the Hambletonian and the Kentucky Futurity are the three trotting races. There have been six winners: Scott Frost, 1955; Speedy Scott, 1963; Ayres, 1964; Nevel Pride, 1968; Lindy's Pride, 1969, and Super Bowl, 1972.

The Cane Pace, the Little Brown Jug and the Messenger are the pacing races. There have also been six winners: Adios Butler, 1959; Bret Hanover, 1965; Romeo Hanover, 1966; Rum Customer, 1968; Most Happy Fella, 1970, and Niatross, 1980.

QUESTION: Which trotter was the top purse winner in 1979? Which filly trotter?

Chiola Hanover won 14 of 20 starts in 1979 and led the trotters with earnings of $553,058. Classical Way earned $217,025 with 16 victories in 20 outings and led the fillies.

QUESTION: Was the famed Hambletonian trotting race ever held at Yonkers?

Once, in 1943. The '43 Hambletonian had been scheduled to be raced at Goshen, N.Y., but, because of the brownout and the gasoline rationing caused by World War II, all New York State racing that year was held at one location, Yonkers, during daylight hours.

QUESTION: Which five harness drivers won the most races in 1980 and which earned the most money?

Races: Herve Filion, 474; Ron Waples, 396; Carmine Abbatiello, 391; John Campbell, 321 and Joseph Hudon Jr., 313.

Earnings: Campbell, $3,732,306; Abbatiello, $3,366,615; Filion, $3,230,276; William Gilmour, $2,576,149, and Ted Wing, $2,226,349.

# Soccer

## Rules of the Game

**QUESTION: In soccer, if the ball strikes the referee during play and goes into the goal, does the score count?**

Yes. Under international rules, the ball is still in play if "it rebounds off either the Referee or Linesmen when they are in the field of play."

**QUESTION: What is a shootout in soccer and how did it originate?**

The shootout, which is used only in the North American Soccer League, was conceived in 1977 in order to end ties and make the sport more exciting for American fans. It takes place if a game is still tied after two sudden-death overtime periods of seven-and-a-half minutes each. Five players from each team challenge the opposing goalkeeper, one on one. Each player starts with the ball from 35 yards out and must take his shot within five seconds. If the regulation shootout results in a tie, the teams continue until there is a winner after an equal number of shots have been taken.

**QUESTION: Please define soccer's version of an "own goal?"**

An "own goal" occurs when a defensive player makes a deliberate play with either his feet, head or body that sends the ball into his own net. No assist can be credited on such a goal. However, when an offensive shot is deflected off the body of a defensive player, and the referee makes such a determination, that goal is credited to the offensive player. An offensive assist can be credited on such a goal.

**QUESTION: In professional soccer, player A of the attacking team centers the ball near the goal. His teammate B, who has been ahead of A near the goal, runs back, gets the ball, dribbles between the defenders,**

who only now are between him and the goal line, and kicks the ball into the cage. Is the goal legal?

No. The attacking team is offside, because, at the moment that A passed, B was in front of the ball and did not have the required two opponents between him and the goal line.

**QUESTION: I have always been a little confused by the point system used by the North American Soccer League. Now I understand changes have been made for the 1980 season. What are the differences?**

Under the old system, a winning team earned six points for a victory and a bonus point for each goal scored, up to a maximum of three for a game. Under the new system for 1980, this still holds true, providing the goals are scored in regulation time; no bonus points will be awarded for winning in overtime or in a shootout.

**QUESTION: Please explain how the British Football League promotes and relegates teams in its divisions. Also, do the players involved in these team changes have their salaries increased or decreased?**

The three First Division teams with the fewest points at the end of the season (if there is a tie, the goals for and against are calculated) are relegated to the Second Division, and the three top teams in that division are promoted to the First Division. The total in each division, therefore, remains the same.

In the Third and Fourth Divisions, four teams are promoted and four relegated in similar fashion.

The contracts of the individual players are not affected by these changes.

**QUESTION: In soccer, as played in the Major Indoor Soccer League, how many men are on a team, what are their positions, what is the size of the playing field and is the ball smaller than the one used outdoors?**

There are six players: a goalkeeper, two defenders and three forwards. Sometimes one of the forwards is called a midfielder. The field is approximately 200 feet long and 85 feet wide, which are the dimensions of a hockey rink. The ball is the standard leather ball, 27 to 28 inches in circumference and weighing 14 to 16 ounces.

**QUESTION: I know that each team in the North American Soccer League must have at least three players from the United States, but how many North American players are there in the league?**

The final 1980 rosters for each team listed 245 North American citizens and 291 players from other countries. Three teams had a majority of North Americans: Dallas (11-10), Edmonton (13-12) and Houston (14-12). Philadelphia and Toronto had 11 North Americans and 11 foreigners.

**QUESTION: What keeps a game in the North American Soccer League moving so briskly? Does the league have a rule that prevents a team from stalling when it is ahead or needs a breather?**

There is no such rule. N.A.S.L. games have no time outs, except those called by a referee for injuries, and a maximum of three substitutions a game is permitted. The action during the 45-minute halves is, therefore, almost continuous with the teams constantly moving up and down the field.

# For the Record

**QUESTION: Who invented the game of soccer? When did the first game between national teams take place?**

The roots of the game extend far back in history, and there have been so many different claims that it is not possible to pinpoint who invented the game and where it happened. There is no question, however, that the English strongly influenced the development of the game as it is played today. The first game between national teams, England and Scotland, took place in Glasgow in 1872.

**QUESTION: Does Pelé hold the record for the most goals scored by a soccer player? I always thought he did, but I have been told that Artur Friedenreich, another Brazilian, is the top scorer. If so, who was he?**

Friedenreich is the leader with 1,329 goals to 1,281 for Pelé. Both registered that total in league play in Brazil, exhibitions and the World Cup, but the Pelé total also includes 31 goals for the Cosmos.

Friedenreich, the son of a German father and a Brazilian mother, was born in 1892 and died in 1969. He scored most of his goals during the 1920's and retired from soccer at the age of 43.

**QUESTION: Which country has won the most World Cup soccer tournaments and which has won the most gold medals in soccer at the Olympic Games?**

Brazil is the leader in World Cup play, having won three of the eleven tournaments, in 1958, 1962 and 1970. Britain, in 1900, 1908 and 1912, and Hungary, in 1952, 1964 and 1968, each has won three of the 17 Olympic titles.

**QUESTION: When was the last time the United States soccer team qualified for the final round of the World Cup? When will the next final round take place and how many teams will participate? What are the chances that the World Cup final round will take place in the United States in the near future?**

The United States last played in Pool 2 in the 1950 final round, which was won by Spain, although Uruguay won the championship. The next World Cup, in 1982, will be held in Spain with 24 countries competing. The United States has asked to be host for the 1990 Cup final, but its application as yet has not been approved.

**QUESTION: Please list the scores of the 11 World Cup finals.**

In 1930, Uruguay beat Argentina, 4–2; 1934, Italy 2, Czechoslovakia 1; 1938, Italy 4, Hungary 2; 1950, Uruguay 2, Brazil 1; 1954, West Germany 3, Hungary 2; 1958, Brazil 5, Sweden 2; 1962, Brazil 3, Czechoslovakia 1; 1966, England 4, West Germany 2; 1970, Brazil 4, Italy 1; 1974, West Germany 2, the Netherlands, 1, and 1978, Argentina 3, the Netherlands 1 (overtime).

**QUESTION:** Is there a chance that the 1982 World Cup soccer final will be televised on one of the United States networks?

According to United States Soccer Federation officials, there is every chance that one of the networks will televise the 1982 final from Spain.

**QUESTION:** There is an annual soccer competition between the winner of the European Cup and the winner of the Copa Libertadores in South America. In 1977 and 1978, the best teams in Europe have been Liverpool and Nottingham Forest. Have they played the South American champions, and who won? Also, have the Cosmos ever played Liverpool, and, if not, do they plan to do so in the future?

The competition you refer to is not mandatory, and Liverpool refused to meet the South American champions in 1977 and 1978. However, the losing European finalist, Borussia Monchengladbach of West Germany, was beaten by the Boca Juniors of Argentina in 1978.

The Cosmos have never played Liverpool, and currently no game is scheduled.

**QUESTION:** There are many foreign soccer stars playing in the United States, but has any American played in professional leagues abroad?

Yes. Recent examples: Ty Keough of the San Diego Sockers and Bobby Smith of the Philadelphia Fury have played in Ireland, and David Brcic of the Cosmos has played in Scotland.

**QUESTION:** How did the United States soccer team fare in the 1979 Pan American Games? Is it true that two of our players were suspended?

In the preliminary round, the United States team beat the Dominican Republic, 6–0, and Puerto Rico, 3–1, but the Americans lost to Argentina, 4–0, and thus were eliminated from competition for the gold medal. In the final round, the United States lost to Cuba, 5–0, but edged Puerto Rico for fifth place on the basis of goals scored. Brazil won the gold medal.

No United States players were suspended, but two, Don Ebert and Joe Morrone, were thrown out of the game against Puerto Rico.

**QUESTION:** Who won the 1979–80 indoor championship of the North American Soccer League? Was this the first season for the league?

Tampa Bay won the title in a two-game series against Memphis. The Rowdies lost the first game, 5–4, but won the second, 10–4, and the minigame, 1–0. It was the league's first season.

# College Sports

## Football

ILLEGAL; SAFETY

**QUESTION: A punt was blocked in a recent college football game, and the ball rolled slowly through the end zone. The punter grabbed the blocker and prevented him from falling on the ball for a touchdown. A safety resulted. The referee apparently missed the infraction of the rules, but if he had seen it, what would have been the penalty? Would it be the same in professional football?**

If the kicker held the blocker in the end zone, the penalty would have been the safety. If the kicker held the blocker on the field of play, the penalty would have been half the distance to the goal line, with no loss of down. Of course, the blocking team could refuse the penalty and take the safety. In either case, a touchdown was averted. The penalty is the same in professional football.

**QUESTION: In college and professional football, do the onside kicking rules apply on a free kick following a safety, permitting the kicking team to recover the ball if it travels at least 10 yards?**

Yes, but since the free kick line after a safety is the kicking team's own 20-yard line, and its failure to recover the ball would provide the receiving team with excellent field position, an onside kick in such a situation is not practical.

**QUESTION: During a recent college football game, a wide receiver in motion reversed his direction when he was behind the center. Is this a legal move in the National Football League?**

It is legal in college and professional football as long as no forward step is taken.

**QUESTION: In the statistics for college and professional football games, what does the item "return yards" mean?**

The item lists the total yards gained in returning punts, interceptions and recovered fumbles; it does not include kickoff returns.

**QUESTION: In college football, was there ever a time when the ball was placed down at a point where the ball carrier was tackled, without regard to how close to the sidelines that point was?**

Yes. The first side zones, of 10 yards from each sideline, were not created until 1933; they were increased to 15 yards in 1938.

**QUESTION: In professional football, a pass is incomplete if the receiver does not land inbounds with both feet on the ground. Is the same true in college football?**

No. If a college receiver lands inbounds with one foot and he has possession and control of the ball, the pass is complete.

**QUESTION: In college football, was there ever a penalty imposed for incomplete passes?**

Beginning in 1926, a penalty of five yards was imposed for each incomplete pass after the first in any series of downs. The rule was eliminated in 1934.

**QUESTION: When was the first intercollegiate football game played, and who won it?**

Football was played among students in what is now known as the Ivy League as far back as the 1820's, but the first game occurred on Nov. 6, 1869, between Rutgers and Princeton at New Brunswick. Rutgers won the game, six goals to four. Before the match it had been decided that the team first to score six goals would be the winner.

**QUESTION: How did the present system of scoring points in football originate? Was it always the same?**

Originally, a field goal counted for five points and a touchdown for one. In the mid-1880's, a safety was one point, a touchdown two, a point-after-touchdown four and a field goal five. Later, the worth of a touchdown was raised to five points, the same as the field goal, the point-after-touchdown dropped to one and the safety became two. In 1910, the field goal was dropped to three points, and in 1912 the touchdown was raised to six.

**QUESTION: When was the huddle first used in football? Was there always an end zone? Was there a time when, to score a touchdown, the ball had to be run between the goal posts? When did colleges adopt the optional two-points-after-touchdown rule?**

Georgia is credited with using the first huddle in 1896 in a game against Auburn. Before 1873, the ball had to pass through the goal posts to score a legal touchdown. The end zone was created in 1912. The two-points-after-touchdown rule was adopted in 1958.

**QUESTION: When was the forward pass made legal in college football? Who threw the first pass?**

In 1903, with the country becoming alarmed at the number of injuries in football, a move was begun to legalize the forward pass. It took until 1906, however, for the pass to be made legal.

There are any number of stories about who threw the first pass. One of the most reliable, as reported in the 1945 "Football: Facts and Figures," by Dr. L.H. Baker (Rinehart and Company Inc.), says that Walter Camp, while playing for Yale against Princeton in 1876, threw the ball to a teammate as he was about to be tackled. Princeton protested, but the referee tossed a coin and the pass was allowed.

**QUESTION: In a 1981 college bowl game, I saw a player on the receiving team signal for a fair catch on a very high, short kickoff. Is that permitted?**

Yes. A fair catch is legal on a free kick or a scrimmage kick that is untouched beyond the neutral zone.

**QUESTION: If a college student who does not participate in intercollegiate athletics transfers to another college, and there decides to go out for a varsity team, how many years of eligibility does he have left?**

According to the rules of the National Collegiate Athletic Association, a student "must complete his seasons of participation within five calendar years from the beginning of the semester or quarter in which he first registered at a collegiate institution." If the student in question, say, is a soccer player and spent two years at the first college, he would have three years of eligibility left, assuming he had not practiced or participated in organized soccer, whether in college or with a club. Even if he graduated in two years from the second college, he could enroll in another baccalaureate program at that college and still be eligible for his third year of varsity soccer.

**QUESTION: Which college was the first to put numbers on football uniforms?**

In 1908, Washington and Jefferson College put numbers on its football players, but soon abandoned the practice. In 1913, Amos Alonzo Stagg, coach at the University of Chicago, instituted numbering and it soon became popular.

**QUESTION: The Rutgers-Princeton football rivalry is the oldest, but is it the series with the most games played? If not, which is? What is the oldest prep-school rivalry and which has the most games played?**

Rutgers and Princeton started playing in 1869 and have suspended their rivalry after 71 games, with the Tigers winning 53, Rutgers 17 and one game a tie. Lafayette and Lehigh first met in 1884 and have played the most games—115—because they met twice a season for 16 years and once, in 1891, three times. Lafayette leads the series, 63–47–5. In Division I-A, Princeton and Yale are the leaders, having played 102 games, with Yale ahead, 55–37–10.

As near as can be determined, Andover and Exeter, who faced each other for the 100th time in 1980, have the oldest prep-school rivalry and have played the most games. The series began in 1878, with Andover ahead, 52–40–8.

QUESTION: Who was the first player to win the Heisman Trophy, what college did he play for and what were his statistics? Has any player won the trophy more than once?

Jay Berwanger, a University of Chicago halfback, was the first winner in 1935. Berwanger was regarded as one of the greatest all-around backs in an era when the regulars played both offense and defense. In 23 games from 1933 through 1935, he carried the ball 439 times for 1,839 yards, an average of 4.2 a carry. He scored 22 touchdowns and kicked 20 points-after-touchdown for 152 points. Berwanger completed 50 of 146 passes for 921 yards and punted 223 times for a 37.3-yard average. He also kicked off 31 times for a 46.3-yard average, and, while playing defensive back, intercepted eight passes.

Archie Griffin, now with the Cincinnati Bengals, won the Heisman Trophy in 1974 and 1975 while at Ohio State.

QUESTION: I am trying to track down the following quotation: "There are three things that can happen when you pass the football, and two of them are bad." Who made the statement, when, and is that the full quotation?

Woody Hayes was the author of the statement when he was coach of Ohio State. According to the sports information officials at the university, that is the full quotation, and it was made in the 1950's. They are not certain as to the specific year.

QUESTION: In college football, did anyone ever win the Heisman trophy as the outstanding player without being a consensus all-American? How many Heisman winners were on the team ranked No. 1 of the same season?

Paul Hornung, the Notre Dame quarterback, won the 1956 Heisman trophy, but was not picked for the consensus all-America team. This is the only time it happened since 1935, the first year the trophy was awarded.

There were seven Heisman winners on the teams ranked No. 1 by the wire services: Davey O'Brien of Texas Christian, 1938; Bruce Smith of Minnesota, 1941; Angelo Bertilli of Notre Dame, 1943; Doc Blanchard of Army, 1945; John Lujack of Notre Dame, 1947; Leon Hart of Notre Dame, 1949; and Tony Dorsett of Pittsburgh, 1976.

QUESTION: How many times has Notre Dame opposed Ivy League teams in football, and what were the results?

The Irish have won nine games, lost one and tied one. The results:
Against Pennsylvania: 60–20 (1930), 49–0 (1931), 7–7 (1952), 28–20 (1953), 42–7 (1954) and 46–14 (1955).
Against Dartmouth: 64–0 (1944) and 34–0 (1945).
Against Princeton: 25–2 (1923) and 12–0 (1924).
Against Yale: 0–28 (1914).

QUESTION: Please list Notre Dame's football records against Southern California for the years that Ara Parseghian and Dan Devine were coaches. Also, how did the Irish fare against the Trojans in the years that Ed (Moose) Krause played for them?

Parseghian, in 11 seasons from 1964–74, won three games, lost six and tied two. Devine, in six seasons from 1975–80, won one game and lost five. Krause played in 1931, 1932 and 1933 and Notre Dame lost all three games.

QUESTION: How many times did the Notre Dame football team face Syracuse and what were the results? Please list the three Irish coaches with the winningest records.

Notre Dame played Syracuse three times, winning twice, 20–0 in 1914 and 17–15 in 1961, and losing once, 14–7, in 1963.

The three coaches are: Knute Rockne (1918–30), 105 victories, 12 losses, 5 ties; Ara Parseghian (1964–74), 95–17–4, and Frank Leahy (1941–43, 1946–53), 87–11–9.

QUESTION: Did Notre Dame ever meet Ohio State in football? If so, when? And who won?

Notre Dame has opposed Ohio State twice and won twice. In 1935, the Irish were winners by 18–13, having trailed by 13–0 at the half and having then scored the winning touchdown in the final minute. In 1936 the score was 7–2.

QUESTION: In 1946, Army faced Notre Dame at Yankee Stadium in a classic confrontation between two unbeaten teams that ended in a scoreless tie. How many Heisman trophy winners, present and future, played in the game?

Three. Doc Blanchard, who had won the trophy in 1945, and Glenn Davis, who was to win it for 1946, were in the Army backfield. Johnny Lujack, the Irish quarterback who was to be named the winner in 1947, also played. However, Leon Hart, the Notre Dame end destined to be the winner in 1949 and who was a freshman that season, was on the roster but never got into the game.

QUESTION: In what year did Carnegie Tech upset an unbeaten Notre Dame football team? Is it true that Knute Rockne, the Irish coach, was not at the game?

Carnegie Tech defeated the Irish, 19–0, on Nov. 27, 1926, in Pittsburgh. Notre Dame, unbeaten in eight games, did not regard Carnegie Tech, which had lost to New York University and Washington and Jefferson, as a serious opponent. Rockne let an assistant, Hunk Anderson, take over, while he scouted the Army-Navy game in Chicago.

QUESTION: At which colleges did the late Frank Leahy coach and what was his record at each college?

Leahy coached at Boston College in 1939 and 1940, and at Notre Dame from 1941 through 1953, except for 1944 and 1945. At Boston College, he won 20 games and lost two; at Notre Dame, he won 87 games, lost 11 and tied nine. He retired after the 1953 season with a career percentage of .864. He had two unbeaten and untied seasons at Notre Dame and one at Boston College. Four other of his Irish teams were unbeaten but tied.

**QUESTION:** Which college has produced the most players to be the first men taken in the National Football League draft, who were the players and which teams drafted them?

Notre Dame, with five selections, is the leader. The draftees were: Angelo Bertelli, quarterback (Boston, 1944); Frank Dancewicz, quarterback (Boston, 1946); Leon Hart, end (Detroit, 1950); Paul Hornung, halfback, (Green Bay, 1957), and Walt Patulski, defensive end (Buffalo, 1972).

**QUESTION:** What were the five longest undefeated and untied streaks by major college football teams? What years did the streaks span, who were the coaches and how did the streaks end?

Oklahoma tops the list with 47 straight victories, between 1953 and 1957. Charles (Bud) Wilkinson was the coach, and Notre Dame ended the streak with a 7–0 victory.

Washington is second with 39 victories between 1908 and 1914. Gil Dobie was the coach, and a 0–0 tie with Oregon State halted the string. In all, counting four ties, the Huskies were unbeaten in 63 games from 1907 to 1917.

Two different Yale streaks, each of 37 games, hold third and fourth spots. The first, between 1887 and 1889, was ended by a 10–0 loss to Princeton. The second, between 1890 and 1893, was also ended by Princeton, 6–0. The coaches during that era were R.W. Corwin, W.C. Rhodes and Walter Camp.

The fifth-longest winning record, 35 games, was set by Toledo between 1969 and 1971. Tampa snapped it, 21–0. Toledo's coaches were Frank Lauterbur and Jack Murphy.

**QUESTION:** Which major college holds the record for scoring the most points against another major college?

Houston holds the record for the most points scored against a major opponent, defeating Tulsa, 100–6, on Nov. 23, 1968. The Cougars scored 14 touchdowns, 13 points after and a field goal.

**QUESTION:** Who holds the record for the longest field goal in college football? Who is the career leader?

Three players have kicked field goals of 67 yards: Russell Erxleben of Texas, on Oct. 1, 1977, Steve Little of Arkansas, on Oct. 15, 1977, and Joe Williams of Wichita State, on Oct. 21, 1978. The career leader is Tony Franklin, a Texas A & M soccer-type kicker, who, from 1975 to 1978, was successful in 56 kicks out of 101 attempts, with his longest three-pointer being 65 yards.

**QUESTION:** Which colleges have won the most Rose, Orange, Cotton and Sugar Bowl games? Also, since the inception of the rivalry between the Big Ten and Pacific-10 in the Rose Bowl, what is the won-lost record of the conferences, and which college has the most victories?

Including the 1981 games, Southern California leads in the Rose Bowl with 17 victories, Oklahoma in the Orange Bowl with 10, Texas in the Cotton Bowl with nine, and Alabama in the Sugar Bowl with seven.

The Big Ten has won 19 times and lost 16 times in its rivalry with the Pacific-10 (which was formerly the Pacific-8 until the addition of Arizona and Arizona State a few years ago), but the Pac-10 has won 10 of the last 12 games. Southern California has the most victories here, nine.

**QUESTION: Did George Welsh, coach of the Navy team that defeated Brigham Young, 23-16, in the Holiday Bowl in 1978, also play on a Navy team that won a bowl game?**

Yes. Welsh was the quarterback on the Navy team that routed Mississippi, 21-0, in the 1955 Sugar Bowl.

**QUESTION: How many consecutive seasons has Alabama appeared in a bowl game? What is Alabama's career record in bowl games?**

The Crimson Tide has played in a bowl game for 21 straight seasons, including the 1981 Cotton Bowl victory over Baylor, 30-2. In 34 bowl appearances, Alabama has won 18 games, lost 13 and tied three.

**QUESTION: Notre Dame was beaten by Georgia, 17-10, in the 1981 Sugar Bowl. What was the first bowl game the Irish played and what is the complete record?**

Notre Dame's first such game was the Rose Bowl of Jan. 1, 1925, a 27-10 victory over Stanford. Because of a subsequent school policy opposing postseason appearances the Irish did not play in another bowl for half a century. The big money of the major bowls ultimately lured them back, and on Jan. 1, 1970, they played Texas in the Cotton Bowl and lost, 21-17. Notre Dame's other bowl games have been:

### Cotton Bowl
Jan. 1, 1971—Notre Dame 24, Texas 11.
Jan. 2, 1978—Notre Dame 38, Texas 10.
Jan. 1, 1979—Notre Dame 35, Houston 34.
### Orange Bowl
Jan. 1, 1973—Nebraska 40, Notre Dame 6.
Jan. 1, 1975—Notre Dame 13, Alabama 11.
### Sugar Bowl
Dec. 31, 1973—Notre Dame 24, Alabama 23.
### Gator Bowl
Dec. 27, 1976—Notre Dame 20, Penn State 9.

**QUESTION: What are the individual season records in college football, as of the end of the 1980 season, for total offense yardage, passing yardage, rushing yardage and scoring?**

Total offense: Jim McMahon of Brigham Young, 56 yards rushing and 4,571 yards passing, for 4,627, in 1980.

Passing: McMahon, 4,571 yards on 284 completions in 445 attempts, in 1980.

Rushing: Tony Dorsett of Pittsburgh, 1,948 yards on 338 rushes in 11 games, 1976.

Receptions: Howard Twilley, Tulsa, 1,779 yards on 134 receptions, in 1965.

Scoring: Lydell Mitchell of Penn State, 174 points on 29 touchdowns, in 1971.

QUESTION: Whenever the traditional Army-Navy game approaches, some questions come to mind: What was the Lonely End concept and which player was noted for playing that position? Also, I recall that an underdog Navy team once snapped a long Army unbeaten streak, but how and when did that happen?

Earl Blaik, when he coached Army, originated the Lonely End in 1958. He stationed the end 15 yards to the right or left of his quarterback. The quarterback, by movements of his feet as he stood behind the offensive huddle, would send the play to the Lonely End. Bill Carpenter was the first and most famous Lonely End.

On Dec. 2, 1950, Navy won, 14–2, ending Army's 28 game unbeaten (but tied) streak. Navy scored two touchdowns in the second period, one by Bob Zastrow, the quarterback, on a 7-yard buck, and the second on a sensational catch of a 30-yard pass by Jim Baldinger, an end, 20 seconds before the end of the half. Army was completely outplayed and only managed a safety in the third period.

QUESTION: In which years were the Army-Navy games played at the Polo Grounds and at Yankee Stadium?

Polo Grounds: 1913, 1915, 1919–21, 1923, 1925 and 1927. Yankee Stadium: 1930–31.

QUESTION: Did Chuck Essegian or Jackie Robinson or Jackie Jensen ever hit a home run in the World Series and score a touchdown in a Rose Bowl game?

No, and neither did anyone else. Essegian had two home runs in three pinch hits for the Los Angeles Dodgers in the 1959 World Series, but he did not score for the Stanford team in the 1952 Rose Bowl game won by Illinois, 40–7. Essegian played guard in that game.

Robinson hit two homers in a total of six World Series for the Brooklyn Dodgers, but the University of California at Los Angeles never made the Rose Bowl while he played football there.

Jensen scored a touchdown for California in the 1949 Rose Bowl, won by Northwestern, 20–14, but he appeared only as a pinch runner for the New York Yankees in the 1950 Series.

QUESTION: When Marshall Goldberg played for the University of Pittsburgh's football team in 1938, who were the other members of the Dream Backfield? Also, where is Goldberg now?

Harold Stebbins, Dick Cassiano and John Chickerneo were the other members of the backfield. Goldberg, now 61 years old, is president of the Goldberg-Emmerman Corporation, a manufacturer of machine tools in Illinois.

QUESTION: George Bork was a college quarterback in the 1960's who set a number of records, but I never heard of him after that. Where and when did he play, and what were his college statistics? Did he ever make it to professional football? What is he doing now?

Bork played for Northern Illinois, a Division II college, from 1960 to 1963. He attempted 902 passes, completed 577 and had 33 intercepted. He gained 6,782 yards and passed for 60 touchdowns. He is tied for third in Division II for career completions, and was the national leader in yardage gained in 1962 (2,398) and in 1963 (2,945). He holds two records: most passes completed in a game, 43 of 68, against Central Michigan on Nov. 9, 1963, and most passes completed per game for a season, 27.1 (244 in nine games) in 1963.

Bork was not drafted by a National Football League team, but played three seasons for the Montreal Alouettes of the Canadian Football League. He attempted 424 passes, completed 219, gained 2,593 yards, was intercepted 27 times and had 12 touchdown passes.

He is now a teacher and a golf coach at Mt. Prospect High School, Prospect, Ill., a Chicago suburb.

**QUESTION: Which college football teams won the Grantland Rice award in 1954 and 1974?**

The award, honoring the top team in the country, is selected by the Football Writers Association of America and was instituted in 1954. The University of California, Los Angeles, won in 1954 and Southern California won in 1974.

**QUESTION: Fordham University's great football team of 1937 had the line that was called the Seven Blocks of Granite. Who were the four men in the backfield?**

The quarterback was Andy Palau, the halfbacks Al Gurske and Frank Mautte, and the fullback Joe Dulkie.

**QUESTION: Earl (Red) Blaik was one of the greatest college football coaches. At how many colleges did he coach and what were his statistics at each? How many all-Americans did he coach?**

Blaik was head coach at Dartmouth (1934–40) and Army (1941–58). At Dartmouth he compiled a record of 45 games won, 15 lost and 4 ties, which included an unbeaten streak of 22 games. At Army his record was 121–33–10, which included six undefeated teams, three national championships (1944–46) and an unbeaten streak of 32 games, the longest in Army's history. Blaik coached 33 All-Americans, among them Feleix (Doc) Blanchard and Glenn Davis, of Army's national champions. Blaik was elected to the Hall of Fame in 1964.

**QUESTION: Miami of Ohio has long been known as the "cradle of coaches." How many graduates of the college have been selected as football "coach of the year?"**

Division I-A: Earl (Red) Blaik, Army (1946); Paul Dietzel, Louisiana State (1958); Ara Parseghian, Notre Dame (1964); John Pont, Indiana (1967); and Bo Schembechler, Michigan (1969).

Division I-AA: Jim Root, New Hampshire (1967).

Division II: Bill Narduzzi, Youngstown State (1979).

**QUESTION: When did Frank Cavanaugh and Jim Crowley coach the Fordham University football team, and what were their yearly records?**

Cavanaugh coached from 1927 through 1932, and Crowley from 1933 through 1941.

Cavanaugh's record: 1927, 3 victories, 5 defeats, no ties; 1928, 4–5; 1929, 7–0–2; 1930, 8–1; 1931, 6–1–2; 1932, 6–2; total, 34–14–4.

Crowley's record: 1933, 6–2; 1934, 5–3; 1935, 6–1–2; 1936, 5–1–2; 1937, 7–0–1; 1938, 6–1–2; 1939, 6–2; 1940, 7–2; 1941, 8–1; total, 56–13–7.

QUESTION: Who holds the Ivy League career record for yards rushing and most touchdowns rushing? Who holds the record for passes completed and yards gained passing? For total points scored?

Ed Marinaro, who played for Cornell from 1969 to 1971, leads in rushing with 3,391 yards and in rushing touchdowns with 34. He also is the scoring leader with 222 points. Marty Domres, who played for Columbia from 1966 to 1968, is the passing leader with 298 completions and 3,624 yards gained.

QUESTION: Did Penn State, in any year between 1969 and 1979, ever have the most players in the National Football League? Which school had the most players in the league during those years? Which 10 schools had the most players in 1979?

Penn State never had the most players in any one year. Southern California, which led each year, Ohio State and Michigan are the only schools to appear in the top 10 every year. The Trojans averaged 31 players a year, the Buckeyes 23 and the Wolverines 20.

The leaders for 1979 were: Southern California, 37 players; Oklahoma, 31; Colorado, 29; Penn State, 26; University of California at Los Angeles, 25; Ohio State, 24; Nebraska, 21; San Diego State, 21; Notre Dame, 19; Alabama, Arizona State, Grambling, Jackson State and Michigan, each with 18.

QUESTION: What were the most rushing yards gained by Gale Sayers in a single game while at the University of Kansas? What is the team record for the most rushing yards in an N.F.L. game?

Sayers, on Oct. 27, 1962, rushed for 283 yards in 22 carries against Oklahoma State in a game won by Kansas, 37–17.

Detroit, on Nov. 4, 1934, rushed for 426 yards against Pittsburgh. The Lions won, 40–7.

QUESTION: What college did Joe Ferguson of the Buffalo Bills graduate from, and what were his statistics there?

Ferguson graduated in 1973 from the University of Arkansas. He attempted 581 passes and completed 324 for 4,230 yards and 27 touchdowns. He was intercepted 25 times.

QUESTION: What were the final statistics of Phil Simms, now the Giants' quarterback, at Morehead State? Did he set any school records? Any Ohio Valley Conference records?

Simms set a number of school and conference marks. His college career records were: 836 passing attempts; 409 completions; 5,545 yards gained; 32 touchdowns; most plays, 836 passes and 403 rushes for a total of 1,239, and 45 interceptions. His college season record was: Most offensive plays, 241 passes and 125 rushes for a total of 366 (in 1976).

His 836 passing attempts, 5,545 yards gained and 1,239 career plays were also conference records.

**QUESTION: Where and when did Joe Piscarcik, the former Giant quarterback now with the Philadelphia Eagles, go to college, and what were his career statistics there?**

Piscarcik played for New Mexico State University from 1971 through 1973. He threw 936 passes and completed 445 (an average of .475) for 5,970 yards and 30 touchdowns. Fifty of his tosses were intercepted. He holds nine passing records at New Mexico State and twice was named to the all-Missouri Valley Conference team.

**QUESTION: In what years were Neill Armstrong, coach of the Chicago Bears, and Jim Hanifan, coach of the St. Louis Cardinals, the leading college pass receivers?**

Armstrong, while at Oklahoma State (then A & M), led in 1943, with 39 catches, good for 317 yards. Hanifan, while at the University of California, led in 1954, with 44 receptions, for 569 yards.

**QUESTION: At 80 years of age, memory becomes a bit uncertain. Could you confirm or deny a recollection of Frosty Peters of Illinois kicking a record 15 field goals in one game?**

On Nov. 1, 1924, Forest (Frosty) Peters, playing for the Montana State freshmen, tried 22 dropkicks for field goals against Billings Tech. He made 17 of them. He later transferred to Illinois, where he played in three seasons and had a career total of 18 field goals. He never had more than three in a game.

**QUESTION: What factors determine the classification of college teams in Division I, II or III?**

The rules of the National Collegiate Athletic Association are complex. Simply put, a college can declare itself a member of any division, but it then must adhere to the requirements set up by the N.C.A.A. For example, Division I-A football teams can offer only 30 financial aid awards each year, and no more than 95 may be in effect in any one year. It must sponsor a minimum of eight intercollegiate sports, including football, and 60 percent of its football games must be against other members of Division I-A. There are other rules and restrictions that are placed on all colleges. In Division III, moreover, no athletic financial aid may be granted except upon a showing of financial need.

**QUESTION: Harvard's loss to Yale, 14–0, in the 1980 football season, brought back many memories of this ancient rivalry, including the famous 29–29 tie in 1968. How many games have been played in this series, and who leads?**

There have been 97 games since the series started in 1875. Harvard has won 36 times, Yale 53, and there have been 8 ties.

QUESTION: Who are the major college rushing leaders on a per-game basis for a single season and for a career? Who are the leaders in rushing yards per carry for a single season and for a career?

Most yards gained per game: season, Ed Marinaro of Cornell, 209.0 on 1,881 yards in nine games (1971); career, Marinaro, 174.6 on 4,715 yards in 27 games (1969–71).

Highest average gain per rush: season: (minimum 150 rushes), Greg Pruitt of Oklahoma, 9.35 on 178 rushes for 1,665; (225 rushes), Billy Sims, Oklahoma, 7.63 on 231–1,762 (1978); (290 rushes), Charles White, Southern California, 6.15 on 293–1,803 (1979); (325 rushes), Tony Dorsett, Pittsburgh, 5.76 on 338–1,948 (1976).

Highest average gain per rush, career: (minimum 300 rushes), Glenn Davis, Army, 8.26 yards on 358 rushes for 2,957 (1943–46); (500 rushes), Billy Sims, Oklahoma, 7.09 on 538–3,813 (1975–79); (650 rushes), Archie Griffin, Ohio State, 6.13 on 845–5,177 (1972–75).


QUESTION: What was the career record of Lou Saban, now the president of the New York Yankees, as a coach in college and professional football?

Saban has been the head coach at six colleges and with three professional teams (twice with the Buffalo Bills) in 30 years. He has resigned his job 10 times. As a coach with Case Institute, Northwestern, Western Illinois, Maryland, Miami (Fla.) and Army, his teams won 45 games, lost 54 and tied 4. As head coach with the Boston (now New England) Patriots and the Buffalo Bills in the American Football League, and with the Denver Broncos (A.F.L. and the National Football League), his teams won 95 games, lost 99 and tied 7. His Buffalo teams won the A.F.L. championship in 1964 and 1965.

# Basketball

QUESTION: At the beginning of the second half in a college basketball game, each team takes the floor promptly but faces the wrong basket. Team A wins the tap, and scores. The scoring desk stops the game and notifies the officials of the error. The officials then award Team B the 2 points, and Team B ultimately wins the game by 4. Does Team A have a legitimate reason for a protest?

No. There are only five correctible errors in college basketball, according to Edward S. Steitz, editor of the Official Basketball Rules and Interpretations book of the National Collegiate Athletic Association. They are: "Failure to award a merited free throw, awarding an unmerited free throw, permitting a wrong player to attempt a free throw, permitting a player to attempt a free throw at the wrong basket and erroneously counting or canceling a score."

The officials' allowing a team to face the wrong basket is not a correctible error. And their taking the 2 points from Team A and awarding the score to Team B would not be an error at all. In this regard the rules say merely, "A goal from the field counts 2 points for the team into whose basket the ball is thrown."

In scoring, by the way, this goal would not be credited to an individual but would simply be mentioned in a footnote.

QUESTION: Spectators at college basketball games interfere more and more with the foul shooting of players by waving pennants, pom-poms or screaming at them. It is unsportsmanlike, yet it appears as though officials never do anything about it. Why?

According to the National Collegiate Athletic Association rule book, "The official may call fouls on either team if its supporters act in such a way as to interfere with the proper conduct of the game." However, the operative word is "may." Officials have the right to call a technical for unsportsmanlike conduct by spectators, but they are not required to do so. Experience has shown that calling a technical on a crowd does not accomplish what it is supposed to, and, in fact, the spectators will react negatively to such a call. The N.C.A.A., therefore, puts the responsibility for the crowd's behavior in the hands of the game committee or management.

QUESTION: Has there ever been a National Collegiate Athletic Association champion in both basketball and football in the same school year?

No, because the N.C.A.A. does not conduct a postseason tournament in football as it does in basketball. There are unofficial wire-service national champions in football, but the closest any school ever came to winning the basketball title and ranking first in football was Ohio State, in the 1961–62 school year when it was second in both.

QUESTION: Has the most valuable player in the National Collegiate Athletic Association's basketball tournament ever been a member of a team other than the championship team?

Yes, 10 times since the award was first made in 1940. In 1953, Indiana beat Kansas in the final, but B.H. Born of Kansas was voted the m.v.p. Others from nonchampion teams were Hal Lear, 1956, for third-place Temple; Wilt Chamberlain, 1957, runner-up Kansas; Elgin Baylor, 1958, runner-up Seattle; Jerry West, 1959, runner-up West Virginia; Jerry Lucas, 1961, runner-up Ohio State; Art Heyman, 1963, third-place Duke; Bill Bradley, 1965, third-place Princeton; Jerry Chambers, 1966, fourth-place Utah, and Howard Porter, 1971, runner-up Villanova.

Porter's award, however, was vacated by the N.C.A.A., because, the association said, he had engaged a professional agent.

QUESTION: Has the circumference of the basketball used by college teams remained the same as originally devised by Dr. James Naismith?

No. In 1891, the circumference was 30 to 32 inches. In 1930, it was reduced to 31 inches, and in 1934 it became 29.5 to 30 inches, as it remains today under National Collegiate Athletic Association rules.

In 1897, the ball weighed 18 to 20 ounces; in 1900, not less than 20 ounces nor more than 23; it now weighs no less than 20 ounces nor more than 22.

Today's ball in the National Basketball Association has a circumference of 29.5 inches and weighs the same as the one the colleges use.

QUESTION: How many college basketball players in Division I finished their careers with an average of 20 or more points scored per game and 20 or more rebounds per game?

As of the end of the 1979–80 season, seven players have accomplished this: Walt Dukes of Seton Hall (23.5 points and 21.1 rebounds); Bill Russell of San Francisco (20.7 and 20.3); Elgin Baylor of Seattle (31.3 and 20.0); Paul Silas of Creighton (20.5 and 21.6); Julius Erving of Massachusetts (26.3 and 20.2); Artis Gilmore of Jacksonville (24.3 and 22.7) and Kermit Washington of American University (20.1 and 20.2).

**QUESTION: How many National Collegiate Athletic Association basketball tournaments have been held, and which college has won the most titles? Who was the first player to participate in four different tournaments?**

There have been 43 tournaments, from 1939 through 1981. The University of California, Los Angeles, leads with 10 titles, Kentucky has won five and Indiana three. Oklahoma State, San Francisco and Cincinnati each has won twice.

Because of the Korean War, freshmen were allowed to play varsity ball in 1952. Gerald Bullard of Oklahoma City played in the tournament that year as a freshman, then again in 1953–54–55, to become the first to play in four tournaments. Oklahoma City never advanced past the regional semifinals, and Bullard, in the five games in which he appeared, scored one goal and five free throws, for a total of seven points.

**QUESTION: Has any player ever been on the championship basketball team in the N.C.A.A., the National Invitation Tournament and the National Basketball Association?**

Only five schools have captured both college tournaments in a span short enough to permit one of their players to be a member of a championship N.B.A. team. Kentucky won the N.I.T. in 1946 and 1947, the N.C.A.A. in 1948 and 1949, the N.I.T. again in 1976 and the N.C.A.A. again in 1978, but none of the players involved was on a league championship team.

The same applies to the players on the City College of New York team that won both college titles in 1950, the only time this was accomplished in one season, and to the Indiana players on the teams that took the N.C.A.A. in 1976 and the N.I.T. in 1979.

Utah won the N.C.A.A. title in 1944 and the N.I.T. in 1947. Arnie Ferrin played on both teams and also on the champion Minneapolis Lakers when they won in 1949 and 1950.

LaSalle won the N.I.T. title in 1952 and the N.C.A.A. crown in 1954. Tom Gola played on those teams, and also on the champion Philadelphia Warriors of 1956.

**QUESTION: How many times has a team from the East won the National Collegiate Athletic Association's basketball title? How many times has a team from the East reached the final but lost? Please list the scores of the championship games won by Eastern teams.**

Holy Cross (in 1947), the City College of New York (1950) and LaSalle (1954) won N.C.A.A. titles. The scores were: Holy Cross 58, Oklahoma 47; C.C.N.Y. 71, Bradley 68, and LaSalle 92, Bradley 76.

Dartmouth (1942), Georgetown (1943), Dartmouth again (1944), New York University (1945), St. John's (1952), LaSalle (1955) and Villanova (1971) all reached the final but lost.

QUESTION: Is there a basketball player who has been a member of a championship team in the National Basketball Association, the American Basketball Association and the National Collegiate Athletic Association?

Tom Thacker was on the N.B.A.'s Boston Celtics in 1967–68, the A.B.A.'s Indiana Pacers in 1969–70, and the University of Cincinnati teams that captured the N.C.A.A. titles in 1961 and 1962.

Rick Barry and Billy Melchionni are two players who have been on teams that captured N.B.A. and A.B.A. championships. Barry was on the A.B.A.'s Oakland Oaks in 1968–69 and the N.B.A.'s Golden State Warriors in 1974–75. Melchionni was on the N.B.A.'s Philadelphia 76ers in 1966–67 and the A.B.A.'s New York Nets in 1973–74 and 1975–76.

QUESTION: Many college basketball teams have spurned the National Invitation Tournament to play in the National Collegiate competition, but has the reverse ever happened?

In 1970 Marquette rejected an invitation to the N.C.A.A. tournament because Coach Al McGuire was displeased by the regional playoff into which the Warriors had been placed. Marquette entered the N.I.T. and won the championship by defeating St. John's in the final, 65–53.

QUESTION: When were the first college basketball games played in Madison Square Garden and what were the scores?

The games that are considered the beginning of scheduled college basketball in the Garden took place on Dec. 29, 1934. In the opener of a doubleheader, St. John's lost to Westminister, 37–33, and in the second game New York University stopped Notre Dame, 25–18. More than 16,000 fans watched the games. However, college tripleheaders for charity occurred in the Garden in 1931, 1932 and 1933. Those were the years of the Great Depression, and the crowds that attended those benefit games laid the foundation for regularly scheduled contests.

QUESTION: In 1950, the City College of New York captured both the National College basketball tournament and the National Invitation Tournament. Who were the five starters on that team?

Ed Warner, Ed Roman, Floyd Layne, Al Roth and Irwin Dambrot were the starters on the only team that has ever won both tournaments in the same year.

QUESTION: When did Dan Kaplowitz play on the Long Island University basketball team and what was his point average? What were the team's won-lost records for those years? Did he ever play professional basketball? What is he doing now?

Kaplowitz was a starter for L.I.U. from 1936–37 through 1938–39. The Blackbirds were a power in college basketball in those years, and the team had season records of 27–3, 23–4 and 23–0. In his last season, L.I.U. won the National Invitation Tournament, defeating Loyola of Chicago, 44–32. Kaplowitz never played professional basketball, because he went on to medical school, eventually becoming a psychiatrist. He still practices in Manhattan. School records for those years are incomplete, but Dr. Kaplowitz says he averaged about 12 points a game. He also notes that he was one of the first players to shoot with one hand, although his was not a jump shot, and that his coach, Clair Bee, tried to discourage him from doing so.

**QUESTION: When did Harry Boykoff play basketball for St. John's? How tall was he and what were his college statistics? Did he ever play professional basketball? Where is he now?**

Boykoff played for St. John's between 1942 and 1947, with time out for military service between 1943–45. In 70 games with the Redmen, he scored 1,029 points. His best game was against St. Francis of Brooklyn on March 11, 1947, when he scored 54 points, then a record for Madison Square Garden. In his first season on the team, St. John's won the National Invitation Tournament, beating Toledo, 48–27.

Boykoff, at 6 feet 9 inches, was one of the first of the great big men, and one of the reasons the goaltending rule was adopted. He played four years of professional ball, with Toledo and Waterloo in the National Basketball League, and then, in the N.B.A., with Waterloo, Boston and Tri-Cities. He scored 2,456 points in 229 games, for an average of 10.7. Boykoff now lives in the Los Angeles area and is in the advertising business.

**QUESTION: What were Albert King's basketball statistics at the University of Maryland? Is he among the top five career scorers there?**

King, in 118 games, made 862 field goals in 1,673 attempts, 334 of 431 free throws for 2,058 points and a 17.4 career average. He had 1,715 rebounds for a 6.1 average and 304 assists. He ranks first among Maryland scorers. John Lucas (1972–76) is second with 2,015 points; Tom McMillen (1971–74) is third with 1,807; Gene Shue (1951–54) is fourth with 1,397; and Will Hetzel (1967–70) is fifth with 1,370.

**QUESTION: Which high school and which college did Althea Gwyn of the New York Stars attend? Which high school did Nancy Lieberman of Old Dominion University go to? Did they both play on their high-school basketball teams? How much money do the players in the Women's Pro Basketball League earn?**

Miss Gwyn attended Amityville (L.I.) High School and Queens College; Miss Lieberman went to Far Rockaway High School. Each played on her high-school team.

The salaries in the W.B.L. reportedly range in general from $5,000 to $15,000, with a few higher exceptions.

**QUESTION: In the National Basketball Association 1980 draft, the New Jersey Nets selected Mike Gminski, Duke University center, and Mike O'Koren, North Carolina forward. What were their primary statistics in college and where do they rank among their schools' career scoring leaders?**

Gminski, in 122 games, scored 901 goals in 1,697 attempts (a percentage of .530) and 521 free throws in 658 attempts (.791). He totaled 2,323 points, an average of 19.0 a game; took down 1,242 rebounds, and made 128 assists. He is the Duke career leader not only in points scored but also in rebounds.

O'Koren, in 117 games, hit on 643 goals in 1,124 attempts (.572) and on 479 free throws in 660 (.725). He amassed 1,765 points, for an average of 15.0; grabbed 815 rebounds, and made 348 assists. He ranks seventh in career scoring at North Carolina and sixth in field-goal percentage.

# Track

**QUESTION: To achieve greater height in high jumping, why not utilize a tumbler's technique of a full somersault at the top of the leap, thus throwing the legs upward?**

Rules of both the Amateur Athletic Union and the National Collegiate Athletic Association require that the high jumper take off from one foot. According to track-and-field experts, it would be physically impossible for the jumper to leave the ground in this way and then execute a somersault at the top of his leap.

**QUESTION: Did Jackie Robinson, the first black major league baseball player, star in the broad jump at college, in addition to being outstanding in baseball, basketball and football?**

Robinson, while at Pasadena Junior College in 1939, jumped 25 feet 6⅓ inches, then a junior college record. The next year, as a student at the University of California, Los Angeles, he won the broad jump at the N.C.A.A. meet in Minneapolis with a leap of 24 feet 10¼ inches.

**QUESTION: I know that Bill Dabney, a track star at Boys and Girls High School in Brooklyn, went on to college, but I don't know where he went or how he fared. Can you tell me? Many observers thought he had the potential to be a world-class runner.**

Dabney went to Adelphi University in Garden City, L.I., and graduated in 1977. As a junior he set several school records: half-mile (1 minute 50 seconds); 800 meters (1:47.1); 1,000 yards (2:08.4) and the mile (4:11). He was hampered by injuries in his senior year, however, missed the indoor season and struggled through the outdoor season.

**QUESTION: Is it true that O. J. Simpson, one of the great professional football players, was a member of a record-breaking relay team while at college?**

Yes. Simpson was on a 440-yard relay team at the University of Southern California that set a national collegiate record, which still stands. He and his three teammates—Earl McCulloch, Fred Kuller and Lennox Miller—raced the distance in 38.6 seconds on June 17, 1967, at Provo, Utah.

**QUESTION: In 1933, Penn ran a mile relay in 3:17, an indoor record at the time. In 1939, Fordham lowered the time to 3:15.2 in a meet at Dartmouth. Were the tracks different, and how long did Fordham's record stand?**

Penn's record was set on a six-lap banked board track at the Kingsbridge Armory in the Bronx. Fordham's mark was set on a six-and-two-thirds-lap track. In 1940, New York University lowered the record to 3:15. This record stood until the Grand Street Boys ran 3:14.4 on an eight-lap flat armory floor in Buffalo in 1953. The current record, on a recognized indoor track of 220 yards maximum, or eight laps to the mile, was set in 1971 at Pocatello, Ida., when the Pacific Coast Club ran the distance in 3:09.4.

# Baseball

**QUESTION:** Which team has won the college baseball world series the most times? Which team has the best record in district playoffs and the world series? Has an Eastern college ever won the title?

Southern California has won the college world series 11 times since 1947 when the first collegiate baseball championship was held. It also has the best tournament record by far, 112 games won and 32 lost. (This does not include from 1947 until 1954, when district playoffs were not considered part of the championships.) Holy Cross is the only Eastern team to win the title, defeating Missouri, 8–4, in the 1952 final.

**QUESTION:** Did Bob Welch of the Los Angeles Dodgers and Bob Owchinko of the Cleveland Indians play on the same college baseball team? If so, when, and how did the team do in the National Collegiate Athletic Association tournament?

Welch and Owchinko played on the Eastern Michigan team in 1976. The team lost to Arizona, 7–1, in the College World Series final game.

# Hockey

**QUESTION:** In hockey, which player holds the record for the most goals in a National Collegiate Athletic Association tournament? The most goals in a tourney game? Which teams scored the most goals in a tourney and in a single game?

Bob McCusker of Colorado College scored seven goals in two games in the 1957 tournament; Carl Lawrence of Colorado College and Gil Burford of Michigan are tied for individual game honors with five goals, a feat both accomplished against Boston College in the 1950 championships.

Colorado College holds the tourney record for most goals, with 23 in 1950. The single-game record of 14 goals is held by two colleges, Michigan (1953) and Minnesota (1954).

**QUESTION:** When did Lloyd Robinson play hockey for Boston University? Did he ever play in the N.C.A.A. tournament? Was he the first black collegiate hockey player in the United States?

Robinson, a left wing, played four years for the Terriers and graduated in 1950. The team reached the National Collegiate playoffs only once during his career, in 1950, and lost to Colorado College, 13–4, in the championship game. That Robinson was the first black collegiate hockey player in the United States cannot be verified, but he was the first at Boston University.

**QUESTION:** Which of the college hockey players chosen in the last 10 years as the most outstanding player in the Division I championship tournament have made good in the National Hockey League?

Two. Dean Talafous, now with the New York Rangers, won the award in 1973 while at the University of Wisconsin. Steve Janaszak, now with the Minnesota North Stars, was chosen in 1979 while at the University of Minnesota.

# Miscellaneous

QUESTION: Which colleges won the most titles in Division I-A in 1978-79? Which five colleges are all-time leaders for team championships before the 1979-80 school year? Which five schools have the most individual champions?

The University of California, Los Angeles, with two team championships in tennis and volleyball, and Texas, El Paso, with two in cross-country and outdoor track, were the leaders in 1978-79.

The five career leaders in team titles are: Southern California (63), U.C.L.A. (38), Oklahoma State (34), Michigan (27) and Yale (25).

The five top individual leaders are: Southern California (241), Michigan (179), Ohio State (161), Oklahoma State (109) and Yale (104).

QUESTION: How many years has the National Collegiate Athletic Association conducted the Division I lacrosse tournament? Which college has won the championship each year and against whom? What were the final season records of each champion?

The tournament began in 1971. The yearly results follow, with the won-lost record of the champion in parentheses:

1971, Cornell 12, Maryland 6 (13-1); 1972, Virginia 13, Johns Hopkins 12 (11-4); 1973, Maryland 10, Johns Hopkins 9 (14-1); 1974, Johns Hopkins 17, Maryland 12 (12-2); 1975, Maryland 20, Navy 13 (11-3); 1976, Cornell 16, Johns Hopkins 13 (16-0); 1977, Cornell 16, Johns Hopkins 8 (13-0); 1978, Johns Hopkins 13, Cornell 8 (13-1); 1979, Johns Hopkins 15, Maryland 9 (13-0); 1980, Johns Hopkins 9, Virginia 8 (14-1).

QUESTION: In women's lacrosse, is the goalie allowed to catch the ball with her hand and then place it in the cradle of her stick?

Yes, though only in the crease area surrounding the goal. This is one way in which the women's game differs from the men's. In men's lacrosse the goalie is permitted to deflect the ball with his hand, but if he picks it up to place it in his stick he will be charged with a technical foul.

QUESTION: When did the National Collegiate Athletic Association begin holding its ski championships and which colleges have won the titles?

The competition began in 1954. Through 1980, Denver has won the title 14 times, Colorado 10 (sharing the crown with Dartmouth in 1976), and Dartmouth has won it once by itself, as have Wyoming and Vermont.

QUESTION: Substitutions in professional soccer are limited, and once a player leaves a game he may not return. What is the rule in college soccer?

Players may be substituted or resubstituted without limitations under the following conditions: on a goal kick, on a corner kick, after a goal has been scored, between periods, in the event of an injury or when a player has been warned by an official about an infraction of the rules.

176

# Olympics and
# Related Sports

## General

**QUESTION: What did the five different color circles stand for at the 1980 Winter Olympics?**

The rings, or circles, that form the Olympic symbol originally represented the five major continents: Europe, Asia, Africa, Australia and America (both North and South). The concept now is that the rings are linked together to denote the sporting friendship of the peoples of the earth. The colors—blue, yellow, black, green and red—were chosen because at least one of them appeared in the flag of every nation on earth.

**QUESTION: With the price of gold being what it is, how much gold is there in the Olympic medals being awarded at Lake Placid, what is the cost of each one and where are they made?**

The Olympic gold medals are actually sterling silver coated with six grams of 22-karat gold. They are being made by Tiffany & Company, which is adhering to its original cost estimate, made two years ago, of $255 for each medal despite the increased price of gold since then.

## Track

**QUESTION: Were track races like the 1,500-meter always run counterclockwise?**

No. The first tracks at Oxford and Cambridge universities in the 19th century were 500 meters, and races in those days were conducted in clockwise fashion. Since 1912, when the International Amateur Athletic Federation was founded, there has been a rule that the curb of the track should be on the athlete's left in the running direction, which means that all races must be run counterclockwise for records to be recognized.

**QUESTION: Can you tell me what happened to Eddie Tolan, who won the 100 meters in the 1932 Olympics at Los Angeles, upsetting Ralph Metcalfe, the favorite, who finished second?**

Tolan also won the 200 meters, with Metcalfe finishing third, and was the only double victor in track and field events in that Olympics. Tolan, a University of Michigan graduate, returned to his native Detroit, where he taught. He died in 1967 at the age of 57.

QUESTION: I know that Henry Rono has simultaneously held four world records, for the 3,000-meter run, the 3,000-meter steeplechase, the 5,000-meter run and the 10,000-meter run. Discounting duplication for short and very similar distances—such as 200 meters and 220 yards—who else has simultaneously held four or more world records in running?

Paavo Nurmi of Finland: 1,500 meters, mile, 2,000 meters, 3,000 meters, three miles, 5,000 meters and 10,000 meters.

Viljo Heino of Finland: six miles, 10,000 meters, 20,000 meters and one-hour run.

Emil Zatopek of Czechoslovakia: 5,000 meters, 10,000 meters, 10 miles, 20,000 meters, 25,000 meters, 15 miles, 30,000 meters and one-hour run.

Sandor Iharos of Hungary: 1,500 meters, 3,000 meters, two miles, three miles and 5,000 meters.

Ron Clarke of Australia: two miles, three miles, 5,000 meters, six miles, 10,000 meters and 10 miles.

Sebastian Coe of Britain: 800 meters, 1,000 meters, 1,500 meters and mile. Coe held four records simultaneously for only 55 minutes. Having broken the 1,000-meter record in Oslo on July 1, 1980, he saw his mile mark of 3 minutes 49 seconds beaten later in the same meet by Steve Ovett, who ran the distance in 3:48.8.

QUESTION: How many Americans are listed among the top 10 runners in the 1,500-meter race and the mile, what are their times and who leads in each?

As of the end of 1978, only one American, Jim Ryun, was included in the 10 best for 1,500 meters. He ran the distance in 3 minutes 33.1 seconds in 1967. Filbert Bayi of Tanzania set the record, of 3:32.2, in 1974. In the mile, three Americans were listed: Ryun, with a mark of 3:51.1 in 1967; Marty Liquori, 3:52.2 in 1975; and Steve Scott, 3:52.9 in 1978. The record was set by John Walker of New Zealand, 3:49.4 in 1975.

QUESTION: When Don Paige swept the 800-meter and 1,500-meter runs in the 1979 National Collegiate meet, another Villanova runner, Ron Delany, was mentioned as having been the last one to accomplish that double. Did Delany ever run a mile in less than four minutes, indoors or outdoors?

Delany ran a 3:57.5 mile outdoors in 1958, but he never broke four minutes indoors.

QUESTION: What is the official time for Bob Hayes's record 100-yard dash, 9.1 seconds, 9.0 or 8.9? I have heard all three figures mentioned.

Hayes ran 9.1 seconds in the Amateur Athletic Union's national championships on June 21, 1963, at St. Louis, setting a world record. That mark was later tied by a number of runners and beaten by Ivory Crockett, who ran 9.0 in 1974, which record in turn was tied by Houston McTear in 1975. Hayes never ran the 100-yard dash in 9.0 or 8.9; in fact, there is no record of anyone's running 100 yards in 8.9, with or without wind resistance.

QUESTION: Would track officials honor a world record at three miles or six miles if it was set during the course of a 5,000-meter race or a 10,000-meter race?

Before 1976 such marks were often recognized, but the rule was changed then. The only such record, called a "linear record," now recognized would be in the mile.

QUESTION: In the late 1930's, at the Princeton Invitation track meet, a distance runner bettered Paavo Nurmi's record for the two-mile run. Who was the athlete and what was his time? What is the present record?

On June 19, 1936, Don Lash of the United States ran the distance in 8 minutes, 58.4 seconds, breaking Nurmi's world record of 8:59.6. Three months later, in Stockholm, another Finn, Gunnar Hockert, reduced the time to 8:57.4. That time was further cut over the years until 1978 when Steve Ovett of Great Britain did 8:13.6. However, since all non-metric distance records, except for the mile, were frozen after the Montreal Olympics in the transformation to metric distances, it is not the official record. That is held by Brendon Foster of Great Britain, who ran the two miles in 8:13.8 in 1973.

QUESTION: Is it true that Frank Dixon was the first black to win the national championship in the mile? What happened to him?

Dixon won the national Amateur Athletic Union mile title in 1943, running the race in 4 minutes 9.6 seconds. He was the first black to win the title, and he went on to capture other mile races as a student at New York University. As a freshman in 1942, he also won the IC4A varsity cross-country championship and the A.A.U. title. His career was interrupted by three years of Army service, and on his return to N.Y.U. in 1946 he never regained his former ability. Dixon died of cancer on Dec. 3, 1977, at the age of 55.

QUESTION: Stella Walsh, the great Polish-American track star, who competed for Poland in the 1932 and 1936 Olympics, was shot to death in Cleveland in 1980. What had she been doing in Cleveland?

Miss Walsh, who competed for Poland under the name of Stanislawa Walasiewicz, lived in Cleveland and was associated with the Polish Falcons, a private athletic club. In an interview some time before her death, she said: "I coach and train about 100 boys and girls from the ages of 6 to 16 in gymnastics, basketball, indoor track, swimming, volleyball and softball."

QUESTION: Who were the medal winners in the 10,000-meter walk in the 1920 and 1924 Olympics?

In 1920, at Antwerp, Belgium, Ugo Frigerio of Italy was first, Joseph Pearman of the United States was second, and Charles Gunn of Britain was third. In 1924, at Paris, Frigerio was again first, Gordon Goodwin of Britain was second and Cecil Charles McMaster of South Africa was third.

QUESTION: Have any high-school athletes in the United States ever run the mile in less than four minutes?

Yes, three. Jim Ryun, then at Wichita East High School in Kansas, was clocked in 3 minutes 55.3 seconds in 1965, Tim Danielson of Chula Vista (Calif.) High 3:59.4 in 1966, and Marty Liquori of Essex Catholic in New Jersey 3:58.8 in 1967.

**QUESTION: Bob Beamon made an incredible long jump of 8.90 meters (29 feet 2¼ inches) in the 1968 Olympics in Mexico City. Do you think that record will ever be broken?**

The cliché, of course, is that all records are made to be broken, and there appears to be merit in it. Often a barrier that appeared insurmountable yesterday becomes insignificant tomorrow. Look at what happened after the four-minute mark was cracked in the mile run.

However, Beamon's record seems to be secure, as the high altitude in Mexico City lent even greater distance to what would have been a remarkable feat in any case.

# Figure Skating

**QUESTION: What is the death spiral in pairs figure skating? The crossover axel lift?**

The death spiral can be performed in four variations: skating backward on the outside blade, backward on the inside blade, forward on the outside blade and forward on the inside blade. (A figure skate is hollowed out in the middle, forming two thin blades.) In the backward-outside variation, as an example, the partners skate backward on the outside blade, and the man performs a pivot. With the hand corresponding to his skating foot, he holds the hand of his partner, who is leaning backward and circling him. Both arms of each partner are outstretched.

In the crossover axel lift, both partners skate in closed waltz position, with the man's right arm around his partner's waist and her left arm around his neck. She is lifted one and a half turns, 540 degrees, and lands backward outside. He skates forward outside.

**QUESTION: Please tell me in what years Ludmilla Belousova and Oleg Protopopov won Olympic gold medals in pairs figure skating.**

In 1964, the two won at Innsbruck, Austria; they won again in 1968 at Grenoble, France.

# Speed Skating

**QUESTION: How fast can speed skaters go?**

Skaters can achieve a speed of 35 to 37 miles an hour for 100 meters, according to the Speed Skating Association. As the distance increases, of course, the speed decreases.

# Skiing

**QUESTION: There were no female ski jumpers during the Winter Olympics at Lake Placid in 1980. I have heard that ski jumping is dangerous for women. Is this true?**

There is no scientific reason for the paucity of female ski jumpers, according to Jim Page, assistant Nordic director for the United States ski team. Because it was always considered a man's sport, like football, women did not participate in ski jumping. However, as women have broken down the barriers in other sports, they are also doing so in ski jumping. There are two or three women active in the sport at present and, Mr. Page says, there are now more girls than boys participating in the junior (for ages 11 and 12) jumping program. At that age, they seem to do better than the boys.

**QUESTION: Now that World Cup skiing is back, please explain what is meant by Alpine skiing?**

Alpine skiing consists of three different types of competition: downhill racing, the slalom and the giant slalom. The term downhill racing involves racing down a mountain at speeds of approximately 80 miles an hour. The slalom involves a complex series of gates through which the skier must pass, at speeds of about 50 miles an hour. The giant slalom is a combination of the first two events, with speeds somewhat less than that reached during the downhill competition.

**QUESTION: How is a ski jump measured: from the front of the ski, from the rear of the ski, or from the jumper's torso as he lands?**

According to rule number 456, page 38, book 111 of The International Ski Competition Rules, "The distances jumped are measured to an accuracy of ½ metre, and measured to where the feet land, normally between the feet."

**QUESTION: Which way should skis be carried on the top of a car, with the tips toward the front or back? Also, why do some people put covers on their bindings in such situations?**

The tips of the skis should be at the back of the car, to reduce wind resistance. Bindings are covered to prevent them from freezing if there is some precipitation while they are being transported in cold weather.

# Marathon

**QUESTION: Please explain how the actual distance for the marathon was determined. Was the distance always the same as it is today?**

According to the Encyclopedia Britannica, in 490 B.C., a Greek soldier, Pheidippides, ran from Marathon to Athens—a distance just short of 23 miles—to bring news of a great Greek victory over the invading Persians. To commemorate that run, a race called the marathon was held at the first modern Olympics, at Athens in 1896. The distance was 24 miles, 1,500 yards. Until 1924, when the distance was standardized at 26 miles, 385 yards, the length varied. The 26-mile-385-yard figure was arrived at in 1908—that being the distance for the Olympic race staged between Windsor Castle and the royal box at the Olympic stadium in London. That distance has only been constant in the Boston Marathon, for example, since 1927. Before that year, the distance was 24.5 miles and then 26 miles, 209 yards.

**QUESTION: Who has won the most Boston Marathons, and who holds the record for the fastest time?**

Clarence DeMar of the United States won the race seven times, the most in history, the first time in 1911, at the age of 22. He did not run again for 10 years, because a doctor had told him that he had a heart murmur. He returned to the race in 1922, at the age of 33, and won. He won again in 1923, 1924, 1927, 1928 and 1930, when he was 41. DeMar's best time for the Boston Marathon at its present distance, 26 miles 385 yards, was 2 hours 34 minutes 48 seconds.

Toshihiko Seko of Japan, in 1981, won the marathon in 2:09.26, the fastest time ever run in the United States.

**QUESTION: Who were the first male and female winners of the New York City Marathon?**

The first marathon, held in 1970, was won by Gary Muhrcke of the Millrose Athletic Association, in 2 hours 31 minutes 38.2 seconds. No women were in that race. In 1971, Beth Bonner of the New Jersey Chargers was the first woman to finish, in 2:55.22.

**QUESTION: When there are more than 10,000 entries in a race like the New York City Marathon, the runners who are placed far back in the pack are under an obvious disadvantage. Is there any provision to compensate them for the loss of time in reaching the starting line?**

No. They have little chance of winning the race and are mainly hopeful of just finishing. The loss of four or five minutes is meaningless when a runner finishes a marathon in four hours or more.

# Tennis

**QUESTION: In what years was tennis a part of the Olympic program, and why was it dropped?**

Tennis was part of the Olympic competition at Athens (1896), Paris (1900), St. Louis (1904), London (1908), Stockholm (1912), Antwerp (1920) and Paris again (1924). By 1924, however, the International Olympic Committee and the International Lawn Tennis Federation were feuding over the definition of amateurism. As a result tennis was dropped from the Olympics, though at the 1968 Games in Mexico City it was played as a demonstration, as opposed to a competition, sport. Olympian tennis never reached the high level of competition of other Games events and did not attract much interest.

# Boxing

**QUESTION: How many fights did George Foreman win in capturing the 1968 Olympic heavyweight title, and whom did he defeat for the gold medal?**

Foreman knocked out three opponents, the last being Ionis Chepulis of the Soviet Union.

# Diving

GAINER / REVERSE

**QUESTION: In diving, what is a gainer?**

A gainer—also known as a Mohlberg, for the German diver who perfected it—is the old term for a reverse dive. The diver runs forward to the end of the board, but after takeoff, having made sure that he is safely clear of the board, he changes direction, curling backward instead of forward, so that he executes the reverse of a swan dive.

# Swimming

**QUESTION: When did the "flip turn" in swimming originate?**

According to records at the Swimming Hall of Fame in Fort Lauderdale, Fla., the first mention of a flip turn, or somersault, in swimming competition was in connection with the 1936 Olympics in Berlin. The swimmer was Katherine Rawls of the United States, who finished seventh in the 100-meter freestyle. Miss Rawls, also a diver, took second place in the springboard event.

QUESTION: In the 1920's many of America's women Olympic swimmers came from the New York area and were members of the Women's Swimming Association. Where was the association's clubhouse situated, who were some of the swimming stars developed there and has a history of the club ever been published?

The W.S.A., founded in 1917, had its first clubhouse on 55th Street between Fifth and Sixth Avenues. About a decade later the association moved to 204 East 77th Street. It stayed there until 1974, its last year. No history of it has been published.

Some of the club's Olympic stars were:

1920—Ethelda Bleibtrey, winner of the 100-meter and 300-meter freestyles and a member of the winning 400-meter freestyle relay.

1924—Gertrude Ederle, third in the 100-meter and 400-meter freestyles and a member of the winning 400-meter freestyle relay, and Agnes Geraghty, second in the 200-meter breaststroke.

1932—Eleanor Holm, winner of the 100-meter backstroke.

1948—Marie Corridon, a member of the winning 400-meter freestyle relay.

1956—Carin Cone, second in the 100-meter backstroke.

Miss Ederle gained even greater fame when, on Aug. 6, 1926, she became the first woman to swim the English Channel. Her time for the endeavor, of approximately 35 miles, was 14 hours 31 minutes, then a record.

QUESTION: Mark Spitz won seven gold medals in the 1972 Olympics, three as a member of swimming relay teams. What athlete has won the most Olympic gold medals for individual performance in a career and in one Olympics?

The record for a career is eight, set by Ray Ewry of the United States in the 1900, 1904 and 1908 Games. Ewry won the standing broad jump and the standing high jump three times each and the standing triple jump twice. He also won two gold medals in the Pan-Hellenic Olympic Games in 1906, but they do not count toward his official Olympic total.

The record for one year is five, held by Eric Heiden of the United States, who won all five gold medals in the men's speed skating events at the Winter Olympics at Lake Placid in 1980. The events were the 500 meters, the 1,000 meters, the 1,500 meters, the 5,000 meters and the 10,000 meters.

QUESTION: In what year did the breaststroke and butterfly become two separate swimming events?

According to the Fédération Internationale de Natation Amateur (FINA), the division was approved in 1952 and took effect on Jan. 1, 1953. The separation was voted because in the early 1930's some swimmers discovered there was nothing in the rules concerning the breaststroke to prevent the arms from being brought back over the water, instead of under. Until the butterfly (a stroke in which both arms must be brought forward together over the water and brought backward simultaneously) was separated, there was much confusion about records in the breaststroke because the butterfly style proved to be much faster.

QUESTION: Did Esther Williams ever hold a national swimming title before she became an aquatic film star?

Miss Williams won the 100-meter freestyle championship in 69 seconds in 1939. If World War II had not broken out and canceled the 1940 Olympics, she would have been favored to win a gold medal.

# Weight-Lifting

QUESTION: When and why was the press event discontinued in weight-lifting contests? Who held the superheavyweight world record when it was dropped?

The International Weight Lifting Federation voted to discontinue the press in 1972, at a meeting in Munich during the Summer Olympic Games. The reason was that the federation no longer felt it possible to correctly judge the lift, which is executed by pulling the barbell to the chest and then pushing it to a locked-arm position overhead, all the while maintaining an erect stance and exerting the strength of only the arms and the shoulders.

Vasily Alekseyev of the Soviet Union held the record, 517 pounds, at the time the press was discontinued.

# Volleyball

QUESTION: Please clarify the blocking rule instituted for volleyball. What constitutes a block, and how many hits are allowed after a block, and is a block a hit?

According to the rule book of the United States Volleyball Association, a block is an action at the net that makes contact with the ball coming from the opponent's side of the net, at or about the time the ball crosses the net. The new rule specifies that after a ball is touched by a block, the blocking team has the "right to three more contacts in order to return the ball to the opponent's area." Thus, a block is not included in the three contacts.

Under the old rule, the ball had to be returned to the opponent's area within two touches after a block.

# Other International Games

QUESTION: How did the United States rowing team fare in the 1979 Pan American Games in Puerto Rico?

The oarsmen did not fare so well as some other Americans. In eight events, they won only one gold medal, plus three silvers and three bronzes. The gold was won in the eight-oared crew race. The Penn Elite Rowing Centre eight, stroked by Bruce Ibbetson, represented the United States. In other events, the Americans' results were: Jim Dietz, single sculls, third; Chris Alsopp and Tow Howes, double sculls, second; quadruple sculls, stroked by Al Shealy, third; pairs with cox, fourth; Rich Cashen and Dave Fellows, pairs without cox, second; fours without cox from Penn Elite Rowing Centre, second; fours with cox, stroked by Steve Christensen, third.

**QUESTION:** In the 1979 World University games in Mexico, athletes who were no longer in college were permitted to compete. What exactly were the eligibility requirements for the event?

College students between the ages of 18 and 27 were eligible to compete, as were graduates who had finished their studies within the previous year.

# Miscellaneous Sports

## Bowling

**QUESTION:** In a bowling match, the ball, on the first roll, knocks down all but one pin, which jumps in the air and lands straight up but not in one of the pin spots. The automatic pinsetter, in clearing the alley, knocks the pin down because it is out of position. Would this count as a strike?

No. If the pinsetter knocks down a pin after the first ball, it has to be set up again, manually.

**QUESTION:** Is it possible to make a 7-10 split in bowling?

A 7-10 conversion is extremely difficult but is often accomplished by professional bowlers, and sometimes by amateurs. A right-handed bowler should aim for the right side of the 7 pin. If it is struck correctly the pin will bounce off the left wall hard enough to come back across the alley and topple the 10. A left-handed bowler should do the reverse, aiming for the left side of the 10 pin, so that it will bounce off the right wall to knock down the 7.

**QUESTION:** Which five bowlers in the Professional Bowlers Association tour had the best averages in 1980?

Based on a minimum of 400 games: Earl Anthony, 218.535; Mark Roth, 216.928; Tom Baker, 214.038; Joe Berardi, 213.550; and Nelson Burton Jr., 213.495.

## Handball

**QUESTION:** Did handball originate in the United States? If not, what is its origin and when did it get to this country?

Handball originated in the 10th century in Ireland, where it at first was called "fives"—five fingers to the hand. In 1882 Phil Casey, an Irish handball star, migrated to Brooklyn and was disappointed to find that there were no courts. He raised the necessary capital and built the first one, 65 feet long and 25 feet wide. It had three walls, the one at the front 30 feet high and those at the sides 25 feet. The court proved popular, Casey invested his profits in the building of others, and the sport took off from there.

## Dog Shows

**QUESTION: Has any dog ever won best-in-show and high in the obedience trial in the same show?**

A golden retriever, Ch. Beckwith's Malagold Flash, a United States and Canadian utility dog tracking (a top obedience degree), owned by Mr. and Mrs. Marv Kvamme of Alderwood Manor, Wash., was the best-in-show at the Kiwanis Club of Kerrisdale fixture at Vancouver, British Columbia, on April 18, 1970, and then won the most points in the obedience trial. This is the only time it has occurred, as far as the records indicate. Rob, as he is called, now is 11 years old.

## Six-Day Bike Race

**QUESTION: When was the last six-day bike race held in Madison Square Garden, and is there any possibility of reviving the sport?**

The last race was held in 1961, and, according to Garden officials, there are no plans at present to revive the event.

## Jogging

**QUESTION: Is there a reason why some joggers wear running shorts over their sweat pants? I notice that women as well as men are now dressed this way while jogging.**

Sweat pants are droopy in the center, and shorts are worn to hold them up.

## Rowing

**QUESTION: What were the dimensions of the boats used in the single sculls at the last world championship regatta? Have those dimensions changed in the last few years?**

Unlike canoe racing, which has set standards, rowing has no such rules. The boats thus vary according to the manufacturer. The average boat for single sculls is about 21 feet in length and weighs 30 pounds, including the outrigger. The lengths have not changed much over the years. The length of the scull, or oar, has been gradually getting longer because of the increased height and weight of the sculler. The sculls now are about 9 feet 10 inches to 10 feet in length, a growth of about six inches in the last 10 years.

# Auto Racing

**QUESTION: I know that the Indianapolis 500 is probably the most famous auto race in the world, but can you tell me where and when the first auto race was held?**

The first automobile race on record, between Paris and Rouen, a distance of about 78 miles, took place on June 22, 1894. No detailed account of it is known to exist.

# Snowshoeing

**QUESTION: The variety of snowshoes offered for sale is confusing for a beginner. What type of snowshoe is best?**

There are really only three basic forms of snowshoes, according to an authoritative book on the subject, "Walk Into Winter" by Gerry Wolfram, published by Charles Scribner's Sons. They are: stubby and oval; longer and medium width, and extra-long and narrow. You also have the choice of four toe designs: rounded front ends with flat or up-curved toes, or pointed in front with flat or up-curved toes. The smallest and lightest snowshoe that will carry your weight is your best choice. Any sporting-goods store that sells snowshoes should be able to advise you on the best one for your weight.

# Polo

**QUESTION: When were left-handed polo players barred from competition, and why was this done?**

As of Jan. 1, 1974, the only left-handers permitted to play in matches sanctioned by the United States Polo Association were those who previously had competed. All new players were required to be right-handed.

The reason for the rule, as explained by the association, was that the polo horses, who can gallop at speeds of up to 40 miles an hour, were at times colliding when a left-handed player and a right-hander were racing for the ball from opposite directions. Under the rules, players cannot cross the line of the ball, so that a horse with a left-handed rider and a horse with a right-handed rider were on a collision course.

# Martial Arts

**QUESTION: Is karate the same as kung-fu, and if not, what is the difference?**

Karate, which is the phonetic spelling of a Japanese word meaning "empty hands," involves punching, kicking, striking and blocking. There are somewhat fewer than 100 variations of karate styles, but basically the moves in that martial art are straight lined.

Kung-fu is the phonetic spelling of a Chinese term meaning expertise. Most kung-fu styles, of which there are more than 400, favor circular motions. In kung-fu, there is a preference for clawing, stabbing hand blows, and a different, stylistic manner.

These two martial arts are complex, and this explanation of their differences is somewhat simplified.

# Sports Medicine

**QUESTION: Please explain what a "charley horse" is and the derivation of the term.**

A charley horse is an aspect of fibromyositis. In lay terms, it is an inflammation involving muscles and their enclosures. Charley horse has now come to mean injuries to muscles as a result of either direct or indirect trauma. In contact sports, a charley horse can result as a direct injury in the collision of players. In non-contact sports, it occurs when muscle fibers or the muscle components have been overstretched or have been subjected to excessive strain. Wherever there is a large muscle group in the body, the same condition can occur. However, in sports, the most common area where a charley horse occurs would be the thigh.

Old lame horses kept for family use many years ago were affectionately called charley horse because of the popularity of the name "Charley." This usage gradually was applied to the inflammation of the tissues in the thighs of human beings.

**QUESTION: I frequently read that an athlete is unable to play because of a hip pointer. What is a hip pointer?**

It is an extremely painful bruise of the iliac crest—the upper ridge of the hip bone. The injury can be severe enough to keep a player out of action for five or six weeks.

# Softball

**QUESTION: In a softball game, a batter bunts a ball down the first-base line in fair territory, but runs toward the bag in foul territory. The pitcher fields the bunt and collides with the runner. Who gets called for interference?**

The runner must give way to the fielder, and he would be called for interference in this case. If the pitcher had not as yet picked up the ball, the runner could have gone outside the three-foot boundary on either side of the base line to avoid him.

WHOSE INTERFERENCE?

**QUESTION: Please compare the top speed of the fastball pitcher in the major leagues with the top speed of a man in fast-pitch softball.**

Nolan Ryan's fastball was once timed at 100.9 miles an hours, which is regarded as a record for major league baseball pitchers.

Ty Stofflet of Ballietsville, Pa., who has been called "the world's greatest left-handed softball pitcher," has been timed at 104 miles an hour. Stofflet is now in his late 30's. In 1976, in the world tournament in New Zealand, he retired 56 men in a row, 33 on strikeouts, before his team, Billard Barbell of Reading, Pa. (it has since been renamed the York Barbells), won the game in the 20th inning on his own single. Stofflet faced 61 batters in that game, one over the minimum, and allowed no hits.

**QUESTION: In softball, is a backspin pitch legal?**

Yes. It is legal in both slow-pitch and fast-pitch softball, but it is used primarily in the slow-pitch game.

# Journalism

**QUESTION: Was William (Bat) Masterson, the famed marshal of Dodge City, Kan., in the 1870's, ever a sportswriter?**

He was a member of the staff of The Morning Telegraph in New York City for 18 years, dying at his desk of a heart attack on Oct. 25, 1921.